THE

**A PRACTITIONER'S GUIDE
TO ACHIEVING LONG-TERM PROFITABILITY
AND COMPETITIVENESS**

SUSTAINABLE
BUSINESS

2ND EDITION

Taking the First Steps Toward Understanding, Implementing
and Managing Sustainability from a Cost/Profit Perspective

JONATHAN T. SCOTT

Greenleaf
PUBLISHING

The first edition of this publication was presented with
'The President's Award for Excellence in a Published Body of Work'
at *Kozminski University* (Warsaw, Poland) on the 5th of May 2010.

© 2013 by the Center for Industrial Productivity and Sustainability, Jonathan T. Scott, and the European Foundation for Management Development.

Published by Greenleaf Publishing Limited
Aizlewood's Mill
Nursery Street
Sheffield S3 8GG
UK
www.greenleaf-publishing.com

Typeset and Cover by OKS Prepress Services, Chennai, India
Printed in the UK on environmentally friendly, acid-free paper
from managed forests by CPI Group (UK) Ltd., Croydon

British Library Cataloguing in Publication Data:
  A catalogue record for this book is available from the British Library.

    ISBN-13: 978-1-906093-83-9 [paperback]
    ISBN-13: 978-1-907643-89-7 [hardback]
    ISBN-13: 978-1-907643-52-1 [electronic]

THE SUSTAINABLE BUSINESS

A Practitioner's Guide to Achieving Long-Term Profitability and Competitiveness

Table of Contents

List of Figures

Foreword

Welcome to this updated and expanded second edition of *The Sustainable Business*.

In the past few years, the issue of sustainability in its widest sense (not just 'green' issues) has been comprehensively and wholeheartedly embraced by the European Foundation for Management Development (EFMD), and its global base of member institutions: business schools, corporations, government and public sector bodies.

This very important book stresses that sustainability is sensible and practical, covering such areas as the legal, financial, economic, industrial, social and behavioural aspects of business. Perhaps sustainability's greatest strength is that it measures and controls costs wherever they arise in a business through the careful use of scarce raw materials and other resources.

We may like to think that we live in a world of relative abundance. But our world is fragile and currently under much pressure. Economic recession, a burgeoning global population and seismic shifts as the economic and political axis moves from West to East all add to that pressure.

As I wrote in the introduction to the first edition of *The Sustainable Business*, we owe it to our children and our children's children not to spend their inheritance on ourselves.

We can do that by adopting sustainable measures, which have the happy side-effect of helping to preserve our environment and creating jobs in the process. This book is one of the most comprehensive and thoughtful guides as to how we might do that.

Prof. Eric Cornuel
Director General & CEO, EFMD

Author's Note

Buyer Beware
(or, All Aboard the Sustainability Bandwagon)

In the autumn of 2011, a former student of mine, who had successfully completed an introductory sustainability program, packed his bags, hopped on a plane, and flew a considerable distance to attend a newly launched university course that claimed to focus on 'shareholder wealth and corporate sustainability'. But his heart quickly sank when he discovered that the 'new' course on sustainability he had paid for was really an old course on corporate social responsibility. 'I wanted to learn more about resource extension,' he (angrily) told me later, 'I didn't travel halfway around the world to attend yet another CSR course.'

Around the same time, a different student of mine, again lured by the promise of a 'new' sustainability program at an institute in another country, signed up and set off to build a portfolio in what she hopes will be a career that involves managing sustainable business operations. But a few weeks after classes started, it became clear that the 'new' program she had set her sights on was little more than a psychology-based curriculum into which the word 'sustainability' had been inserted. 'Its emphasis is exploring the emotional issues behind sustainability,' she told me afterward – with more than a hint of disgust in her voice.

> 'Sustainable development is like teenage sex – everybody claims they're doing it, but most people aren't, and those that are, are doing it very badly.'
> Dr. Chris Spray,
> Northumbrian Water Group

As I write this, an announcement has been made by yet another acclaimed university proclaiming that an 'International Sustainability Conference' will soon be held on its campus. A brief background check of the people involved, however, reveals that none of the nine academics who comprise the organizing and program committees has ever conducted research in the field of sustainability, nor have any of them published a paper on the subject. Further investigation reveals that none of these people has ever worked with a business or other organization in any sustainability-oriented capacity.

And so it goes as an increasing number of business schools and their opportunistic staff rush to capitalize on a subject that many of them rather aggressively turned their backs on for decades. 'For years we couldn't interest a single business school into considering sustainability as a viable academic subject,' confided one of the directors of a prestigious business school accreditation body last year, 'now they're suddenly all experts.'

So who is to blame for this? Is it the growing number of higher-learning institutes that are eager to cash in on a subject that their solipsistic academics and cash-starved departments have finally realized is as important as it is popular? Or should we blame naïve business students who can't be bothered to conduct a basic investigation before they spend their money? (An example of this is seen with, a student who came to me complaining that she was drowning in advanced chemistry and physics [read: material science] at a reputable sustainability program in a renowned university.) One cannot help but be reminded of the adage 'caveat emptor'.

Needless to say, as everyone rushes to jump aboard the sustainability band wagon a lot of unnecessary confusion results (e.g. highly regarded sustainability curricula become lumped together with unscrupulous claptrap – and/or-subjects such as forestry, material science, CSR, the law, etc. are somehow seen as unrelated to sustainability.

This book was written, in part, to help clear up the confusion and I hope it does so without resorting to the 'three common habits of the most irritating management gurus'. According to *The Economist*, these habits are: (1) presenting old ideas as new breakthroughs, (2) over-relying on 'model firms' that we are told we should all emulate, and (3) flogging management tools off the back of numbered lists of bullet-pointed principles.

My fact-checker and sounding-board is, once again, Walter Stahel, who has over 35 years of experience in the field and is one of sustainability's true pioneers. We hope you find this publication useful.

Introduction: What is Sustainability?

It is a sad fact that much of the world is dominated by short-term thinking. And an in-depth look at the numerous problems that humanity now faces often reveals that the downside of allowing individuals or groups to do whatever they want (without considering future consequences) usually results in all of

In the 1980s, the *Brundtland Commission*, a UN investigative body, defined sustainability as development that meets the needs of the present without compromising the ability of future generations to meet their own needs.

us paying dearly for it. Equally as true is that an increasing number of people and their governments are waking up to the fact that producing high levels of costly waste and pollutants does not equate with freedom, nor is it a basic human right. Indeed, it seems fairly safe to assume that the era of privatized profits boosted by socialized costs will soon be drawing to a close. Hence the growing interest in **sustainability**, a catch-all concept that can be as difficult to comprehend as it is to define.

So what exactly is sustainability and why is the word 'green' attached to it – particularly when most definitions of the verb *sustain* don't mention the word 'green'?

To be sure, most definitions of *sustain* describe the following: *processes or acts of long-term continuance; causing or allowing something to continue over a period of time;* a *process or action that keeps something up or keeps something going.* It is therefore easy to conclude that, in a business context, sustainability involves the processes and actions that keep a firm solvent over time.

Following this logic it is also easy to assume that an *unsustainable* process or act is destined come to an end sooner rather than later. In business terms, this obviously translates into financial loss, even if the business makes a bit of money in the short term. So why, you might still ask, is the word *sustainability* synonymous for 'going green'?

The answer is that countless awareness campaigns created by far-sighted environmentalists have gone a long way toward educating the public about the consequences of short-term thinking. And when one group successfully dominates the discourse of a multifaceted issue it is their tune that is most often heard.

Broadly speaking, however, *the capacity for continuance into the long-term* (sustainability) is about more than the environment. Make no mistake, the environment should be of paramount concern to all of us for the simple reason that every business (and life) resource comes from it. That being said, focusing only on the environmental aspects of sustainability – particularly in a business context – is both short-sighted and partial. It's like claiming that good health is solely about vegetables. It is therefore important to note that business sustainability also embraces the legal, financial, economic, industrial, social, material (science) and behavioural arenas.

To add to the confusion, each of these arenas (or fields of study) propagates its own language, customs and culture, which don't often mix in business circles and/or the halls of academia (see FIGURE A-1). Fortunately, however, there is common ground: waste elimination and resource extension. Simply put, the core of sustainability is comprised of waste elimination and resource extension. This is so important that it's worth repeating: *the mechanism of sustainability is waste elimination (and prevention) followed by resource extension*. From a business viewpoint, sustainability is therefore about reducing expenses – including *future* expenses – in every conceivable form so as to facilitate profitability, competitiveness and longevity. These expenses consist of the costs of short-term thinking, the problems and costs associated with waste, the spiralling cost of raw materials and resource deficits (resulting from an increasingly affluent and growing population all of whom are competing for the world's finite supply of resources), costs created or exacerbated by poorly designed products and production processes, the costs of climate change (e.g. property damage and crop failure), and the costs of unemployment and underemployment – to name just a few (in 1994, British business consultant John Elkington condensed these areas into three categories and referred to them as the 'triple bottom line': the *financial*, *environmental* and *human* aspects of business).

In other words, to understand sustainability it is essential to begin by first comprehending the big picture – i.e. to acknowledge that sustainability is about well-being and longevity and to develop an awareness of what that encompasses before analytic thought does its necessary reductive work. Rather than building up from particulars to generals (the empiricist method), one must begin with generals – an in-place, intuitive wisdom of the logic behind thinking in the long term, what it entails, and why it's important. Once that is obtained, most people instinctively gain a better idea as to where to direct their analytic attention. Again, it's difficult to expect progress by focusing only on one area (e.g. the environmentalism aspects of sustainability). The problem with this (the empirical) approach is that once a few facts become clear it's tempting to believe that they possess an independence all their own and to rest in them and believe that they are the foundation of what is being sought (theologians call this 'idolatry').[1] Obviously, dividing the world into parts is something we all do to ease understanding, but in doing so something is always devalued – and what is diminished is often an awareness of and contact with that which can only function as a whole.[2]

This book is an introductory guide. It explains the fundamentals of sustainability (waste elimination and resource extension) from a business application angle. To facilitate comprehension, an easy-to-understand format is used that consists of seven categories each of which begins with the letter P. To be sure, alliterations are rarely perfect, and reducing any broad-ranging topic into categories usually ends up neglecting something that others see as valuable; however, the 7-P model has proven to be helpful both in and out of the classroom so it is used here as a framework. Briefly, the 7-Ps are as follows (an overview of this model is shown in FIGURE A-2):

Preparation – accepting the breadth and depth of sustainability (e.g. particularly the financial implications) and understanding that sustainability is not solely about the environment or being independent. Equally as important is a full recognition of what the reformer is up against when trying to implement profitable, long-term practices (e.g. apathy, ignorance, short-term thinking,

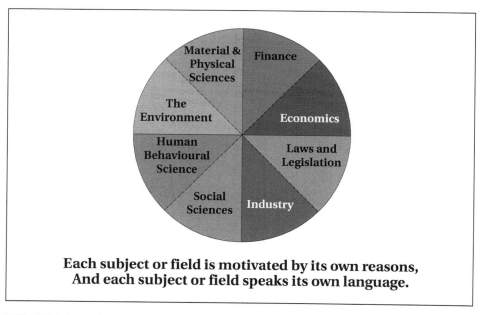

**Each subject or field is motivated by its own reasons,
And each subject or field speaks its own language.**

FIGURE A-1: Sustainability is comprised of numerous subject areas and fields

and what Machiavelli called 'the incredulity of mankind, who do not believe in anything new until they have had actual experience of it.').

Preservation – encompasses two areas: *internal* (collecting and displaying real-time measurement) and *external* (keeping ahead of laws, pending legislation, trends and developments).

Processes – sustainable belief systems, philosophies, business models, and thought patterns that help match a business with customer demands, core capabilities and best practices.

People – accepting the importance of training and education and working diligently to avoid the wasting of people, specifically: *employees* (who seek security and motivation), *stakeholders* (who want a return on their investment), *customers* (who want safe, value-laden products), and the *world community* – including the two-thirds of humanity who are currently left out of the global economic loop (who desire jobs and inclusion) and who represent an economic force all their own.

Place – the buildings and places where work is performed and/or products are sold.

Product – goods and services that are free from unnecessary waste ('non-product') and toxins – and designed so that the materials, energy and manpower that comprise them (and their packaging) are treated as investments and continuously reused.

Production – the physical, mechanical, biological, and chemical processes used to transform raw materials into products or services – as well as the transportation of raw materials and finished goods.

To be sure, there is so much overlap amongst the different fields and categories that comprise sustainability that it can often be quite difficult to determine where one category or field begins and another ends. Again, my advice is to focus on the big picture rather than any perceived boundaries.

If you wish to go beyond the pages of this publication, you are welcome to download the free books, videos and other teaching and learning materials available on the website of the *Center for Industrial Productivity and Sustainability* (www.cipsfoundation.com) and the website of the *Product-Life Institute* (www.product-life.org), Europe's oldest sustainability-based think-tank and consultancy. The free materials on both these sites are continuously developed for classroom use and employee training programs.

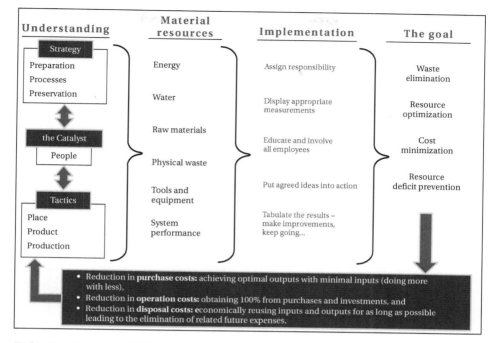

FIGURE A-2: The 7-P Application Model (toward sustainability)
© 2008 Jonathan T. Scott

PREPARATION

... the act of making ready (i.e. putting or setting in order in advance of an act or purpose). Before beginning the sustainability process it's important to: (1) learn what sustainability entails, (2) articulate why the pursuit of it is important, and (3) establish the groundwork that will instil both managers and non-management employees with enthusiasm, answers and support. Without this foundation, most attempts at sustainability are prone to confusion, suspicion, disorganization and dwindling motivation – as well as wasted time and efforts.

1
Fundamentals

Twenty years ago, the *DuPont* corporation decided to transition from a progressive focus on internal safety and environmental regulations at the company's various factories, to a more holistic approach that could be fully integrated into the business models of its numerous branches and subsidiaries. The result produced a reduction in absolute energy use by 6%, increased production by 40%, and saved the firm over $6 billion. In 2011 alone, a three-year effort from the company's *Building Innovations* business (which provides products and services for residential and commercial construction) not only achieved a goal of zero waste to landfill, it also created revenues of $2.2 billion from the sale of waste products at a cost savings of $400,000. Further sustainability-based activities at other subsidiaries generated over $1.6 billion in revenue; particularly from products that help customers (or the final consumer) reduce *their* energy use and greenhouse gas emissions. 'Sustainability consistently delivers both top-line and bottom-line growth for *DuPont*,' says Dawn Rittenhouse, business director for sustainability at the company. She further added (in an interview for this publication) that 'Sustainability makes it possible to create value for business, society and shareholders as well.'

Despite *DuPont*'s successes, however, sustainability is still not an easy sell in the business world. For example, when *General Electric* made the decision in 2004 to have its business operations become more sustainable, many company managers were not impressed (many thought it was just environmental gobbledygook). Four years afterwards, however, the decision delivered $100 million in cost savings to the company's bottom line while yielding a portfolio of 80 new products and services that generated $17 billion in annual revenues (greenhouse gas emissions were reduced by 30%). '[Sustainability is] 10 times better than I ever imagined,' says the company's CEO Jeffery Immelt.[1]

For the most part, what Rittenhouse and Immelt are talking about is eliminating and preventing waste (a.k.a. non-product) in all its forms while extending the life-cycle of the business's resources – both of which resulted in each company becoming more innovative in the process (GE's commitment remains very much in line with the firm's Six Sigma mantra from the 1980s).

Taken as a first step toward sustainability, waste elimination (and prevention) may not seem very glamorous; however, it has proven, time and again, to not only increase quality, facilitate innovation, and lower resource and disposal costs, but also reduce pollutants and the expense of pollution in the bargain (which is why environmentalists are so enamoured with the subject). Electricity consumption provides a good example. The American EPA estimates that a typical data centre consumes 10 to 100 times more energy per square metre than the average office building. Yet a 2,300 m^2 data centre spending $2.6 million annually for power can still enjoy electricity savings of more than 20% per year simply by reducing its energy demands (approximately $1.2 million over a four-year period).[2] A recent IBM study dug even deeper, concluding that less than 4% of the energy going into a modern server farm actually processes data; 40% is needed to cool the room where the servers are located, another 40% is used to cool the interior of the machines, and over 16% is used to keep the servers idling in case a sudden increase in processing occurs.[3] This means that 96% of the costs of operating a server area are used to perform activities that are unrelated to data processing. Moreover, the extra electricity needed results in more coal being burned (coal is the most common fuel used to produce electricity), which produces more pollution, which results in health and clean-up costs being added to the mix, and so on. The problem is exacerbated when one takes into account that up to and over 50% of the overall energy a business consumes is usually wasted.

And the more a business wastes, the more it has to purchase.

For a growing business, an energy-intensive business, or a business suffering through the difficulties of a recession, waste creation is clearly not a sustainable path. The good news is that many of the business costs associated with waste can be reduced with long-term sustainable solutions that are so simple they defy belief. For example, *Yahoo* saves 60% of its electricity costs by opening the doors and windows where its servers are located and letting the hot air out. *Intel* states that similar efficient air-cooling can cut the power costs of a 10 megawatt data centre by $3 million thereby eliminating hundreds of thousands of tons of greenhouse gases and their costly damage.[4]

10 reasons for a business to become sustainable

Following is a look at several market force trends that are currently impacting businesses either directly or indirectly through suppliers and supply streams and are redefining how businesses compete.

1. Volatile energy prices

Between November 2010 and April 2011, oil prices rose from $82 to over $112 a barrel (in 2004, the price of a barrel of oil was below $20), which leads to the inescapable conclusion that as the world's population increases, becomes more affluent, and ages, the cost of oil due to increasing demand escalates accordingly. Insulated windows and walls, and efficient machines and equipment are obvious ways to fight higher fuel costs, but other solutions involve little more than changes in behaviour. Firms like UPS teach their drivers to reduce left-hand turns, pack trucks tighter with more packages, and drive fuel-efficient trucks more efficiently. As a result the company saves millions of dollars every year in petrol and maintenance costs.[5] Investing in more sustainable energy sources (e.g. wind, solar and hydrogen) goes even further in helping businesses avoid the rising costs of non-renewable energy sources. For example, the *Sierra Nevada Brewing Company* in Chico, California, purchased solar panels that produce 203 kilowatts of electricity in addition to four 250 kilowatt fuel cells.[6] Thanks to rebates, tax credits and other financial incentives, a 100% return-on-investment is expected in six to seven years – after which time the company will have few in-house energy costs. More to the point, the company has now protected itself from the numerous power cuts and brownouts that plague its region. Switching shipments and deliveries from trucks to trains is another move that slashed the business's dependence on oil and saves around $2 million a year[7] – money that is used to fund additional cost-saving projects.

2. Increases in raw material costs

Raw materials are increasing in price for the same reason as oil prices (currently, 20% of the world's population uses 80% of the planet's resources). This is somewhat bizarre when one takes into account the enormous number of goods that consumers throw away daily, which still contain all the materials, labour and energy that went into making them (in the USA, for example, 2.5 million plastic bottles are discarded every *hour*[8]). One sustainable solution is 'extended product life', which turns waste into assets via reuse, remanufacturing and recycling. For example, *Stewart's Ice Cream Shops* in the USA has been using refillable bottles (over 12 million annually) in its over 200 shops for more than four decades thereby saving millions of dollars a year.[9] Elsewhere, *Caterpillar*, the world's largest manufacturer of construction equipment, delivered years of record profits due to a manufacturing business model that makes high-quality components, collects them after they've been used, cleans them up, and reincorporates them into new products at a cost 30%–60% less than making them from scratch.[10] Many of these parts are made once and sold three times (think of the profit margins involved). And *Interface Inc.*, the world's largest manufacturer of commercial carpets has, for 14 years, been using old carpets to make new carpets instead of sourcing petroleum as a raw material. As a result, profits doubled, employment almost doubled, and the company's stock price increased 550% over a five-year period.[11]

3. Increases in waste and disposal costs

Simply put, there aren't enough landfill sites to dump the world's increasing amounts of garbage (approximately 2 kilos per person per day and rising[12]) so prices rise accordingly. In the USA, between 1985 and 1995 the average cost of disposing one ton of garbage into landfill rose 425%.[13] The bottom line is that throwing stuff away costs money – and the bigger the business, the greater the costs. The *Sierra Nevada Brewing Company* (mentioned above) saved $1 million in landfill fees and $2 million in waste haulage fees by finding ways to reuse or recycle what it used to throw away.[14] Meanwhile, *Wal-Mart* issued an edict to its distributors demanding that they reduce their packaging by 5%. As a result, the retail giant is now saving $3.4 billion a year in waste disposal costs.[15] Another example is *3M*. After sifting through its waste bins to discover what was being thrown away, the *3M* company developed a profitable new product made entirely from waste.[16] Now that's sustainability!

4. Changes in waste legislation

Banning wasteful incandescent light bulbs to help lower national energy demands and reduce CO_2 emissions is merely the beginning. Paper, plastic and other recyclable materials are increasingly being turned away from landfill sites to avoid waste and encourage recycling. Similar waste legislation examples include the USA's *Toxics Release Inventory*, which some claim was America's first intelligent step toward waste legislation, take-back laws that make manufacturers legally responsible for their products *after* they've been sold to encourage reuse and remanufacturing technologies – and directives such as WEEE (*Waste Electric and Electronic Equipment*), which took effect in 2005 (designed to mitigate the incineration and dumping of electronic waste) and RoHS (the *Restriction of Hazardous Substances*), a 2006 law that bans electronic equipment containing certain levels of cadmium, lead, mercury and other toxic substances. Further regulations include the 2007 EUP directive (*Energy Using Products*), which requires producers to design and track products according to closed-loop waste reduction practices, and the REACH authorization (the directive on *Registration, Evaluation, and Authorization of Chemicals*), which requires manufacturers to publicly display toxicity data and to prove that the chemicals used to make products are safe.[17] Additionally, the 2008/98/EU directive, which went into effect in December of 2009, categorizes waste prevention as a first priority, resource reuse as a second priority, and makes material recovery, in almost all its forms, mandatory. Rest assured that more such legislation, all of which is designed to mitigate future waste problems and expenses, is on the way.

5. Increases in environmental laws

Digging up the earth and turning it into pollution is not a sustainable business model; it's a sign of costly waste. Legislation that classifies CO_2 as a pollutant merely adds weight to this argument (think 'cap and trade'). Company administrators sometimes claim ignorance, but astute shareholders know what is at stake. In 2008, for example, the *Securities and Exchange Commission* was petitioned by representatives of seven American states to force companies to reveal the actions they're taking to deal with climate change. This was not due to a sudden interest in the environment, but rather a belief that investors should have the opportunity to 'avoid investing in companies that are ignoring the spiralling costs of a changing environment'.[18] A year earlier, the CEOs of several corporations had called on the American president to enact mandatory reductions in carbon emissions. The group consisted of chief executives from *Alcoa, BP America, Caterpillar, Duke Energy, DuPont, the FPL Group, General Electric, PG&E, PNM Resources* and others. 'We felt it was better to be in the formative stages of legislation,' said Jim Owens, who was then the CEO and Chairman of Caterpillar, '[otherwise we] could cost [ourselves] out of the market.' By banding together to avoid a patchwork of costly and conflicting regional regulations, far-sighted CEOs are trying to work with lawmakers to set goals and targets that allow businesses time to make changes and implement solutions that will improve the environment and energy efficiency, protect the economy and national trade, and deliver a one–two punch to waste-filled competitors and products.[19]

6. Changes in customer demands and expectations

'Don't go into business to sell what you want to sell,' I regularly tell my students, 'go into business to sell what customers want to buy – and that includes where they want it, how they want it, when they want it, and why they want it.' In 2007, a major telecom manufacturer stated that it had received 50 request for proposal bids (out of 400) asking for information on the company's sustainability initiatives. In 2008, the number increased to 125, and in 2009 it was over 200.[20] It doesn't take a rocket scientist to deduce that B2B customers and B2C customers want lower costs, fewer toxins, less guilt, more incentives, and less packaging associated with the products they buy. Even retailers are watching over their supply chains (where most of their environmental footprint is located) in order to reduce unnecessary expenses that result from wasteful practices. Energy and material price rises are bad enough, but when they're added to supply chains they create even more costs. Firms such as *Planet Metrics* collect information on raw material sourcing, production methods, delivery systems and energy use – indeed all aspects of a product's life-cycle – to provide a clearer picture of what might happen if oil prices increase, or water becomes scarce, or a law changes, or a higher price is placed on CO_2, and so forth.[21] In other words, it's possible for major buyers to now know ahead of time which products they purchase are more likely to experience cost increases (or get hit by new legislation) – as well as the names of alternative (lower-cost) suppliers. If that's not enough to scare the hell out of a wasteful business, I don't know what is.

7. Competitive advantage

During the 2001–2003 recession, global carpet giant *Interface* faced a 36% world-wide slump in carpet sales. Nevertheless the company *gained* market share during this period because of its commitment to low-cost sustainable operations.[22] More recently, the *Tennant* floor maintenance company introduced a commercial floor cleaner that electrically charges tap water to behave like a heavy-duty cleaner.[23] The safe, toxin-free result cleans floors better than anything else on the market, thereby enabling customers to forego the expenses of purchasing cleaning solvents and the cost and time of training employees how to use them. In addition, valuable storage space that once held toxic cleaners is now a thing of the past for *Tennant*'s customers. That's bad news for cleaning supply companies that choose to merely make their chemicals more environmentally friendly. The message couldn't be clearer. Going green isn't enough – and companies that sit on the sustainability sideline may discover that when they finally decide to take action their competitors have already passed them by.

8. Transparency issues

The more secretive a business is the more likely it is to be shunned by customers. So companies like outdoor clothing manufacturer *Patagonia* use transparency to their advantage by making it easy for customers to follow products online from conception to the sourcing of materials to manufacture and delivery.[24] *Clorox* and *SC Johnson* take a similar route by posting online lists of every ingredient in their products. Business writer and environmental speaker Andrew Winston says it best: transparency comes in two flavours: voluntary (information donated by the company) or involuntary (information donated by a consumer watchdog group or disgruntled customers).[25] Guess which one is best for your business?

9. The acquisition, retention and motivation of astute employees

To be sure, money is important to employees, but there are other things that some employees think about as well. For these folks, the ability to make a difference, feel a sense of accomplishment, work with pride and purpose and other intrinsic motivators can be infinitely more powerful than money. Ray Anderson, founder and former CEO of *Interface* carpets, said that nothing galvanizes his employees more than the company's commitment to sustainability.[26] 'In the competition for the best business school graduates and other high-flyers, especially once the economy starts to recover, companies that show they were not mere fair-weather friends of sustainability will be at an advantage,' wrote the *Economist* magazine. As if to prove the point, sustainability pioneer *Patagonia* receives, on average, more than 1,000 CVs for every job position available. Think about how that minimizes talent search and recruitment costs.

10. The cost of procrastination

The longer a business takes to act the higher the cost of change and the further behind it can fall in terms of profitability, innovation and market share. Delayed action also ensures that additional costs – many of which are hidden – continue to accrue. For example, according to the American *Environmental Protection Agency* (EPA), building-related productivity losses and illnesses resulting from poor lighting, poor ventilation and/or indoor pollution (a.k.a. 'sick building syndrome'), cost American businesses $60 billion.[27] And that's just from indoor pollution. Outdoor pollution creates costs as well. For example, the EPA estimates that it will take $1 trillion to clean up America's trichloroethylene residues (trichloroethylene is a toxic substance used to remove grease from metal) and that $100 billion is spent in the USA on medical expenses related to polluted air alone. Meanwhile, a 2001 survey of nearly 600 children found that perfluorooctanoic acid – a substance found in food wrap, Teflon and stain-resistant fabric coatings – is swirling in the blood of 96% of the children it sampled[28] (one of dozens of toxins now found as a matter of course in human bodies[29]). Traces of arsenic, mercury and benzene also show up regularly in the human body alongside heavy metals such as lead, cadmium, zinc, chromium and copper. In river sediments and estuaries these substances are ubiquitous. Escalating levels of polycyclic aromatic hydrocarbons (PAHs), polychlorinated biphenyls (PCBs), and pesticides (each of which can take hundreds of years to degrade) make matters worse[30] – as do residues from billions of doses of prescription drugs now found as a matter of course along shorelines and in wetlands. Swallowed to combat cancer, pain, depression and other ailments, most medications do not harmlessly dissolve into patients and disappear. Instead, they exit the body, leak from sewage pipes, and work their way into the environment.[31] Researchers in Canada found a dozen different toxic drugs in water samples taken from the St. Lawrence River in Quebec, while across the border in the USA a vast array of pharmaceuticals (including antibiotics, anti-convulsants, mood stabilizers and sex hormones) were found in the drinking water supplies of 41 million Americans.[32] Added to this is the belief of many scientists that toxin build-up in air, soil and water is more costly and damaging than climate change – which is one reason why environmental crimes committed by negligent company directors can now result in fines of over $1 million and jail time of up to ten years.

Additional costs that result from waste

Unemployment and underemployment (i.e. the wasting of people) provide further examples of the cost of waste. Expenses associated with laying off employees (or negative job growth in general) include loss of investment in human capital and skills (particularly in individuals that have been unemployed for a long time), social and economic deprivation (rises in crime, depression, divorce, family break-ups, poor health,[33] lower life expectancy, etc.), and a reduction in regional and national economic growth potential (particularly from the one–two punch of fewer tax revenues along with increased government spending designed to spur growth). When poverty is added to the mix these problems only intensify.

Stuart Hart, author of *Capitalism at the Crossroads*[34] and a pioneer in the field of 'Inclusive Commerce', discovered through his research that most business strategies focus exclusively on the 800 million or so people that make up the industrial world while effectively ignoring the 4–5 billion people that comprise the bottom of the economic pyramid. Contrary to popular belief, the world's poorest countries have had zero or negative economic growth since the early 1980s[35] and the years between 1990 and 1999 mark the slowest growing decade the world economy has seen in the past 40 years.[36] Of particular concern are the approximately 1 billion people that live on $1 a day or less, the 16,000 children that die daily from malnutrition, and the fact that the number of people suffering from chronic malnutrition has almost doubled since 1970. Meanwhile, in the world's poorest regions (areas like sub-Saharan Africa) $25,000 is spent every minute servicing the debt owed to rich countries. Today, the *World Bank* estimates that the developing world spends around $13 in debt repayment for every $1 it receives in grants.[37] Clearly, this is not a sustainable path.

Connecting the dots

We know what happens when the world and its businesses are run in an unsustainable manner. The ten-year period between 2000 and 2010 has been described as the 'most dispiriting and disillusioning decade in the post WWII era'.[38] The millennium began with a dotcom bust and a Wall Street crash, both of which were overshadowed by major terrorist attacks. In the years that followed there were even more large-scale terrorist bombings. Then came the worldwide financial meltdown of 2008 brought about by irresponsible deregulation and monetary policies. Large swathes of the globe are now beset with high unemployment, huge amounts of debt, and growing unrest. An increase in catastrophic storms, floods and droughts – and the increasing acidification of the world's oceans – merely adds to overall costs and malaise as well as a profound feeling that humanity is moving in the wrong direction. Further-more, potable water is now at such a critical low level that wars over this cru-cial commodity are predicted to break out within 10–20 years while the Earth's resources (of which there are finite supplies) continue to be captured, abused, concentrated to industrial (toxic) levels, and discarded at an alarming rate.

Meanwhile, on the 24th of July 2004, the American senate abandoned plans to establish a cap-and-trade policy for the United States. Ironically, the day before this decision was made, Lew Hay (CEO of one of the country's largest utility owners) stated that setting a price on major pollutants and laying down requirements for renewable energy could create the certainty to – among other things – make big next-generation investments that would create 'roughly 50,000 jobs over the next five years'. Around the same time, as if to capital-ize on the inability of American politicians to think in the long term, China reported that it was establishing a five-year plan based on placing a price on costly pollutants as a means of shifting to a less expensive and more sustain-able economy.

Even military strategists are jumping on board the sustainability band-wagon. Retired Brigadier General Steve Anderson (who was General David Petraeus's senior logistician in Iraq) stated, '…over 1,000 Americans alone have been killed in Iraq and Afghanistan hauling fuel to air-conditioned tents and buildings. If our military would simply insulate these structures, it would save billions of dollars, and, more importantly, save the lives of truck drivers and their escorts… [while taking] lots of big fuel trucks (i.e. Taliban targets) off the road [thereby] expediting the end of the conflict.'[39]

'We have seen the enemy,' said Walt Kelly's satirical character *Pogo*, 'and he is us.'

There is a better way. It is possible to abandon the costly, cancerous actions that constitute short-term thinking. It is possible to do more with less, obtain more from purchases and investments, reuse industrial inputs and outputs, and minimize future problems and expenses. To be sure, sustainable business practices will not solve all of the world's ills – the complex, multi-dimensional configuration of sustainability ensures that there is no silver bullet that can be relied upon to hit every target. Equally as true is that no known business on Earth can call itself 100% sustainable (those that are interested are, for the most part, merely experimenting with the concept). That being said, eliminat-ing waste, thinking whole-system, and acting in the long term is a big step in the right direction. Businesses in the manufacturing, retail, financial and serv-ice sectors are benefitting in astonishing ways. If you wish to take part in this phenomenon, (to paraphrase Mahatma Gandhi) you will have to be the change you want to see in your business. Translation: clean your own house first. Let your competitors spend their money on lawyers and lobbyists. Rather than make excuses and continue with delays, start thinking long-term…

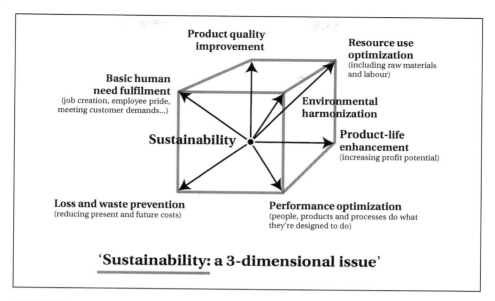

FIGURE 1-1: The areas where sustainability leads
Adapted from Walter Stahel's 'Quality Cube'

2

Understanding Waste

Imagine a business taking 30%, 40%, 60% or more of its hard-earned revenues, placing this money on a pyre, and burning it. If that is too difficult to imagine, try to picture a business flushing its revenues down a drain or throwing them away as if they were garbage. As preposterous as these scenarios may seem, businesses around the world perform the equivalent of them every day – and because discarding money is not conducive to long-term business success, it is here that the story of modern-day sustainability begins.

Back in the 1970s, the United States was wracked with a growing number of costly problems that were often explained away as a necessary component of conducting business. For example, in the state of New York, children living in an area named Love Canal began developing rare forms of cancer and other illnesses at a rate that far exceeded what was considered normal (the residents eventually learned that their community had been built on top of a toxic waste dump). In other cities across the country people were told to stay indoors to avoid the harmful effects of increasing levels of smog. And in Ohio, the Cuyahoga River, one of the state's main waterways, caught on fire after becoming saturated with oil, chemicals and garbage.

Further south, in Chattanooga, Tennessee, a similar story had been unfolding for years. According to the *World Resources Institute*, Chattanooga was once renowned for its natural beauty, but as a means of facilitating job growth and economic prosperity the city decided to attract a variety of industries (including textile mills, chemical plants and coke foundries) into its confines without first considering the short-term profit models that drove these businesses. As long-term planning continued to be thrown to the wayside, the region slowly morphed into a thriving industrial waste site. Soon the city's riverfronts were clustered with factories and its mountains were reduced to what looked like stains behind thick clouds of industrial smoke.

By the late 1960s, companies were dumping toxic waste into the area's rivers at an increasing pace and the air quality was, according to federal authorities, the worst of any city in the United States. People driving cars had to turn their lights on in the middle of the day and the mountain ridges often could not be seen from the city below. Girls covered their heads with scarves so that soot would not get in their hair on the way to school. Meanwhile, tuberculosis cases grew to three times the national average and other problems began to emerge. As times changed and industries refused to change, a significant number of manufacturing jobs became obsolete – and in what became a familiar pattern across numerous American industrial cities, unemployment grew, bringing crime, social unrest and racial tensions, followed by flight to the suburbs and the abandonment of downtown areas.[1]

Faced with these and other mounting problems, as well as the unprecedented nationwide healthcare and pollution clean-up costs resulting from them, the federal government introduced a series of laws that restricted the amount of pollutants a business could dump while making companies responsible for cleaning up the messes that they created. And, needless to say, the majority of America's business communities angrily reacted by claiming that these laws would greatly damage the nation's businesses as a whole, resulting in massive employee lay-offs, huge rises in the cost of products and services, and a decline in the economic prosperity and competitiveness of the country.

Imagine the surprise then when the *3M Corporation* publicly stated that it not only welcomed the new clean-up laws, but that it would voluntarily go beyond them by setting higher standards. *3M* administrators confidently made this announcement because one of their managers, a Chinese immigrant named Joseph Ling, had successfully explained to them that the truckloads of garbage the company regularly sent to landfill sites, and the smoke billowing from its factories, and the discharges flowing from its drainage pipes were nothing more than signs of waste – and that waste is irrefutable proof that a business is haemorrhaging money (today, waste is defined as not obtaining 100% from purchases and investments). Ling went on to rationalize that if 3M made efforts to reduce its waste, substantial cost savings could be enjoyed in terms of lower raw material expenses, fewer disposal expenses, and reduced pollution clean-up costs.

Further shockwaves were created when the company declared that it would rely on two pioneering methods to eliminate its waste. First, rather than collect and treat waste after it was created (as the law stated), 3M declared that it would prevent waste at its source before it became a problem. Second, the company insisted that front-line employees would play an integral role in obtaining this objective (the usual method at the time was to employ engineering specialists and pollution control consultants).

Ling's ground-breaking waste elimination program began simply enough by asking employees to stop being wasteful. Leaks, spills and other forms of material waste were reduced or eliminated; scrap material was recycled back into production processes; products were reformulated using less toxic and more sustainable substances; and equipment and manufacturing processes were redesigned so that they required fewer raw materials and less energy to produce.

Fifteen years and hundreds of improvements later, *3M* discovered that its efforts had lowered overall waste and emissions by 50% and had resulted in the company saving over $500 million in costs. In fact, the program was deemed to be such a success that the company launched an improved version of it in 1990 with the intent of reducing additional waste and emissions by a further 90% in ten years.[2] Dozens more efficiency projects were launched and millions more dollars were saved before employees and managers figuratively stepped back and wiped their brows, firmly believing that there were no cost-effective projects left to pursue. Unbeknownst to them, however, an independent *3M* plant in Midland, Michigan, thought differently. Entrenched in the belief that eliminating waste is a never-ending process, plant administrators set two new objectives designed to push themselves and their employees further. The first objective was to cut waste and emissions an additional 35%. The second was to integrate local health and environmental experts into the program – a move that introduced workers to different perspectives and provided them with new ways of thinking. Working with the community in which the plant was located – as well as with outside environmental activists and pollution control specialists – employees were able to initiate 17 more projects that lowered costs an additional $5.4 million.[3]

Shortly thereafter, in 2005, 3M's program celebrated its 30th anniversary with enough accumulated data to reveal that Joseph Ling had saved the company over $1 billion in costs.

Waste is defined as not obtaining 100% from purchases and investments

How much waste is out there?

Joseph Ling's legacy includes not only looking for symptoms of waste, but also determining the causes (imagine a patient with a hacking cough going to a doctor and being treated for the cough rather than the cancer that is causing it and the value of understanding symptoms and causes becomes apparent). Just as important, Ling's whole-system approach asks every employee to get involved in finding and eliminating waste and its causes – which also includes non-physical forms of waste such as fraud, risk, damage, investment losses, human error, weaknesses (or redundancies) in processing systems, poor service, lawsuits, bad customer relations, etc.

A good way to explore waste and costs and how expensive the overall waste picture becomes is with motors. Every business contains motors; some have thousands. Even offices contain scores of motors because motors come in a breath-taking array of sizes from the enormous to the minuscule and are behind just about everything that moves mechanically (e.g. a fan in a computer, a coolant pump in a refrigerator, or a machine on an assembly line). Combined, a business's motors can account for up to 60% or more of its overall fuel costs. Indeed, motors consume so much electricity that the amount they use over their lifetime *always* costs more than the purchase price of the motors themselves. For example, a new electric motor purchased for $1,500 can cost as much as $13,000 a year to run and a typical 100 horsepower AC induction motor purchased for $5,000 can require $35,000-worth of electricity to operate annually (some motors actually consume more than the amount of their purchase price in electricity costs every *week*). Taking the time to purchase an efficient motor should therefore be an integral part of the motor-buying process because just a 4% increase in efficiency can amount to more than $20,000 in electricity savings over the life of a typical 100 horsepower motor. That being said, these costs represent only one part of the complete picture.

Further 'big picture' costs that need to be added to the equation include those associated with operations waste. The diagram below reveals the amounts of waste inherent in a common industrial pumping system. As much as 70% of the energy produced from burning coal is lost in the power plant due to poorly insulated and poorly designed furnaces. From the amount of electricity that emerges from the plant, 10% is lost due to inefficiencies in the transmission lines. From what emerges out of the transmission lines, 10% is can be lost because of inefficiencies in the motor, and so on.[4] It all adds up to huge financial losses for businesses and consumers because the more that is wasted, the more has to be purchased. And as the picture broadens, an even greater amount of avoidable costs becomes apparent.

All together, the amount of electricity motors consume totals around 40% of the world's electrical power or roughly 75% of all industrial electricity usage. And since most electricity is derived from burning coal, an examination of the costs behind coal must be taken into account. A good example is a 2011 Harvard

University medical study by Paul Epstein ('Full Cost Accounting for the Life Cycle of Coal') which concluded that coal mining and the use of coal for generating electricity costs the United States economy between $140 and $242 billion a year. These costs include premature deaths associated with coal mining, the expenses of lung and heart disease, the cost of climate change and other environmental impacts as well as the negative financial effects on local economies from lost business and tourism in dirty coal-mining areas. What has not yet been factored in to this data is the effect coal consumption has on groundwater pollution including benzene, arsenic, mercury, lead and other coal-producing carcinogenic materials that typically find their way into household water supplies. The study concluded that these and numerous other unseen pollution-related health impacts could raise the total costs of mining and burning coal to $500 billion annually.[5] Indeed, clean-up costs for a 2009 rupture of a fly ash containment area in Harriman, Tennessee, alone (fly ash is a toxic residue left over after coal is burned, which is often mixed with water to keep it from dissipating into the air) are estimated to be over $1 billion (this particular disaster flooded over 300 acres of forest, wiping out roads and railroad tracks and destroying several homes, thereby making it one of the worst industrial accidents in American history).[6]

Obviously, as the demand for electricity (and other forms of energy) increases, such large amounts of waste and costs become difficult to ignore. Just as important, governments cannot afford to continue building power plants to compensate for wasteful infrastructure, nor can they continue to ignore big-picture externalized costs that are traditionally dumped onto consumers.

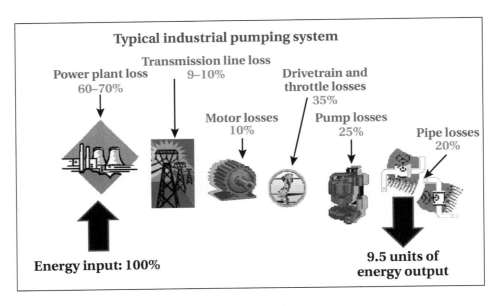

Typical industrial pumping system

Power plant loss
60–70%

Transmission line loss
9–10%

Drivetrain and
throttle losses
35%

Motor losses
10%

Pump losses
25%

Pipe losses
20%

Energy input: 100%

9.5 units of
energy output

FIGURE 2-1: First steps towards sustainability: a lesson in waste
Source: Jonathan T. Scott, *New Standards for Long-Term Business Survival* (ed. Walter R. Stahel; 2011; www.sustainbusper.com): 8.

Lastly, disposal costs must be included in the mix. Motors are heavy, which means that throwing one away can be expensive (landfill disposal costs are usually based on weight). It's therefore necessary to know how much it costs to discard a motor when it reaches the end of its product life – particularly if the local landfill site is full, or if it's discovered that the motor contains toxins that render it impossible to dispose of in a straightforward manner. One business throwing away its toxin-filled motors may seem insignificant, yet when hundreds of thousands of businesses do the same, serious problems can arise – and a similar tale can be told about virtually every tool, piece of equipment, production process and product in business.

Putting the infrastructure in place: a call for new standards

A common argument against change raises the question of costs – particularly when those who choose to protect their investment in antiquated or outdated processes insist that change should be feared. The change-should-be-feared argument almost always relies on a 'change is always and only an expense' supposition that incorporates 'top-down' economic models without considering 'bottom-up' models that take in to account the added savings and potential earnings that new practices and new technologies can produce. For example, before the passage of the American *Clean Air Act Amendments* of 1990, 'top-down' theorists predicted that meeting sulphur emission targets would cost businesses $1,500 (or more) per ton of emissions. Instead, sulphur allowances traded at less than $100 per ton by 1996 and fell to $66 by 1999. According to Stephan DeCanio in *The Economics of Climate Change*,[7] sulphur emissions then subsequently dropped across the United States by 37%. Just as important, electricity rates, which were predicted to rise to astronomical heights (power plants are one of the chief creators of sulphur emissions), *fell* by one-eighth. Ironically, the reason why the worst-case scenarios of the top-down theorists never materialized is because making waste more expensive resulted in the power companies becoming more efficient, more competitive and more innovative.

The 'change is only and always an expense' argument continues with the supposition that the infrastructure for necessary changes rarely exists and that significant amounts of capital will therefore be required to introduce sustainable activity on a large scale. Although this is true, it is not a valid argument. Consider the light bulb. When the light bulb was perfected in the late 1870s no electrical power plants existed, no transmission lines criss-crossed towns and countries, no houses or businesses were wired for electricity, and no lamps were being manufactured. Nevertheless, the financial (and other) benefits of the light bulb outweighed the cost of the infrastructure needed to support it so the necessary capital and investment was eventually – and willingly – put forward. For the same reason, new, government-mandated standards, coupled with financial support (as well as the nurturing of a network of cooperating businesses), must play a critical role in creating and promoting a more sustainable future.

In 2011, author Roger A. Pielke reiterated the principle behind this belief when he stated in an article for the *New York Times* that pioneering inventions and innovations are not enough to guarantee economic progress. As he put it, few people remember that in the United Stated during the 1800s, a nationwide lack of standards meant that weights and measures – including measured units of electricity – could have as many as eight definitions, which overwhelmed industry and consumers with a confusing array of incompatible choices. Meanwhile, Germany's standards agency, established in 1887, was busy setting rules for everything from the contents of dyes to the process for making porcelain – with other European countries following suit. The result was higher-quality products that helped Germany's trade growth exceed that of the United States in the 1890s. Pielke goes on to state that in 1901, the United States became the last major economic power to establish an agency to set technological standards and that afterwards, a boom in product innovation occurred in almost all aspects of life. These technological standards not only promoted innovation, they also helped protect national industries from falling behind those of another. Similarly, today, China, India and other rapidly growing nations – including those in the European Union – are adopting new standards that speed the deployment of new technologies and products. Companies that cannot compete risk losing overseas markets while innovative goods from other countries flood their domestic markets. A good strategy, therefore, is for a nation to not only continue developing higher standards and better infrastructure, but also to devise a strategy to apply its new and tougher standards consistently and quickly. This approach is taken by Japan's *Top Runner* program, which sets energy-efficiency standards by identifying technological leaders in a particular industry and mandating that the rest of the industry keep up with its innovations. As technologies improve, higher standards are therefore established that enable a virtuous cycle of improvement. At the same time, government should be working with businesses to devise further multi-dimensional standards and incentives to ensure that consumers don't balk at products because they sacrifice cost for efficiency.[8]

One more time: why is waste elimination important?

It is unrealistic for businesses to expect their hard-earned profits (not to mention taxpayer money) to indefinitely cover the expenses associated with waste.

Simply put, economic prosperity and job security are compromised when the financial damage from the waste a business creates exceeds the good that the business generates. Moreover, businesses and industries that fail to comprehend the issue of finite resources and increases in resource prices should elicit no sympathy when they claim they 'didn't see it coming'. No manager wakes up and suddenly discovers that his or her business can no longer afford its raw materials, or that consumers will no longer tolerate wasteful practices and toxic products, or that a new law has made certain chemicals or dangerous forms of production illegal. Instead, what usually happens is that management chose to ignore the warning signs – and now it can no longer afford to sit passively on the sidelines and do nothing.

3

What the Reformer is Up Against

With large corporations saving more than $1 billion from waste elimination and resource extension – and countless smaller businesses adding tens of thousands of dollars a year (or more) to their bottom lines by doing the same – one would think that businesses around the world would be rushing to adopt sustainable practices that reliably deliver long-term results. Unfortunately, this is not the case – and a major reason why this appears to be so lies within the complexity of the human brain.

The *Center for Research on Environmental Decisions* (CRED) is a research organization based at *Columbia University*. For the past several years, sci-

Some time between 1513 and 1532, Niccola Machiavelli, author of *The Prince*, wrote, 'There is nothing more difficult to carry out, nor more doubtful of success, nor more dangerous to handle, than to initiate a new order of things. For the reformer has enemies in all those who profit from the old order, and only lukewarm defenders in those who would profit from the new order – the lukewarmness arising partly from fear of adversaries who have the laws in their favour, and partly from the incredulity of mankind who do not believe in anything new unless they have had actual experience of it.'

entists at CRED have been working to understand the mental processes that shape human choices, behaviours and attitudes. Understanding why people behave differently when presented with simple choices is a field of study located at the crossroads of psychology and economics, which sprang from the work of Nobel Prize-winning psychologist Daniel Kahneman and his colleague Amos Tversky, both of whom discovered that humans often carry a number of biases that greatly affect decision-making.[1] For example, we are generally more averse to losses than gains and we repeatedly use short cuts to solve problems (a process called *heuristics*). Moreover, most of us have an inert dislike of delayed benefits. Placed in an everyday context, this means that given a choice we will more often take €20 now as opposed to waiting a year to collect €100.

People are also extremely susceptible to how questions are posed. For example: would you adopt cost-free procedures that resulted in your company saving €29,000 annually; or – would you adopt cost-free procedures that cut carbon emissions by 139,000 kilos per year? The result (from turning off unneeded lights in a business one of my students examined) in both cases is the same, yet, depending on who is being questioned, the answers vary considerably.

Further examples of biases that affect human decision-making processes include:

- A finite pool of worry – being able to focus on only a limited number of problems at any given time.

- Single-action bias – the belief that performing one act or task is enough to solve a complex problem.

- Focusing more on what is unknown rather than what is known – for example, endlessly debating the **exact** amount of money that a sustainable procedure will save (€200,000 or €500,000) rather than the fact that the procedure will save more than it costs.

- The expectation bias – making a judgment based on what the outcome is expected to be (or, as Henry Ford is credited with saying, 'Whether you believe you can or believe you can't, you're absolutely right.')

- The anchoring bias – the belief that things are as they appear to be, or: as they have been **taught** (in other words, an individual's powers of estimation, frequencies, probability and sizes are heavily influenced by his or her surroundings, background and education; this helps explain why people are incensed by flag-burning or the kind of sex others have in private, even though these issues don't really affect them – yet when an issue like toxin build-up comes along, which does affect them, their reaction is negligible).[2]

Compounding these biases are a number of additional shortcomings that influence behaviour including poor communication skills (especially those of scientists, academics, managers and teachers), prevention avoidance (e.g. only being able to defuse a bomb *after* it has exploded), and the constant misinformation spread by moneyed interests, sceptics or out-and-out liars (a situation exasperated by a common perplexing belief that the truth is whatever anyone says loudly or fervently enough).

Mixed messages, as well as messages expressed in ways that motivate the messenger more than the receiver, create additional obstacles to long-term thinking – and a quick search through the proliferation of websites promoting green business practices provides a case in point. Many of these sites earnestly document the amount of greenhouse gas emissions a company can eliminate in a bid to become 'greener', but all too often there is little or no mention of the financial savings that will be achieved in the process. This is puzzling for the simple reason that finance is the language of business – *not* CO_2 emissions. Is it any wonder so many businesses are not interested in sustainability?

Manifestations

How do the above biases and shortcomings manifest themselves in academic institutions and workplaces? Usually in the following ways:

- Lack of awareness. Without question, ignorance is the greatest enemy of sustainability. Most people simply don't know about the cost of waste, the numerous negative situations that can be alleviated by eliminating it, and the money that can be saved by eliminating it (e.g. 3M's 'Pollution Prevention Pays' program saved the company more than $1 billion over a 30-year period). Just as important, most people never consider that pollution and over-production are among the easiest signs of waste to spot. Added to this is the common misconception that just because a system, machine or product is functioning, it is operating at 100% efficiency, or that traditionally low-end costs (such as water and electricity) don't amount to much and are therefore not worth examining.

- Waste acceptance. Some people believe that waste is a natural and acceptable part of business. Common variations of this theme include defeatism (e.g. saying sustainability is not worth the effort) or the belief that sustainability doesn't apply in (our) part of the company or in (our) industry. As harsh as it sounds, the more short-term a person's thinking is, the more likely it is that he or she will feel this way.

- The cost myth. 'How much is this going to cost me?' is the first question managers usually ask when the basics of sustainability are explained – and the question is often put forth in a pessimistic tone implying that the cost will be too high. Unfortunately, it misses the point. It's not the costs, but the savings and potential profits that should be considered first. Yes, in many cases some capital is required to start a sustainable process, but the point of sustainability is that it can pay for itself – with the added benefit of additional savings year after year that can be used to fund further improvements. Energy-efficient light bulbs provide a good example. Efficient bulbs can cost anywhere from $6 to $20 (or more) per unit whereas regular light bulbs cost around 75 cents (or more) per unit. Most folks assume that 75 cent bulbs are the less expensive option, yet if one takes into account that energy-efficient bulbs last years longer and can save $30–$60 in electricity costs over the life of the bulb, the 'cheaper' bulb becomes the more expensive alternative. Unfortunately, too many people don't think in the long term and end up choosing the more expensive option. This is especially true with 'stranded capital' (businesses that invest millions of dollars in inefficient equipment and machinery and can't afford to change).

- The dimes-not-dollars argument. Those who have looked into efficiency sometimes find it difficult to become enthusiastic because they assume it only leads to small-time savings. Most of the businesses my students assess, for example, initially scoff at the notion that they can save money by implementing basic efficiency procedures – until estimates show that many of them can save thousands of dollars per year just by turning their lights and computers off when not in use. In several cases we revealed that annual savings of up to and over half a million dollars could be obtained by incorporating a few more inexpensive (and risk-free) solutions. The moral of the story is that the savings from efficiency don't just add up – they tend to multiply. For example, to continue with the light bulb example above, the overall savings from installing energy-efficient light bulbs includes: (1) reduced electricity costs (efficient bulbs consume less electricity), (2) reduced replacement bulb costs (efficient bulbs last longer), (3) lower cooling costs (heat from inefficient light bulbs can increase a building's heat load by 30%), (4) a reduction in air-conditioning needs (with heat levels cut by 30%, a smaller, less expensive air-conditioning system is needed), (5) reduced HVAC energy requirements (smaller air-conditioning systems require less electricity), and so on.

- The hassle factor. Many people don't want to add more work to their day no matter how much time or money they can save. The message to remember here is that sustainability is not about sacrifice. It's about eliminating wasteful practices and replacing them with more cost-effective alternatives that make work easier, more enjoyable and less expensive.

- Scepticism and/or obstinacy. In a world where prices are regularly taken into account, but long-term value rarely is, sustainability is a difficult concept for many people to accept. Sceptics, for example, often think that the amount of cost savings a business can achieve are impossible to prove (especially if no measurement is taking place). Estimations therefore become easy to dismiss with an unmovable conviction that the amount of time and money invested will be less than what is received. Stated differently, since much of sustainability falls into the realm of prevention, and the predicted savings from most preventative measures can't be proven until after a practice has been implemented, predictions become easy to ignore.

- Social loafing. Almost every business or industry has within its ranks those who reduce their efforts when they see that others are more than pulling their own weight. This practice is called social loafing and it's anathema to sustainability – particularly when the lowered input of one or two individuals has the ability to reduce the work or aspirations of an entire operation (or industry). Social loafing tends to be pervasive in under-regulated industries and/or in companies that have untrained or unsupervised employees. As a result, since employees feel that the company (or industry) that employs them doesn't care about costs – why should they?

- 'Let's wait and see'. Businesses (or managers) that wait to see how other companies react first before they themselves take action probably suffer from a lack of education, direction and training. Ironically, because of the virtually risk-free nature of efficiency and the rapid financial improvements it brings about, when a decision to become more efficient is finally made those that sat on the sidelines may discover that their competitors have already passed them by.

- The solutions are too simple. A British efficiency consultant in France once relayed to me that almost every manager he spoke with about sustainability rolled his or her eyes when the first suggestion he made was to turn off unneeded lights (this practice alone saved one factory that my students assessed €28,800 a year). Although there is no data to suggest that complexity legitimizes business solutions, many people apparently seem to need the false reassurance that they feel complexity provides. Therefore, because many sustainable solutions are simple and low-tech, they're rejected out of hand.

- 'We're already doing as much as we can. These self-deceiving words are usually uttered by managers and employees who: (1) mistakenly believe that they've done it all, or (2) wish to avoid additional work, or (3) are placating customers, their shareholders or the media with false information. According to the Scottish Environmental Protection Agency, the true cost of a business's waste is often 5–20 times more than what the business assumes. Think about that for a moment. An office manager once told my students that it was highly doubtful they could find more than $300 in efficiency savings ('We're already efficient,' she said). The students found over six times that amount in two hours. Another group of students found over $4,000 in savings in a restaurant which claimed beforehand that it too was as waste-free as it could be thanks to the policies set by its head office. Managers and employees take note: proclaiming that your business is as good as it's going to get is tantamount to claiming that it has no further need of new thinking, training, input or ideas.

- Group-think or a 'committee mentality' results when laziness or the smug air of superiority creeps into a business and it refuses to consider what it feels are strange or different viewpoints from others. For example, students I have trained to conduct waste evaluations have been called 'tree-huggers', 'crackpots' and a host of other names when they mention that sustainability also helps the environment by dramatically lowering green-house gases. This type of behaviour is mostly a hangover from the 1970s when businesses and environmentalists clashed (sometimes physically) on a regular basis.

- Additional obstacles include: fear of change, lack of leadership, an inability to accept criticism, poor management and poor decision-making – all of which will be examined later.

The illusion of control

Humans often have a strong desire to feel in control – so much so that acquiring a feeling of control is usually deemed essential for survival. Psychologist Bruno Bettelheim concluded (from first-hand experience) that survival in Nazi death camps depended on a person's ability to preserve areas of independent action and to maintain some control over certain aspects of one's life. Eliminate control and people experience depression, stress and even the onset of disease.[3] In an academic study of elderly nursing home residents, for example, a group of individuals was told that it could decide how their rooms were decorated and that each person had a choice over what type of plant he or she could have (the subjects were also told that they were responsible for caring for the plant). A second group had everything done for them. Eighteen months later, 15% of the subjects in the first group had died compared with 30% in the second group.[4]

Although research shows that satisfying the human need for control can create a powerful sense of purpose and direction, the irony is that too much control can generate problems. Few people enjoy the company of control freaks, for instance, and having one person in a group (or business) make every decision often results in the group being vulnerable to bad choices – particularly when it comes to money. Studies have shown, for example, that people feel more confident when they toss a set of dice rather than if someone else makes the toss for them.[5] Most people will also value a lottery ticket more if they choose it rather than if one is chosen for them at random.[6] A similar study revealed that well-educated subjects actually thought that they could improve their prediction of coin tosses through practice.[7] Obviously, in all of these examples the subjects had no control over the outcomes of the acts described, yet as psychologist Leonard Mlodinow reports,[8] on a deep, subconscious level they must have felt they had some control because they *behaved* as if they did. The conclusion is that sometimes a false sense of control can promote a false sense of well-being by allowing an individual to maintain the hope that a bad situation can be improved.

So what, you may ask, does a false sense of well-being (i.e. the illusion of control) have to do with sustainability?

In the introduction it states that sustainability embraces the legal, financial, economic, industrial, social, behavioural and environmental, arenas – and most of the examples provided in this document offer proof that this is so. Now take a minute to thumb through this guide while asking yourself the following question: *how much control does the business in which I work have over these issues*?

Battling the illusion of control

Because of the enormous breadth and depth of sustainability – and because too many people believe (or want to believe) that the issues comprising sustainability are distant both in time and place – the astute manager has his or her work cut out trying to implement sustainable practices in the workplace. Over the past few years it has become fashionable to describe the kind of focused, collaboration-induced communication needed to break through these barriers as having the proper frame, explains Jon Gertner, author of the article 'Why Isn't the Brain Green?'[9] However, in our haste to mix jargon into everyday conversation, frames are sometimes confused with another psychological term: 'nudges'.

Frames and nudges are powerful tools that help mitigate biases, reduce individual shortcomings and clarify mixed messages. A frame is a method used to get people to behave or think a certain way by using sophisticated messages that resonate or take advantage of cognitive biases (such as placing a message in a financial context rather than an environmental context). Nudges, on the other hand, direct the intended recipients toward a preferred action and are designed to follow frames by structuring choices so that cognitive shortcomings don't drive desired actions off course.

For example, if a business has been told that it can save €2,000,000 in costs by reducing wasted electricity (the frame), a nudge that can encourage employees to reduce those costs could take the form of an electricity monitor displayed so that every employee can see how much electricity is being used or wasted in real time (see FIGURE 2-1). Nudges therefore appeal to the human need for short-term satisfaction as well as the desire to be rewarded for improvement. So, placed in a management context, a 'frame' is the ability to communicate a message to others in a way that they understand and a 'nudge' refers to the feedback and measurement that enables the targeted group to see if their actions are achieving desired results.

Establishing a resonating frame for businesses

To date, in an ongoing survey, my students have asked 127 business managers and 530 employees in eight countries (Belarus, Canada, China, Peru, Poland,

Russia, the United Arab Emirates and the United States) what aspects of sustainability most interest them. Top ratings are almost always given to: the cost savings involved, profit potential, market share increases and job security (i.e. the financial aspects of sustainability). Environment concerns are usually ranked least important – often by margins of 8 to 1. Why then, when trying to win over businesspeople, are the aspects of sustainability that appeal most to business constantly forced to take a back seat to environmental facts and figures?

The importance of collaboration

Apart from frames and nudges, group collaboration (i.e. the input of employees as well as different departments, customers, suppliers, and so on) appears to be another key component to achieving success when sustainability-based changes are introduced into a business. Why? Because when an individual is reminded that he or she is part of a group, the group tends to become the decision-making unit – and groups are often more patient than individuals, especially when considering long-term or delayed benefits. Equally as important is that armed with good information, the freedom to speak out, and strong leadership, the calibre of group work can usually be expected to exceed the sum of that which each individual could normally produce on his or her own. Experiments conducted at the CRED research centre, for example, show that giving subjects a blue sticker and telling them they are on the 'blue-star team' increases cooperation from 35% to 50%. Just seating the 'team' together at a table increases participation rates by 75%.[10] These outcomes suggest that collaboration can be used to set long-term sustainable goals *before* individual biases and misinformation have the chance to set in – which is important because, as the next section reveals, setting clear, understandable goals and objectives that everyone can agree on is a cornerstone of the sustainability process.

4

Establishing Sustainability as an Objective

Not long ago, an administrator at a prominent UK business school pulled me aside and explained that her university had just bought a hybrid car (coloured green, of course) and had painted the words '(Our) university is going green!' on its side. 'What will the car be used for?' I asked. 'That decision hasn't been made yet,' she replied. 'Who'll be driving this car?' I responded. 'We haven't figured that out yet either,' she answered, 'but we're really serious about this sustainability thing so we're also going to knock down two of our buildings and rebuild them so they're greener.'

Obviously something is wrong here. Few grandparents try to connect with their teenage grandchildren by using 'gangsta' hand gestures, saying things like 'peace out', and wearing snorkel jackets and trousers that hang down around their knees. Yet too many business schools (and businesses) fail to see a similar sense of irony when they announce that they're 'going green' – with the result that their efforts end up looking like nothing more than a misplaced marketing exercise. Put another way, it's probably not in the best interest of a business or business school to tackle the subject of sustainability from its weakest point (environmentalism) – particularly when a wealth of other vitally important skills and abilities are within its grasp.

The role of the astute manager

For the past five years, companies considered to have good social, environmental and governance policies have outperformed the MSCI world index of stocks by 25%. Indeed, it has been shown that 72% of companies that adopt sustainable policies regularly outperform their industry peers.[1] What this suggests is that if sustainable practices are a proven way to improve business operations they should be strongly considered – and since the role of a manager is to serve customers[2] (see FIGURE 4-1) perhaps the best way to implement sustainability is through service. Serving external customers (e.g. paying customers) involves finding out what they want – as well as how, when and where they want it – and then moving heaven and earth to provide it (see Section 14: *Understanding the Importance of Customers*). Serving *internal* customers (employees, colleagues, suppliers, contractors, shareholders and other stakeholders) includes finding good people, educating (training) them, and giving them what they need so that they know the needs of the business, the business knows their requirements, and the two can serve each other. Any other decision on the part of the manager merely serves the manager (in a nod to the *Four Horseman of the Apocalypse*, I refer to the four major managerial weaknesses depicted in FIGURE 4-1 as 'the Four Horseman of the Managerial Psyche'). For example, if an employee approaches a manager with a sustainable cost-saving idea and the manager says 'no', the manager is probably serving his or her ego (few words show that a manager has superiority over a subordinate than the word 'no'). If the manager says 'no' because he or she is not sure if the idea will work, insecurity is perhaps to blame (a manager's job is to find out how or if new ideas *will* work). If the manager says 'no' because implementing the idea will involve

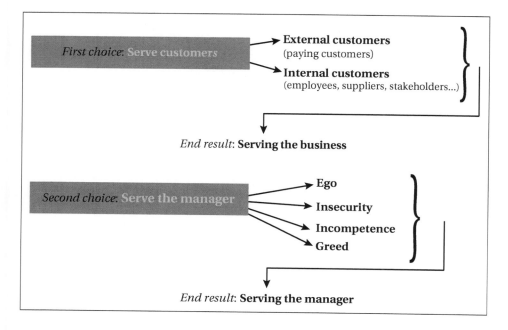

FIGURE 4-1: Scott's 'Two Choices of Management'

additional work (as new practices often do in their initial stages), the manager is probably serving his or her incompetence. Lastly, if the manager says 'no' because he or she is just being stubborn, or the idea will allow someone else to shine, the manager's greed (or selfishness) is most probably being served.

Sustainability: make it an ongoing mission and make it known

A common refrain heard from employees and managers in many organizations is that they don't know the aims of the company in which they work and they have never been taught their employer's values and priorities (if they have any) – a situation that usually boils down to a lack of communication. Poor communication results in employees not performing to the utmost of their ability and the organization as a whole not pulling in one direction. Simply put, people work better (1) when they know *exactly* what it is they're supposed to be doing, (2) when they've been told (and have accepted) what is expected of them, and (3) they're provided with regular real-time feedback.[3]

Ensuring that proper goals and objectives are established

When establishing its sustainability objectives, *Dow Chemical* could boast support from the company's CEO as well as shop-floor workers, clients, suppliers and environmentalists.[4] Excluding input from any one of these groups was seen as asking for trouble – something the *Monsanto* corporation discovered only too well during the 1990s. Around this time, *Monsanto* developed a bold new vision of providing sustainable agricultural products that could resist pests and diseases without the use of chemicals. The company's objective was to aid the environment and provide a level playing field for poor farmers around the world who could not afford the latest fertilizers and pesticides and other high-end technologies. This seemed to be an admirable objective from the viewpoint of business administrators; however, the company started developing genetically modified seeds to achieve its aims without first asking its customers what they thought about this plan. The resulting violent reaction against *Monsanto* and its genetically modified products shook the GM industry to the core, caused the company's stock price to collapse, forced its CEO to step down, and ended with the company being merged with another. In other words, by giving its customers what it *thought* they wanted instead of asking what they actually wanted, *Monsanto* set off in the wrong direction and paid a heavy price for it.[5]

Four steps to achieving optimal objectives

1. Create a vision

A vision is a clear and vivid idea of how things should be. In the UK, *HSBC Holdings PLC* decided to motivate its external and internal customers with a vision of reducing waste by becoming carbon neutral (which is something both groups desired). *Reckitt Benckiser*, a British manufacturer of household goods has developed similar plans. In the USA, the *Bradley Corporation*, a manufacturer of commercial washroom fixtures, proclaimed a comparable vision which led to its products becoming 'environmental solutions instead of environmental problems'.[6] Computer maker *Dell Inc.* has announced that it is committed to becoming the greenest technology company on the planet. Organizations like these have discovered through research and close client relationships that a commitment to sustainability not only reduces waste, pollutants and costs, it also promotes responsibility and respect – attributes that attract the attention of customers and help create an inspiring vision for employees to fulfil.

2. Decide on a mission

Mission statements individualize a business by defining its purpose and uniqueness. For example, *ST Microelectronics* pledged to obtain a forty-fold increase in production and become virtually waste-free by 2010. Figuring out how to do this took the company from being the 12th-largest microchip manufacturer in the world to the 6th – while saving a billion dollars in the process.[7] Meanwhile, *Ben & Jerry's Ice Cream* declares as its mission a dedication 'to make, distribute, and sell the finest all-natural ice cream… [with] a 'continued commitment to incorporate wholesome, natural ingredients and promote business practices that respect the Earth and its environment'.

3. Break the mission statement down into *achievable* objectives

Objectives are blueprints for achieving a mission that incorporate concepts of time and measurement, address financial and non-financial issues, and are more concrete and action-oriented. For example, sustainable carpet manufacturer *Interface* jump-started its employees by setting the following objectives and then asking everyone how to achieve them:

1. To drive waste out of the company completely,
2. To emit only benign emissions,
3. To harvest old carpets into new carpets rather than use virgin raw materials,
4. To only utilize renewable energy in production processes,
5. To transport products from the factory to customers as efficiently and cleanly as possible,

6. To sensitize people and communities about sustainable practices, and

7. To reinvent commerce itself using improved leasing services.[8]

4. Formulate strategies to achieve objectives

The final stage of the objective process is to identify short-term goals for unit, departmental or individual use, along with timelines to avoid procrastination as well as forms of measurement to ensure that progress is being made (e.g. the production department will reduce waste by 60% in nine months and energy consumption by 25% in three months…). Methods for achievement can include providing better employee training, replacing raw materials with recyclable materials, investing in clean energy, replacing outdated equipment and machinery with efficient alternatives, redesigning products and so on. Tapping into the workforce is essential because involving employees yields ideas and solutions and builds motivation and commitment. For example, on the 4th of May 2004, the *Subaru* car manufacturing factory in Lafayette, Indiana, made history by becoming the first auto assembly plant in North America to become waste-free thanks to the ongoing commitment and input of workers and managers. 100% of the waste steel, plastic and other materials coming out of the plant are now reused or recycled. Even paint sludge is dried to a powder and shipped to a plastics manufacturer where it ends up as parking lot bumpers and guardrails. What can't be reused – about 3% of the plant's trash – is incinerated to generate electricity.[9] In another example, a *Kozminski University* student who was assessing a business approached a worker and asked him if he had any ideas that would improve efficiency. The worker suggested moving two machines closer together so that one person could operate them both, thereby freeing up a second worker to focus on other tasks. Hearing this, the shop foreman expressed surprise that the worker hadn't spoken up earlier. 'No one asked me earlier,' the worker replied.[10]

Putting it all together: frames, nudges, objectives and control

For a manager interested in 'selling' sustainability to colleagues, success or failure often hinges on an ability to speak the language of the people being addressed. This is the world of selling, where putting the needs and interests of customers ahead of one's own is considered by many pros to be the most winning of strategies. The key to successful selling lies in understanding customers and their motivation. Two factors are involved. The first is moving toward a goal or reward. The second is moving away from a fear or loss. According to sales guru Tony Parinello, if you can work out which one of these motivates your customers (or can figure out how both of them can), you're on your way to making a sale.[11] Don't assume that merely talking about financial savings and profit increases will win a financially minded audience over to sustainability. Yes, this type of information can be made interesting and intriguing; however, it doesn't always instigate action – and *action* (e.g. approval, the granting of authority, and funding) is what most managers are after. Before pitching any proposal, it is imperative that research is done beforehand to identify a specific problem the audience faces. Once that information is known, a proposal can be tailored to show how it will help the audience as well as those who have the power to act. For example, if a seller is pitching first-aid kits to a factory, rather than explaining the low cost of the kits, the advanced materials the kits contain, the lives they've saved or the design awards they've won, it would be in the seller's best interest to first find out the most common injuries suffered by employees in the factory. In a chemical factory where employees are prone to burns this information could then be used the following way in a sales pitch: 'Studies show that, thanks to our first-aid kits, chemical burn scars are reduced by 63% and pain is reduced by up to 80%. Furthermore, by having our kits on your premises, your insurance premiums can be lowered by up to 14% *and* your company will save an additional $2,000 per year because of the current discount we're offering. Our kits, and the support system behind them, will even help you sail through your next health and safety inspection.'

This type of approach helps the seller target three objectives: (1) It gets the customer emotionally connected to the product or idea, (2) it targets the real problems of the customer with real solutions, and (3) it shows the customer what is at risk by not implementing the idea. In other words, in one fell swoop it shows how the customer can (a) move closer toward a goal or reward and (b) move away from a fear or loss.[12] In a sustainability setting this could mean explaining how the $25,000 that can be shaved from the business's yearly electricity bills would be used to pay the wages of a part-time worker needed in a production department. $40,000 in fuel savings can be pitched as a perfect way to purchase new computers. If the shipping department needs a new vehicle or operations is desperate for a more advanced extrusion machine, the $82,000 a year saved by incorporating sustainable waste recovery practices could be explained as a no-capital, non-risk way to begin paying for what is needed. Likewise, if the region, state or country is poised to adopt new environmental legislation that might cost the company a fortune, show how taking action now will save $125,000 *and* reduce carbon emissions by 30,000 tons over the next five years. Proposals presented this way are difficult to ignore.

One more time

In 2005, employees at *Hewlett Packard* managed to keep 84% of the company's trash out of landfills around the world as part of the business's sustainability drive. At *Xerox*, a company that credits sustainable activities as having helped save it from financial collapse, employees reuse, remanufacture and recycle over 90% of company waste. Workers at three of *Toyota*'s manufacturing plants in the United States have reached a 95% recycling level – as have the employees at *Fetzer Vineyards*, one of America's largest wine makers.[13] The point here is that sustainable waste-minimization practices mesh beautifully with the fundamentals of business: to serve the needs of customers, to reduce costs, and to streamline the business toward making a sale (not to mention the protection and creation of jobs). To be sure, the examples mentioned in this and other sections represent only a fraction of the overall sustainability picture – and it is important to note that sustainability is like quality in that one sub-par or out-of-sync component often diminishes the entire end result. Staying on track involves acknowledging the big picture by continuously honing and developing an awareness of what sustainability encompasses (e.g. understanding the interplay of every component; see FIGURE 4-2) *before* analytic thought, personal interests, negative experiences and biases begin their reductive work. Equally as true is that after a few goals have been achieved it's tempting to believe that these successes possess an independence all their own and to rest in them and believe that they are the foundation of what is being sought. This is the time to note that a pledge to sustainability is a pledge to ongoing improvements across the board along with complete acknowledgment that there is always room for improvement.

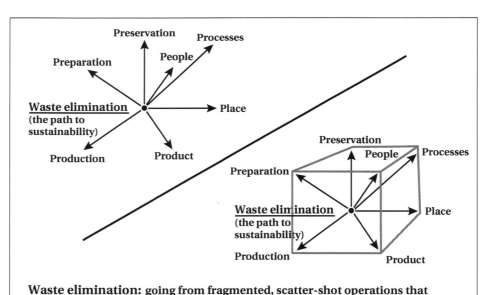

Waste elimination: going from fragmented, scatter-shot operations that foster an *'It's not my job'*, *'That's not my area'* or *'I don't know'* attitude to a responsible mindset that promotes long-term, whole-system, three-dimensional unity and stability.

FIGURE 4-2: Sustainability in your business: connecting the dots

PROCESSES

A *process* is defined as: (1) a series of progressive, interrelated steps or actions from which an end result is attained, or (2) a prescribed procedure or a method of conducting affairs. Either way, processes form the belief systems, philosophies or thought patterns that constitute the work environments in which goods and services are manufactured (seen from this angle, a business process can also be referred to as a 'business model' or 'the way we do things around here'). Most practitioners agree that for any business process to function properly, total commitment from all involved is mandatory. Success is also reliant upon a perfect fit between the process, its product, and the business's customers.

5

Resource Extension Part 1: Service and the Performance Economy

In 1973, several far-sighted individuals working for the *European Commission* (EC) made two important observations: (1) oil prices are probably going to continue to rise due to increasing demand, and (2) no matter how many jobs are created in the coming years they will probably not be enough to satisfy the continent's growing population. Not knowing how to resolve these challenges, the *EC* called upon the academic community to investigate these issues – which resulted in more than a few unreadable academic papers coupled with requests for additional funding.

Eventually, Walter Stahel, a Swiss architect working out of Geneva, Switzerland, approached the problem by examining the relationship between energy use and manpower. Sometime earlier, he had discovered that in the construction industry, roughly three-quarters of all industrial energy consumption is associated with the extraction and/or production of basic building materials (e.g. steel, wood, glass...). The remaining one-quarter, he observed, is used in the transformation of these materials into buildings. Conversely, he noticed that the opposite is true of labour. About three times the manpower is used to convert basic materials into buildings than is required in the extraction and production of basic raw materials. Stahel's award-winning discovery, however, was proving that this insight also accurately described the energy/manpower ratio of most products and their production processes (see FIGURE 5-1).

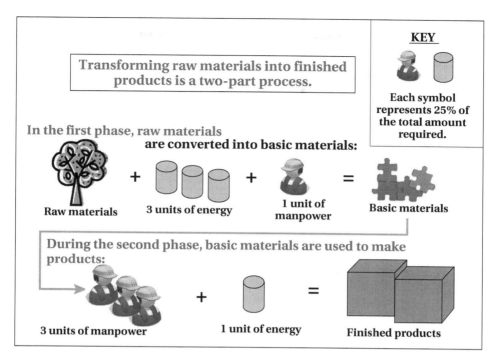

FIGURE 5-1: Stahel's ratio for manpower and energy use in production
© 2008 Jonathan T. Scott

Stahel then took his observations one step further. Being an architect, he knew that it is less wasteful and more cost-effective to remodel an old building rather than tear it down and construct a new one – and that's because extending the life of a building draws out the value of the labour, materials and energy that went into constructing it (i.e. increasing the use of a building to twice its intended life means that the original costs of its materials and energy are halved and the cost and subsequent waste of constructing a new structure are avoided). With products, the same principle applies. Stahel thus showed that reuse, repair, remanufacturing and recycling is financially advantageous in industrial settings (see FIGURE 5-2). Of course, this is nothing new. Stahel still readily admits that our ancestors were masters of reuse, repair, remanufacturing and recycling concepts (for example, the 18th-century maxim *waste not, want not*; and the early-19th-century adage *use it up, wear it out, make it do, or do without*).

Of course, the most important aspect of Stahel's discovery is that in the first stage of many manufacturing processes more money is usually spent on energy than labour *when it could be the other way around*. In other words, by extending the life of the materials that go into a product, or extending the life of the product itself, less energy is used, less waste and pollution is created, and more

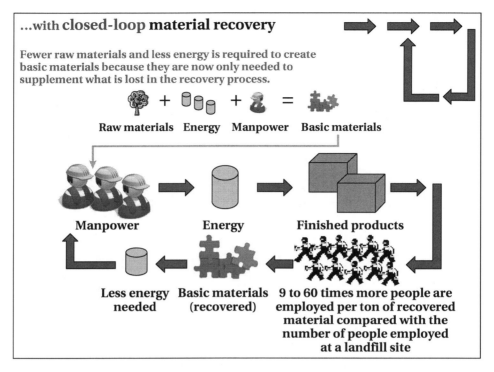

FIGURE 5-2: Closed-loop material recovery

people are employed – with no long-term increase in costs. Indeed, manufacturing costs tend to *decrease* with product life-extension practices.

To expand and build upon this discovery, Stahel and a colleague (Orio Giarini) founded the Geneva, Switzerland-based *Product-Life Institute* (www.product-life.org) to research and promote what they call a *service economy* (also known as a *lake economy* or a *functional economy*) with the idea that goods and materials should be used as long and as often as possible to promote a healthy, sustainable economy (the opposite of a service or lake economy can be likened to a *linear* or *river economy* in which raw materials, manpower and energy continuously flow along an insatiable manufacturing stream, are used for a short period of time, and end up as landfill).

Over thirty years of research has shown that there are two ways a more efficient 'lake economy' or 'service economy' can be created. The first is to reuse, repair or remanufacture products (including buildings), which facilitates job creation, and ultimately recycles materials and molecules (again, see FIGURE 5-2). The second is to optimize the performance a product provides by converting the product into a service so as to keep its materials in the hands of the manufacturer for as long as possible so they can be reused.

Benefit perception and service

Most people, when they purchase a product, are not interested in owning the product per se. Instead, they're seeking the *benefit* the product delivers. For example, when an airline passenger purchases a ticket, he or she seeks the benefit of traveling from one place to another; no one expects to purchase part of the plane. Similarly, when consumers buy home heating oil, most of them don't want to own and deal with a dirty, toxic and expensive liquid fossil fuel. Instead, they want the *heat* the oil provides – not the substance itself and certainly not the expense or the involvement of delivering, containing and burning the oil.

Adding service to the equation makes this concept even more intriguing.

Personalized service not only keeps customers coming back, it can also help a business keep track of the benefits its customers seek. For example, studies have shown that a business can lose 20% of its customers if its products are of poor quality; yet 66% can be lost if the service itself is perceived as being poor. Additional statistics claim that it costs five to ten times more to attract new customers than it does to retain old ones – and that the average company can lose half its customers every four years if it's not careful. Good service, therefore, is a powerful competitive advantage.

Putting benefit perception and service together

Safechem, a division of *Dow Chemical*, is a solvent distribution company that incorporates benefit perception and service into a portfolio range offered to general industries across Europe.[1] These services include waste collection and refinement, parts washing, oil collection, and chemical recovery and disposal. In short, *Safechem* is a service company. Its customers do not have to purchase the solvents they need to conduct their operations nor do they have to pay for costly application equipment or high disposal fees. Instead, *Safechem* focuses on the benefits its customers seek by travelling to the place where its customers work and applying their needed solvents for them. Afterwards, *Safechem* cleans up the work site, transports the used solvents back to *Safechem*, and cleans and/ or recycles everything that was used – including the solvents, the washers, the spray guns and the steel drums – in preparation for the next customer. By selling 'square metres of cleaning' rather than gallons of solvents, *Safechem*: (1) extends the life of its materials, (2) focuses on the benefits its customers seek, and (3) reduces waste and costs by reusing its materials instead of having to make (or buy) more. *Clean Harbors Environmental Services* in North America offers its customers similar services.[2]

The payoff for customers

Why would a customer want to choose a service (or the benefit a product provides) over a product itself? The incentives include:

- Only having to pay for what is actually needed,
- The avoidance of major equipment purchases,
- The avoidance of maintenance costs,
- The elimination of end-of-life equipment and waste disposal costs, and
- A reduction or elimination of inventory.

The payoff for the service provider

In 2004, the Austrian government commissioned two studies that looked into the potential profitability that chemical companies have in regards to offering a service rather than selling a physical product. Both studies concluded that over half of the 4,000 chemical companies in Austria would benefit by adopting a service program. Moreover, because of the efficiency inherent in a service system, it was estimated that chemical consumption in Austria could be cut by a third and the average company could expect cost savings equivalent to over $12,000 per year.[3] Bear in mind that although the chemical industry is being used extensively as an example in this chapter, chemical companies are not the only businesses that can benefit from a product-to-service arrangement. Similar schemes have been devised for home washing machines (the customer only pays for the number of washes), computers, cars, refrigerators – almost any product that is traditionally bought, used and thrown away.

The *Michelin* tyre company, for example, has moved into selling the *performance* of truck tyres rather than just tyres, because it can produce a long-life tyre that's easy to re-tread, thereby earning a higher profit. If a re-treadable tyre sold as a performance service can travel twice the distance (e.g. the distance the tyre can travel is sold rather than the tyre itself – with the tyre remaining under the control of the company), the company earns more money; whereas, if it produces and sells a longer-distance tyre, the buyer would probably not pay the higher price involved (to pay for R&D and disposal costs) and company turnover would decrease.

The hotel industry has benefited from a similar practice for years thanks to linen suppliers that provide a service rather than sell a product. Many hotels do not own their linens (sheets, towels, etc.). Instead, these items belong to a textile company that does the washing and repair with an average economic break-even point of around three years per item. In other words, the linens have to last at least three years before the company can make a profit so the company is driven to lease high-quality textiles that last longer. A similar example, called pay-by-the-hour, is found in the gas turbine industry. Once again, the benefits enjoyed by the service provider include:

- Control over the maintenance of the product and its equipment, which translates into long product life,
- The quality of the product increases (quality always increases with product-life extension for the simple reason that low-quality materials and products cannot be continuously reused),
- The lowering of unit production costs because not as many units have to be produced (which reduces material and energy consumption),
- Wastage is reduced to very low levels because money saved in waste reduction means lower costs and more profit for the provider,
- Revenues either increase or are solidified because services are usually needed by customers continuously throughout the year, whereas equipment purchases, particularly big-ticket items, are often only made during times when customers can afford them,
- A new dimension is added to the service provider's product portfolio package, which can provide a much-needed boost in company competitiveness,
- Skilled jobs are created (workers not needed on production lines can be trained as service appliers),
- The product itself is no longer moving as quickly toward landfill.

Resource extension is not just for manufacturers

Extending resources to maximize revenues can be applied in almost any setting – not just manufacturing – for the simple reason that the word 'resources' doesn't only refer to 'raw materials'. Indeed, 'resources' also pertains to information, labour, markets (customers), furnishings, machinery and so on. Seen this way, examples of resource extension can also involve:

- Reducing employee turnover,
- Extending the life and use of a building, office or workplace (including renting or subleasing areas or equipment that are not used or are only partially used),
- Locking in customers or markets with optimal customer service or other value initiatives,
- Expanding market share (perhaps via 'inclusive business' practices [see Chapter 14]),

- Finding new ways to use old or current data, and/or
- Creating or extending value in the long term by reusing, reworking (modifying) or adapting what your business currently has instead of throwing it away or abandoning it.

The hurdles

Obviously, turning a product into a service is not a one-size-fits-all concept nor is it a practice that can be adopted overnight. The standards, operations and procedures of the service provider must be adapted to work hand-in-glove with those of the service buyer to avoid dysfunctional conflict. Agreeing on a service fee is another formidable task that requires a full understanding of all operations and their costs. Additional service challenges exist in changing outdated behaviors and old ways of thinking; both the service provider and the customer may find it difficult to overcome institutional and personal stubbornness. Customers, for example, must break the habit of what Jonathan Chapman, senior lecturer at the *University of Brighton* (UK), calls 'adulterous consumption'. Chapman compares the possessions that consumers purchase with the idea of adultery. 'We make a commitment to one thing and then become distracted by a younger model,' he says, '[because nowadays] everything is temporary if we want it to be.'[4] What Chapman is referring to is the human desire to own products – even though this attachment often vanishes when a newer version becomes available. This throw-away-and-buy-another addiction is difficult to stop, not least because many businesses profit from, and promote, it. Indeed, the entire concept of 'Industrial design was specifically invented to convince people that their washing machine, their car, or the refrigerator they had was out of fashion,' says Walter Stahel.

When one takes into account the low prices of everyday durable goods the concept of closed-loop practices can become even more difficult to implement. 'You can't find anybody who will work on a microwave oven now,' laments Steve Cruciani, owner and operator of *Steve's Appliance Installations* in Berkeley, California. 'What's the point? For $65 you can get another one.'[5]

But the main reason why service concepts are of little interest to so many businesses (particularly small to mid-sized businesses) is the initial costs that can incur. Without a minimal density of goods on offer, turning products into a service can be difficult and expensive (examples of the costs incurred include: collecting, taking apart and remanufacturing used products – otherwise known as reverse logistics). Selling a product outright avoids these challenges because it delegates disposal responsibilities to the buyer. Even big companies can be turned off by turning a product into a service not least because it requires a uniquely different mindset. Large production-oriented businesses, for example, traditionally invest more in capital expenditures because they are geared toward a production setup that is intent on making as many products as possible. Service businesses, on the other hand, tend to invest more in research and development. A service setup can therefore pose difficulties in terms of resource allocation to an organization that wishes to do both. More to the point, becoming service-based requires long-term thinking and commitment, which goes against the short-term production strategy of many companies.[6]

Lastly, although a service-oriented selling system is applicable to more products than most manufacturing-oriented businesses would admit, sometimes turning a product into a service does not make sense. For example, a hardware store that sells drills may find it difficult to market and sell a hole-drilling service because the less expensive a drill is to buy, the more impractical and obsolete a hole-drilling service becomes. Moreover, a hole-drilling service may not be available when it's needed – or customers may want to drill holes on their own and conclude that owning a drill and having it on hand is more cost-effective than paying for a service. In these situations, equipment rentals can handle short-term customer requirements. In the long term, however, an alternative is needed that maximizes the benefits that turning products into services provides while avoiding the perceived stigma of non-ownership. And that, say several pro-service advocates, can be found in leasing.

6

Resource Extension Part 2: Leasing and the Performance Economy

'If it appreciates, buy it.
If it depreciates, lease it.'

John Paul Getty,
Billionaire

Some time after publishing his 'energy versus manpower' production ratio observation, industry analyst Walter Stahel coined the phrase 'cradle to cradle' to help explain his concept of a closed-loop or 'lake economy' (also known as a 'circular economy'). According to Stahel, in an ideal cradle-to-cradle (or closed-loop/circular) system, waste would not exist because waste would be seen as an asset in transition and be used as a raw material. In other words, when a well-designed product reaches the end of its useful life it would be returned to its manufacturer to be reused, repaired or remanufactured to facilitate job creation, reduce waste and further its profit potential. Today, many researchers credit the *Xerox* corporation with pioneering cradle-to-cradle practices in the 1980s by leasing photocopiers instead of selling them. The idea was to provide the company with a reliable source of parts and materials that could be used in remanufacturing 'closed-loop' processes.

Elsewhere, the *Collins & Aikman Floorcovering* company (now part of the *Tandus Group*) is widely considered to be the first business in the carpet industry to take the closed-loop plunge by collecting and breaking down old carpets into material for new carpets. Much to the company's surprise, making carpet backing from reprocessed carpet waste not only proved to be much cheaper than that made from virgin raw materials, the end product also turned out to be more stable, softer and easier to clean. This pivotal discovery reduced the company's raw material costs, resulted in a new and inspiring company motto ('Mining buildings rather than resources') and allowed *Collins & Aikman* to enjoy double-digit growth in both revenues and profits when the entire carpet industry was growing at about 4% a year.[1]

With old carpets proving to be a superior raw material source, it wasn't long before another multinational carpet maker, *Interface*, got in on the act. *Interface* makes 40% of all the carpet tiles sold on Earth, has manufacturing centres in 33 global locations, and sells carpets in 110 countries on six continents. This activity consumes a lot of raw materials and produces a lot of waste. Since most carpet-manufacturing processes require approximately one kilogram of fossil fuel to make about half a kilogram of carpet material, and because carpets can take up to 20,000 years or more to decompose, the head of *Interface*, Ray Anderson, decided that it would be in the best interests of his company to become both sustainable and restorative (i.e. to replenish the resources his company uses).

According to *Interface*, color, texture, comfort underfoot, acoustics, cleanliness, ambience and functionality are the reasons why most people wish to have a carpet. Since it's not necessary to own a carpet to obtain these benefits, *Interface* looked into how it could retain ownership of its products and the value of the materials, labour and energy that went into making them. To achieve this goal, *Interface* developed what it calls an 'Ever-Green Lease' in which the company focuses on leasing what a carpet is supposed to deliver rather than selling the carpet itself. Turning a product into a service demands a close relationship with customers in order to discover what they want in terms of service (also, the company needed to establish a steady supply of recyclable raw materials to make its leasing concept feasible) so employees at *Interface* realized they had to do some work. Through in-depth research, they discovered that most carpet wear occurs in heavily trafficked zones leaving areas around furniture and walls virtually untouched. This is good news for customers because it means that when a leased carpet begins to show wear, *Interface* will come in, pull up the worn areas, and immediately replace them (a service that is part of the lease arrangement). Customers are thereby relieved of the expense of purchasing a new wall-to-wall carpet as well as the time and bother of shutting down an entire work area while a new carpet is installed. Moreover, the customer is not responsible for the costs of disposing the old carpeting because *Interface* takes it back to its factory and uses it to make new carpets. Further cost reductions for *Interface* and its customers have come about as the company substituted oil-based carpet fibre materials with more environmentally friendly fibres that use less materials (and energy) and create less production waste.[2]

Although *Interface* admits that customers still balk at the misperceived notion that leasing a carpet is more expensive (the company insists it isn't), the payoff from its improvements have been enormous. By changing from a carpet-selling business to one that more resembles asset management and reclamation, *Interface*, which claims to be halfway to achieving its sustainability goals, nearly doubled company employment, doubled its profits and increased its stock price 550% over a five-year period.[3]

Not to be outdone, *DuPont* has developed a similar carpet-leasing program to enhance its carpet manufacturing subsidiary. *DuPont*'s leasing service includes free consultations, quick installation that minimizes business disruption, professional cleaning, and on-the-spot spill and stain removal. Furthermore, because *DuPont* runs several different manufacturing operations, fibres from its carpet reclamation process can also be used to manufacture auto parts and sound insulation products.[4]

It's not just photocopiers and carpets

Electronic equipment, paint, cars, wood pallets, reusable totes, furniture, rags and linens, parts washers, almost anything – including temperature – can be leased. The *Carrier* air-conditioning company in the USA, for example, leases cooling services to its clients rather than air conditioners.[5] As with any leasing arrangement, ownership of *Carrier*'s air-conditioning equipment is maintained by the company, which means that *Carrier* is highly motivated to keep its products in optimum condition. This means they last longer (which reduces costs). *Carrier* is further driven to ensure that the building where it administers its cooling service is energy-efficient because the more efficient the building the better and more cost-effective its product will be, which translates into higher profits for *Carrier*. Customers love the arrangement because *Carrier*'s commitment to increasing efficiency, reducing waste and lowering costs ultimately means lower all-around heating and cooling prices for consumers.

In a similar fashion, the *Bank of Japan* collaborated with Japanese power companies to facilitate the leasing of energy-efficient automobiles, home appliances and water heaters to everyday consumers. The aim is to encourage and promote the development of energy-efficient appliances while reducing the nation's energy requirements, carbon emissions and waste. Appliances that aren't efficient are not allowed into the program, which encourages the manufacturers of wasteful products (who want to be included in the program) to make their products more sustainable.

Does leasing always close the manufacturing loop?

Unfortunately, no. Sometimes a customer will purchase a leased product at the end of the lease term and never return it to the manufacturer. Similarly, after a transfer of ownership, the customer may sell the leased product on the second-hand market. Both of these practices can break the closed-loop cycle needed for leasing to provide its benefits. Additional problems include the fact that some products – such as inexpensive goods and short-lived consumables – are not seen as compatible with leasing. In this regard, products may need months or perhaps years of redesigning or rethinking before leasing can become profitable.[6]

Conclusions

Leasing is a long-term profit strategy that demands long-term thinking. Customer needs and desires must be ascertained, insurance and liability issues must be addressed, employee training must be ongoing, and an incentive must be provided for customers to return leased products to the lessor after use. If these issues are not addressed, the demands of EPR legislation (Extended Producer Responsibility), which requires manufacturers to take back their products (including packaging) after use or face legal consequences, can be difficult to achieve. With careful forethought and planning, however, under the right circumstances, leasing has proven to be a good way for companies to move closer to sustainability while lowering production costs, increasing revenues and decreasing waste.

7

Cooperative Networking

In Scotland, a construction business asks for (and receives) the ash waste from a nearby coal-fired electric plant, which it uses to manufacture building materials. In Australia, a building designer teams with a rival architectural firm, a renewable energy supply business, and a construction company to discuss affordable, energy-efficient homes. In the United States, a business that produces merchandise from wood enters into talks with a plastics injection firm to discuss recyclable packaging ideas. Further north, a consortium of northeastern and mid-Atlantic states discuss a cap-and-trade program to curb carbon emissions. What in the world is going on?

Cooperating businesses

Anyone who thinks sustainability is about being independent could not be more wrong. With increasing frequency, businesses (and governments) are discovering that by working together with carefully chosen partners each can accomplish what was impossible for just one on its own. This is particularly true with small businesses that need help with large-scale projects or those that lack the funding to take on more sustainable activities. The term used to describe the process of different businesses working compatibly with one another is *cooperative networking*.

The notion of working together to achieve a common goal has been around for thousands of years and is similar to what we call today *cooperatives*, *co-ops* or *collectives*. The purpose of this allows for a group of individual entities to join together to undertake an activity for the mutual benefit of all. One or more businesses can combine forces with either a competitor or a seemingly unrelated business (or both) to work together on a temporary or permanent basis. Several years ago, I conducted a survey in 14 countries which revealed that 42% of the small business operators questioned stated that they had at one time or another joined with other businesses (including competitors) in order to maximize profits; 7% of those who had not done so said they would like to do so in the near future.[1]

For the most part, the reason for joining a cooperative network is because going it alone requires considerable cost, effort and risk – all of which can be reduced when others get involved. In practice, the number of businesses cooperating together can range from two to over 100. Common goals include:

- Joint purchasing projects (purchasing materials in bulk as well as purchasing capital-intensive machinery, tools, production facilities and/or solar panels and wind turbines),

- Sharing resources and skills (sharing equipment or facilities, or pooling information, expertise or systems),

- Identifying and researching market opportunities (finding and tapping into customer bases previously not considered or combining one or more products or services with those of another business),

- Banding together to ask suppliers to produce sustainable or eco-friendly products and materials,

- Combining marketing resources and expertise (promoting the services and products of cooperative partners in advertising schemes, trade shows and promotional schemes),

- Combining logistics and operations (offering coordinated deliveries, designing new products, services or event packages, improving production capacity by sharing production lines, and so on), and

- Creating reuse or recycling programs (e.g. pooling waste to collect enough to make recycling feasible) and/or using the waste or discharge from one business as a raw material in another.[2]

Getting over the hurdle

The notion of cooperative networking often becomes more palatable once it's understood that cooperating is not about giving away trade secrets or merging with another business. Rather, it's about working with others in a complimentary fashion. The idea is to enhance the competitiveness of members, reduce costs, create new capital bases, increase advantages of scale, scope and speed, and open up new markets. For example, the *Recycled Products Purchasing Cooperative* operating out of Encinitas, California, works to promote the use of recycled paper in both the public and private sectors by running a purchasing cooperative that offers members information on services, prices, shipping, and the cost benefits of reusing paper waste.

Of course, as with most 'new' business practices, joining a cooperative network requires a different way of thinking – one that debunks the traditional go-it-alone business mindset, which dictates that every company must supply its own research, product design, marketing, office support, supply routes, financial functions, production processes, and management. For example, a sizeable number of agricultural producers have discovered that by working together they can purchase and share expensive planting and harvesting equipment, decide which crops should be farmed, work to reduce water usage, and even set a fixed price for wholesalers. This prevents having to needlessly compete against other growers. It also lowers costs, decreases risk in the marketplace, and ensures a fair outcome for each participant. The reported success and stability of cooperative networks, however, is perhaps the most enticing factor to those that join. Although cooperative networks are not infallible, businesses that cooperate are more apt to satisfy social and entrepreneurial objectives, avoid ethical and legal lapses, and, in general, be more economically vigorous and competitive, especially against larger rivals.[3]

What type of businesses prosper most?

The foremost indicator of a successful business network is a common purpose. For example, the *Tokyo Metropolitan Government*'s 'Municipal Environmental Protection Ordinance' in Japan developed a series of cooperative networks one of which involves a shared delivery system enjoyed by 15 different retail companies. By consolidating deliveries to the 30 stores owned by the 15 companies, the network reduced the amount of delivery vehicles on Tokyo's roads by 50%, which eased traffic congestion and reduced carbon emissions by 4,000 tons per year.

Getting started

How do networks begin? Two methods seem to dominate. The first method uses a third party such as a business development centre or a chamber of commerce to bring different entities together and propose working in unison. The *Chamber of Commerce* in Henrietta, New York, for example, initiated an education and assistance program with the *Audubon International Sustainable Communities Program* to help foster energy and waste reduction programs between local government, business and the community. *The San Francisco Bay Area Green Business Program* offers similar networking support.

The second approach to the creation of a network is more personal and involves the introduction of two or more like-minded businesspeople at a social gathering or a personal agreement between long-term acquaintances. Either way, the ingredients for a successful cooperating network revolve around mutual interests (and trust) combined with a can-do attitude.

Advantages and disadvantages of business networks

Of course, not every cooperative network is filled with sunshine and smiles. As with any group endeavour, cooperative networks are susceptible to people problems. For example, a network can collapse when a key player leaves or if members grow too like-minded and become immune to new ideas and new ways of thinking. Similarly, networks can contain some participants who take more than they give or there might be a general falling-out between individuals that results in the taking of sides. Claims have also surfaced that state that business networks can take a great deal of time to make decisions.

Supporters counter these arguments by insisting that it's easy to dismiss unproductive or disruptive participants and that the more brains that are brought to the table for the purpose of making a decision the better the resolution. Moreover, proponents of cooperative networking say that once decisions are made they're often carried out quicker and with more enthusiasm than those made in big corporations. This is because commitments and involvement tend to be stronger when they come from people who share a mutual interest and reach an agreement together.

By most accounts it appears that cooperative business networks operate under much the same principles, and therefore need the same forms of maintenance, as those required by teams. Additional advantages include:

- The establishment of improved communication pathways (if communication pathways are nurtured and encouraged),
- Increased human development and innovation (from the sharing of skills and experiences),
- Better long-range planning and experimentation due to the spreading of financial risk,
- The satisfying of social needs (i.e. cooperating business owners and managers do not feel alone),
- An increased feeling of openness and learning, which is fostered by a genuine interest in what other members have to offer,
- Strength in numbers,

- Increased feedback from customers, employees, and participants (usually because cooperating partners demand it),
- Improved problem solving due to in-depth discussion and implementation – particularly when it comes to servicing niche or specialized markets,
- Improved motivation (ample research shows that close personal business ties heighten empathy and increase altruistic behaviour[4]).

The rules of cooperative business networking

Most cooperative business networks rely heavily on relationship building. In other words, the same elements that create and foster human relationships (honesty, communication, straightforwardness, integrity, wisdom, honour, etc.) appear to be no different from those needed to maintain successful business relationships. Unfortunately, with marital divorce rates as high as 50% (or more) around the world, many people seem to be in the dark when it comes to relationship building. Perhaps the expectation is that a good relationship can unfold on its own with no real effort from the parties involved. The following suggestions are therefore put forward to help avoid problems:

1. *Be prudent and careful as to whom you wish to do business with.* Check the backgrounds of proposed partners and consult with others before shaking hands or signing on a dotted line.
2. *Be a good partner.* Instead of adopting a single-minded 'what's in it for me' attitude, balance the needs of your business against those of cooperating partners.
3. *Be honest and sincere.* Always try to exceed the expectations of your partners. Never inflate your business's abilities and never steal ideas or clients from cooperative partners.
4. *Take the initiative.* Rather than wait for partners to come to your aid, be the first to plan meetings, raise issues, tackle problems and introduce needs.
5. *Stay committed.* Enthusiasm, or the lack of it, are contagious. Offer referrals and information on a regular basis. Such actions tend to ensure that partners reciprocate in kind.
6. *Be reasonable.* Cooperative business networks are professional relationships and should not be considered as friendships. Keep partners close yet still at 'arm's length'.
7. *One step at a time.* Before joining a long-term cooperative business venture test-run the partnership by partaking in one or two short-term preliminary projects.

8

Lean Thinking

Lean thinking (also known as *lean manufacturing*) is a business philosophy that demands the total and systematic elimination of waste from every process, every department and every aspect of an organization. With lean thinking, however, waste is not defined as 'not obtaining 100% from purchases and investments'. Instead, waste is defined as 'the use or loss of any resource that does not lead directly to what it is that customers want' – and what customers want, say the advocates of lean thinking, is *value*. Any act or process in a business that a customer would balk at paying – or any process or act that can be eliminated without the customer noticing the difference – is often interpreted as having no value in lean thinking.

The *Dell Computer Company* is a classic example of a company that embraces the lean-thinking concept. *Dell* became a computer-manufacturing powerhouse by allowing customers to personalize their purchase before a sale was made. In other words, *Dell* produced its products *after* it received a customer order. Before it decided to branch out into retail markets, *Dell* had a paying customer for every product it sold. No expensive inventory of computers was stacked away in a warehouse awaiting transportation nor were any shop shelves filled with unsold products. *Dell* never got stuck with an unsold computer because only what its customers asked for was ever made. From the onset, one of *Dell*'s major production expenses involved maintaining a supply of parts to manufacture its products, but since these parts are designed for use in a variety of configurations every single one is always used sooner or later. Along with a focus on made-to-order merchandise, this allowed the company to decrease its overheads and concentrate on client-oriented matters[1] – all of which are hallmarks of lean thinking.

The wasteful practices inherent in businesses

According to the *Cardiff Business School*, only 5% of most business production operations are comprised of activities that directly relate to what customers want in a product or service.[2] This means that up to 95% of the activities in most businesses add no customer value at all.

Activities classified as 'non-value' can be split into two categories. The first, *necessary, but non-value adding activities*, constitutes as much as 35% of most organizational work and is comprised of actions that do not directly contribute to what customers want in a product (e.g. payroll, behind-the-scenes cleaning, the fulfilment of government regulations, and so on). The second category, *non-value adding activities*, can comprise up to 60% of work activities, yet these activities add no value to customers in any way, shape or form (e.g. production line snags, waiting periods, unnecessary paperwork, end-of-line quality inspections, etc.). The aim of lean thinking is to find and eliminate the wasting of time, labour, materials and money in both categories.

The origins of lean thinking

Lean manufacturing goes back a long way. In 1926, Henry Ford was reported to have said that one of the greatest accomplishments in keeping the price of his automobiles low was the shortening of their production cycle. The longer a product takes to manufacture, and the more it's moved about, he said, the greater the cost.

After the Second World War, Eiji Toyoda (of the car company that bears his family's name) took Ford's words to heart. Toyoda visited American car manufacturers to learn about their production methods and returned to Japan intent on practising what he'd learned. With the assistance of his colleagues, Taiichi Ohno and Shigeo Shingo, Toyoda spent years refining and continuously improving upon waste reduction. Eventually he hit upon the idea of trying to eliminate all the non-value tasks in his business for which customers were not willing to pay. Ohno in particular, became so good at eliminating waste while streamlining operations that the concepts and techniques he developed are now widely known as TPS (the *Toyota Production System*). Having witnessed American supermarket systems in the United States, Ohno came to realize that the scheduling of work should not be driven by production targets, but rather by sales. TPS concepts and techniques have since been reintroduced back into America under the umbrella of lean thinking or lean manufacturing.[3] In service firms such as banks, restaurants, hospitals and offices, lean-thinking concepts are referred to as 'lean enterprise'.

It is worth noting that in the mid-1990s *Toyota* more or less abandoned its model of focusing almost solely on solving customer issues and instead decided to embrace a common view in business (and business schools) that 'if you're not growing you're failing' and that being biggest is best. The subsequent strategy the company developed of borrowing huge amounts of money to become number one in production resulted in *Toyota* making itself extremely vulnerable to steep declines in demand, which is not akin to being 'lean'.[4] It has been said that *Toyota* is now returning to its original lean strategies.

Why go lean?

According to James Womack and Daniel Jones, authors of the book *Lean Thinking: Banish Waste and Create Wealth in Your Corporation*,[5] the lean process is highly supportive of human dignity and begins by reassuring employees that no jobs will be lost. Once that fear has been eliminated companies have been known to enjoy 400% *increases* in production and 400%–1,000% *decreases* in delays, inventories, accidents, defects, errors and scrap. Womack and Jones go on to claim that if a business cannot (1) quickly reduce its product development time by half, (2) cut its order processing time by 75%, and (3) decrease production times by 90%, then the business is doing something wrong.

Why does lean thinking elicit strong emotions?

Lean thinking contradicts a number of established production theories taught in business schools because it advocates making a shift from conventional 'batch and queue' production practices (i.e. the mass production of large lots of a product based on anticipated demand) to a 'one-piece flow' system that produces products in a smooth, continuous stream based on customer demand.[6] This means that customer wants must first be identified before manufacturing begins. Customer demand then 'pulls' a product or service through the manufacturing process rather than having the business push its mass-produced goods onto the market. Anything that does not contribute to the pull of customer demand is considered waste.

Typical forms of waste

Aichi Toyoda and his colleagues originally identified seven common forms of waste, but over time two more have been added. Today, the nine forms of waste that lean manufacturing seeks to reduce or eliminate are:

1. *Over-production*: which is defined as producing more information or product than a customer requires, or making the product or its components earlier than is required, or making it faster than required.

2. *Waiting*: the time spent waiting on materials or information.

3. *Moving items*: needlessly shifting, storing, stacking or filing materials and information, or needlessly moving people, materials and/or information from one point to another.

4. *Over-processing*: the time and effort spent processing information or material that does not add value to the product (e.g. unnecessary paperwork or employees and managers seeking approvals).

5. *Inventory*: any and all materials or information awaiting processing.

6. *Unnecessary motion*: any activity that does not add value to a product or service.

7. *Defects*: the unnecessary repairing, scrapping or reworking of material or information.

8. *Employee resistance*: the political posturing, stalling or passive resistance taken by employees in the hope that 'this project will also soon pass'.

9. *Under-utilizing people*: not involving all employees and not using everyone to their full potential.[7]

Starting the journey

Lean thinking is based on five principles that must be thoroughly understood and agreed upon before work can begin. They are as follows:

1. *Specify what the customer defines as value.* Anything that does not add value from a customer perspective should be reduced or eliminated.

2. *Draw up a value map.* A value map is much like a process map with one distinct difference: a value map starts from the customer end and makes a clear distinction between value-added activities (transformational activities for which the customer is willing to pay) and non-value-added activities (activities that add cost without adding customer value).

3. *Place all value-creating steps in a tight sequence so the product flows smoothly toward the customer.* On the shop floor, this may involve moving machines and equipment into a tight assembly-line sequence to minimize material and product movements. An additional explanation of this stage is often explained via the '6-S' model below.

   - *Sort.* Determine exactly what employees need to create customer value (tools, equipment, supplies, materials, etc.). Eliminate all other clutter.

Tools, production equipment and information systems should be right-sized so they produce exactly what is needed – no more, no less.

- *Stabilize* (or *Set-in-order*). Place tools, equipment, supplies and materials in logical sequences where they are needed rather than in off-to-the-side areas (in lean-thinking terminology this is called *Point-Of-Use-Storage* or *POUS*). Employees must take part in ensuring that the design, selection, correction and maintenance of every machine, tool and process is accurate and ready to perform without interruption.
- *Shine.* Inspect work areas and eliminate physical barriers so that everyone can see (literally) what is going on. This allows for further introspection and observation.
- *Standardize.* Reduce all variations, integrate processes, use standardized parts and materials where appropriate, establish uniform delivery schedules, make performance measures transparent, and empower each manufacturing unit so that it has the capability to produce exactly what is required without having to move along multiple work centers.
- *Safety.* Develop and maintain a strict adherence to safety concerns, teachings and practices.
- *Sustain.* Enforce a continuous commitment to change with robust planning, regular inspections, much patience, trial-and error allowances, and a good reward and recognition program.

4. *As flow is introduced, let customers pull value from the next upstream activity.* While wasteful activities are being reduced or eliminated, shift the business's efforts toward letting the customer determine production quantities. Remember, the point of lean thinking is to create an enterprise that is responsive solely to providing what paying customers want, when they want it. No more, no less. This type of setup demands:

- The building and maintenance of strong relationships with customers and suppliers,
- A streamlining of entire systems – not just parts of the system,
- The removal or reassigning of anchor draggers (people or processes that slow down operations),
- Immediate results from everyone,
- Informing people that two steps forward and one step backward is okay; no steps forward is not okay,
- The circulation of lean-thinking strategies in every department and procedure,
- The creation of a lean accounting system,
- Paying employees in relation to their performance, and
- Asking suppliers and customers to also think lean.

5. *Keep going.* Just as with quality and efficiency, there is no finish line associated with lean thinking. Never stop observing, analyzing, questioning and improving.[8, 9, 10]

Ready to begin?

Many experienced lean thinkers suggest kick-starting the lean process via the following:

1. Find a leader who is willing to take responsibility for the lean transformation.
2. Research lean-thinking practices and inform *everyone* about them (i.e. initiate a training program).
3. Find a change agent (a wasteful practice or a bottleneck area) or locate (or create) a crisis for which action must be taken, or select a pilot project and run it for a few months during which time you can evaluate, review, and learn from, your mistakes.
4. Involve others and begin making changes as soon as possible. Don't procrastinate and don't waste time establishing any grand plans. Just do it.

The role of the manager

According to lean-thinking advocate Jim Womack, the manager's role in lean thinking is to eagerly embrace the role of problem-solver. This means visiting actual situations, asking about performance issues, seeking out root causes, and showing respect for lower-level managers (as well as colleagues) by asking hard questions until good answers emerge. Most importantly, the lean manager realizes that no manager at a higher level can or should solve a problem at a lower level (Womack calls this one of the worst abuses of lean management). Instead, the role of the higher-level manager is to help the lower-level manager tackle problems through delegation and dialogue by involving everyone involved with the problem. The lean law of organizational life is that *problems can only be solved where they exist, in conversation with the people whose actions are contributing to the problem* (which requires support, encouragement and relentless pressure from the higher lean manager). The lean manager also realizes that problem-solving is about experimentation by means of 'plan–do–check' with the expectation that mistakes do happen and that experiments yield valuable learning that can be applied to the next round of experiments. Lastly, the lean manager knows that no problem is solved forever. New things generally introduce more problems – which is necessary to enable probing minds to continue the perfection process.

Lean-thinking weaknesses

Despite much positive press, lean thinking has inherent weaknesses (both physical and behavioural) that must be prepared for. The good news, advocates say, is that these weaknesses can be avoided if addressed in advance.
Physical weaknesses include making lean changes in production when:

- The design of the product or service is not ideal,
- The product or service is not economical,
- Customers are not satisfied with the current design of the product, and
- The product's configuration does not fulfil the functional requirements of the market or the consumer.

Behavioural weaknesses include:

- Management does not support and nourish change,
- Measurement is not taking place,
- Lean-thinking methodology is seen or addressed as a tertiary or secondary issue,
- Managers and employees are not rewarded for the improvements they make, and
- The values of the business are not in sync with lean-thinking concepts.[11]

Lean thinking summarized into ten concise steps

1. Eliminate waste.
2. Minimize inventory.
3. Maximize flow (streamline processes).
4. Determine and meet customer requirements.
5. Pull production from customer demand.
6. Do everything right the first time.
7. Empower workers.
8. Allow for changes to be made rapidly.
9. Partner with suppliers.
10. Create a culture of continuous improvement.[12]

For more information about lean thinking visit the *Lean Thinking Institute* at www.lean.org. The international arm of the *Lean Thinking Institute* is located at www.leanglobal.org.

9

The Waste-First Rule: Resource Extension Begins with Waste Elimination

Every one of the practitioners interviewed for this publication (including sustainability pioneer Ray Anderson, the founder of *Interface* carpets, who died in 2011) stated that before a business begins 'closing its loops', it must first establish a thorough and permanent waste elimination and prevention program at the core of its operations. My students hear this so much from me that they have christened it 'Scott's Law'. The following examples (the first is theoretical, the second is real) explain why eliminating and preventing waste as a first step toward sustainability is so important.

Imagine that a business has decided to reduce its energy costs by investing in renewable energy equipment (see 'Volatile energy prices' in Chapter 1, and all of Chapter 19). Imagine also that the company needs 1,000 kilowatt-hours of electricity per month to run its operations. If the business wants to become energy-self-sufficient, this means that it will have to purchase enough solar voltaics, wind turbines or fuel cells to produce 1,000 kilowatt-hours of electricity every month. Or maybe not.

Keep in mind that 1,000 kWh per month is what the business needs now. After it conducts a waste elimination program it may discover that it can get by using much less electricity. Indeed, according to David Klockner, vice-president of *ENERActive*, 'During the nineteen years I've worked to help businesses lower their energy consumption, I've conducted thousands of energy assessments and have found that it's quite possible to reduce the energy needs of buildings and factories by 35% or more.'[1]

Using Klockner's observations, we can therefore realistically estimate that if the business conducts a waste-energy elimination program *before* it purchases its new renewable energy equipment, it might lower its energy consumption (by 35%) to 650 kWh per month, which means that it now needs fewer solar panels, or a smaller wind turbine, or fewer fuel cells to meet its energy requirements.

In their seminal book *Natural Capitalism* (Little, Brown & Company, 1999), sustainability pioneers Paul Hawken, Amory Lovins and Hunter Lovins relay the true story of an 18,581 m^2 office building in Chicago which replaced its 20-year-old windows with energy-efficient 'super-windows' that let in more daylight and reduced solar heat. As a result, the cooling load of the building was reduced by 85%. The old climate control system was then replaced with a more efficient model that was three-fourths smaller and a quarter of a million dollars cheaper – and required 75% less energy to operate – thereby saving the building hundreds of thousands of dollars annually in energy costs. The same principle applies to production processes.

If a waste assessment is conducted before a business purchases new production equipment or machinery, it may be discovered that less machinery requiring less energy can be used and that fewer resources and support materials are needed (see the *Boeing* examples in Chapter 24). In fact, eliminating and preventing waste as a first step before resource extension often leads to profitable, previously unforeseen results as the following examples demonstrate.[2]

A team of employees at *DuPont*'s Edge Moor, Delaware, plant established a goal of zero waste and in the process developed a new iron-rich co-product from a former waste stream. When the goal of zero waste was obtained, the plant's 100 acre landfill site was shut down leading to cost savings of $5 million annually. The old landfill site has since been converted into a wildlife habitat.

A printing-and-publishing and integrated-operations team from Parlin, New Jersey, designed, tested and implemented a new system to recycle acetone/water waste solvent back into a production process for manufacturing toners. As a result, waste from drum disposal was reduced by 95%, $180,000 in capital expenses was avoided, the business saved $150,000 in annual costs, and the potential for worker spills and exposure to toxins was reduced.

In Brazil, a worker at a *DuPont* subsidiary developed an industrial process that converted a solid chlorinated organic residue into two commercial products (propanil and 3,4 diochloro aniline). $10 million was thus saved annually by eliminating waste storage and incineration of the original residue. Moreover, the commercial products pulled in revenues of $7 million per year, and 35 full-time jobs were created.

A specialty chemicals team at one of *DuPont*'s Delaware plants identified, characterized, tested and implemented a novel form of carbon from Russia that proved to be a much better production catalyst for phosgene then the previous carbon catalyst. CC14 emissions were thereby reduced by 84%, operating costs were lowered by $300,000 annually, and the new process saved the business $2 million because it did not have to build a special incinerator to destroy the plant's previous emissions.

The moral of the story? A thorough waste elimination and prevention program should *always* be implemented before 'improving' a production process or program or purchasing new machinery or equipment. Ignoring this rule can result in wasted purchases, higher operating costs and unnecessary disposal costs. Also keep this in mind when improving supply chains and customer use stages.

Waste comes in all shapes and sizes

Waste (not achieving 100% of purchases and investments) can take many forms, including: lost time, missed opportunities, unseen benefits, and resources (including people) not being used to their full potential. For example, in his book ***Stepping Up: How Taking Responsibility Changes Everything*** (Berrett-Koehler, 2012), author John Izzo states that when employees are excluded from decision-making, innovation, and idea creation they tend to withdraw from improvement processes, but when they are listened to and get involved, they can contribute significantly to productivity, retention and innovation. An example of this is seen in the development of the *Starbucks* frappuccino. The idea for the drink was suggested by front-line employees, yet the corporate office rejected it out of hand until one store manager decided to follow the instincts of the employees and experiment with the idea. The result was a billion-dollar product for *Starbucks*. Viewed through the prism of waste elimination leading to resource extension, this series of events clearly demonstrates that by recognizing and acting upon the potential of employees (read: not wasting people), *Starbucks* got more use out of its equipment, its labour force and its stores (read: extending its resources) in the form of producing and selling a profitable new product.

In a similar vein, researchers at the *Massachusetts Institute of Technology* are working to double the battery life of smartphones by reducing the electricity needs of the phone rather than focusing on the battery (read: eliminating waste to extend the life of the battery rather than making the battery bigger). *Eta Devices*, an offshoot of MIT, discovered that the power amplifiers in most smartphones waste as much as 65% of the energy they use because, when the phone transmits data, the amplifiers jump from standby mode to a high-power output signal mode, which can cause signal distortion. Standby power is therefore set at a high level, which helps reduce the distortion. The downside is that setting standby power on high saps the battery – and, with some phones (e.g. Apple's iPhone 5) using as many as five amplifiers, the result is a battery that needs constant charging. The proposed solution (called 'asymmetric multilevel out-phasing') works by having a special chip automatically select the right level of voltage needed by certain inner workings at any given time, which minimizes power consumption. In other words, by working to eliminate unnecessary electricity use within the phone, the phone's most critical resource (electricity storage) is extended.[3]

One more time...

Not long ago, I was teaching entrepreneurship and business plan writing to a group of executives at the *Rotterdam School of Management*. One day after class, two attendees approached me to discuss a business idea that involved encasing inefficient furnaces and boilers in factories with low-grade technology that converted wasted heat into electricity. Their research had concluded that the number of poorly designed and badly insulated furnaces and boilers around the world was staggering so the target market was huge. I asked them how much the wasted energy was worth compared to the amount of electricity it generated – and at that moment they realized the fault in their idea. Without question, the raw material (wasted fuel) was worth more than the envisioned end product (electricity). Once again, the moral of the story is that it's usually far more profitable for a business to stop wasting its resources than to try and sell or convert the results. Such is what all too often happens when a business tries to 'close its loops' before eliminating its waste.

Please refer to the 'Production' section of this publication for more examples of how eliminating and preventing waste can lead to dramatic (and often unforeseen) cost savings in production processes.

PRESERVATION

Preservation is defined as:

- The process of keeping something in existence,
- To keep up or maintain something,
- The act of protecting or safeguarding something from harm or injury,
- Keeping possession of, or retaining, what currently exists.

Any way it's looked at, preservation is not about standing still. In a business context, sustainability demands that two forms of preservation take place. The first is *internal* and involves the collection and analysis of real-time measurement in production processes and product use. The second form is *external* and includes keeping ahead of laws and legislation, industry improvements, directives from customers (e.g. 'scorecards' insisting that packaging or toxins be reduced), disruptive trends, and other forms of change.

10

Mapping the Waste-Elimination Process

Trying to eliminate waste in an organization without first conducting some form of reconnaissance is comparable to hacking one's way through a jungle without a map. Put another way (as one practitioner explained it), without in-depth knowledge of what you're looking at and what you want to do, trying to find wasteful practices in a business is akin to wandering around in circles pointing out superficialities. For this reason, Walter Stahel and I both advocate creating a sustainability *process map* (also known as a *process flow chart*) to help lay a strong foundation before application begins.[1]

Almost any production setup or work process in any organizational setting will benefit from being mapped. including service businesses, factory assembly lines, farms, offices, schools and food production. When done correctly, a process map usually reveals clarifying facts and figures about consumption and waste, including:

- *Raw materials* (including the amounts of whatever is needed to collect, process, and ship them),

- *Manufacturing processes* (including manpower needs, material use, energy use, and waste creation),

- *Packaging requirements* (the amount of paper, plastic, Styrofoam and other materials being consumed),

- *Transportation needs* (the amount of energy used to shift materials from one place to another),

- *Maintenance* (the chemicals, energy and water needed to use, maintain, and/or clean whatever is being produced), and

- *Use and disposal methods* (a description of how the product is thrown away as well as the current and future costs involved).[2]

Because gathering and mapping an organization's production activities requires effort and usually involves more participation and time than originally envisioned, obtaining the input of the many different people involved in the activities being examined is crucial. Henri Miller, a famous American painter and novelist, once said that 'in this age, which believes that there is a shortcut to everything, the greatest lesson to be learned is that the most difficult way is, in the long run, usually the easiest'. Keep Miller's words in mind when mapping a work process.

Laying the groundwork

Don't worry if you or your employees have no experience putting together a process map. Practice makes perfect. Experienced practitioners suggest using post-it notes to start the process. Displaying work processes on post-it notes and rearranging them on a big board makes it easy to move and add new information. Again, remember to obtain input from as many people as possible. You're bound to miss something if you go it alone. FIGURE 10-1 shows how a mapping process can start.

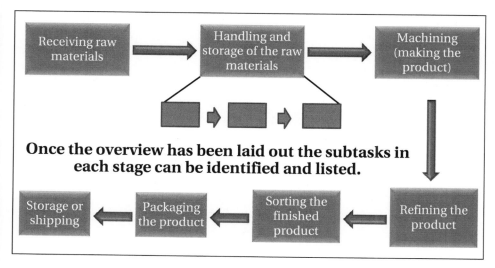

FIGURE 10-1: Overview of a seven-stage manufacturing process
© 2008 Jonathan T. Scott

Analyzing every stage of production

After every stage of production has been laid out, the next phase is to break the stages down into subtasks for further analysis. List and describe every activity in the order that it occurs. Examine how these activities impact one another and measure and record the amount and costs of *every* production unit input and output (see FIGURE 10-2). Measuring and recording all inputs and outputs includes weighing or counting (in terms of units or financial amounts) how much is consumed as well as how much is produced and discarded. Use this information to create baseline statistics against which future measurement can be judged. Nothing should be seen as trivial. For example, one of my students visited a company to conduct his waste reduction research and discovered that employees used mobile phones to communicate with one another in different parts of the plant. A quick search on the Internet revealed that the mobile phones could easily be replaced with cheaper walkie-talkies, powered by rechargeable batteries, which would drastically cut the business's phone bills. 'Everyone stopped laughing at my waste reduction suggestions after that,' the student said.

Examples of waste measurement statistics include: utility and fuel bills, the number of trash bags the business fills daily (placing similar items of garbage into separate containers makes this process easier), water consumption figures, raw material invoices, and so on.

A common way to measure (and appreciate) the amount of physical waste a department or business disposes is to 'dumpster dive' (i.e. collect and examine what has been thrown away).[3] 'Once you've seen your garbage up close its hard to ignore it,' says Shira Norman, a research consultant with *YRG Sustainability*. As if to prove her point, for over 12 years, the *Bentley Prince Street* carpet company (a division of *Interface*) has forced employees to record what they toss in the trash by sifting through company rubbish (a different department is selected to do this every month). Examining the company's rubbish makes it easy to determine what can be reduced, reused, reincorporated back into production, or sold to a recycler. The company now only orders snacks from vending machine suppliers that take back their packaging – a move that has greatly reduced the amount of rubbish in office bins.[4]

Keep it simple

The term 'process mapping' is not normally used by practitioners when they describe the activity of investigating and recording inputs and outputs of work processes for waste minimization purposes. 'We just study our utility bills and look in our garbage bins to see the amounts of waste being produced,' one practitioner explained to me, 'then we make a note where it comes from. We don't

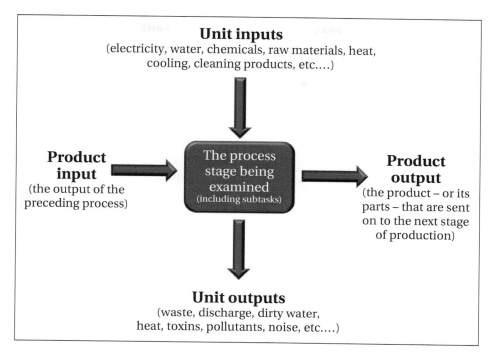

FIGURE 10-2: Production unit analysis
© 2008 Jonathan T. Scott

make maps.' When it was suggested that collecting waste data, determining its origins, and recording it (to make improvements) is indeed a form of process mapping, he (and several others) conceded. The message? Don't overload your waste-reduction process map with symbols, technical jargon or academic markings that render it incomprehensible. Most business will find it difficult to profit from a map that only a handful of employees understand.

Calculating carbon footprints

Calculating a 'carbon footprint' (i.e. the amount of carbon dioxide a process creates) is a trendy way to measure carbon emissions with the added benefit that, when lowered, the numbers can be used in public relations campaigns or to prove compliance with emissions legislation. Employees usually enjoy seeing how their efforts help reduce environmental degradation so displaying carbon emission reductions alongside other relevant data can help create motivation and a strong sense of achievement. For more information about carbon footprints and their calculation, consult the free online calculators available on the websites of reputable environmental organizations, government departments and/or reliable energy organizations (note: make sure that your calculations take into account the energy practices and energy sources of your specific country or region).

Involve everyone and examine everything

After the data from measurement is collected, it's time to sit down with colleagues and ask some tough questions. What types of waste are being produced? How much waste is there? Why does the waste exist? What can be done about it? Note that these questions are merely the beginning. The resulting answers (and additional questions) as well as any perceived disruptive changes should not be considered as painful obstacles, but rather as the path to success. The idea is to stay ahead of the rising bar being set by astute competitors, increasing legislation, and other exterior influences. Being reactive and playing catch-up is not a viable business strategy. Your business's never-ending goal is to stop paying for more resources than it needs and to stop producing stuff (i.e. non-product) it can't sell. Everything the business does should be questioned. If your business is a financial institution you'll need to discuss whether or not you want to buy from, invest in, or lend money to, businesses that ignore the financial advantages of sustainability. If your business is in the manufacturing sector, what affect will rising raw material and energy costs have on production? What will happen when oil hits $150 a barrel – or $200 – or $300? What will you do if a tax is put on carbon emissions or a chemical you use? What will happen if the local landfill site suddenly refuses to accept the waste your business produces? What if a cleaner, more efficient system or process is invented in the industry? What will happen when local and/or national environmental laws tighten?

Don't make the mistake of assuming that your business (or industry) is exempt from the need for waste elimination and sustainability-based (long-term) thinking. An example of this was vividly brought to life in 2012 when I was invited to speak to a group of insurance company executives about sustainability. During the presentation, I showed a picture of a house that had been swept away by a sea of toxic fly ash when the lake-size containment area it was being stored in ruptured after several days of rain.

'What does this have to do with us?' asked one of the executives in attendance, 'this is an example of an externalized cost. It has nothing to do with us.'

For several seconds I stared at the man in disbelief. 'Technically speaking there's no such thing as externalized costs,' I replied, 'because someone, somewhere eventually has to internalize them.' I pointed again at the picture on the screen, which depicted in graphic detail what is widely considered as the second-worst industrial accident in the history of the United States. 'Who do you think was the first person the owner of this destroyed home phoned after the dust settled?' I asked.

Several seconds of silence followed before one of the executives at the far end of the room replied in a low voice, 'His insurance broker.'

Needless to say, the attendees became much more interested in waste elimination after that.

Taking it to the next level

Once you've examined your business from top to bottom, it's time to start searching for similar weaknesses up and down your supply chain and in the customer use stage (FIGURE 10-3). Higher fuel prices, increasing raw material costs, and changes in legislation may not affect your business directly, but what happens when your suppliers are hit hard? Working with suppliers and paying customers on a regular basis to eliminate waste can help lower costs for everyone concerned both in the short term and long term.

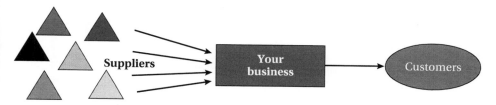

FIGURE 10-3: Map and examine the entire supply and demand picture

For example, as stated in a previous chapter, *Wal-Mart* has cut $3.4 billion from its annual waste disposal costs by ordering suppliers to reduce their packaging by 5%.[5] At the other end of the spectrum (the customer use stage), *Procter & Gamble* discovered that 85% of the energy required to use its laundry products occurred at the customer end and involved heating water. As a result the company developed a new product (*Tide Coldwater*) that enables customers to reduce their energy costs by cleaning their clothes with cold water. An added extra is that this innovation makes the product more environmentally friendly.[6] It is one of seven sustainable products that helped the company generate more than $7 billion in sales within one year.

Don't make the mistake of believing that your business is exempt from waste elimination and prevention. You may not be manufacturer, but that doesn't mean you can't reap the benefits of eliminating and preventing waste. As mentioned in Chapter 2, waste can acquire countless non-physical forms including: fraud, unnecessary risk, damages, preventable financial claims, investment losses, human error, weaknesses (or redundancies) in processing systems, poor service, lawsuits, bad customer relations, etc. – all of which can, and do, waste huge amounts of money.

11

Ongoing Measurement and Record-Keeping

In 1979, *Sierra Nevada Brewing Company* founders Ken Grossman and Paul Camusi cobbled together a brewery using second-hand dairy tanks, equipment salvaged from defunct beer businesses, and a soft-drink bottling machine. Today, *Sierra Nevada* employs over 450 people and produces nine award-winning types of beer, ale and stout. According to *Sierra Nevada*'s sustainability coordinator, Cheri Chastain, regular measurement helps determine where the company is wasting water, electricity and other resources as well as where physical waste is being produced. After a waste source is revealed, Cheri then works with teams of company employees to reduce it. 'Record keeping is absolutely critical for keeping track of progress,' she explains. 'I keep detailed spreadsheets for all of our sustainability related programs. Without records, there's no way to know what whether or not we're improving and reaching our goals.'[1]

Typical measurements recorded by *Sierra Nevada*'s waste reduction program that have helped the company save millions of dollars annually include:

- The amount of material that is recycled through the company's various vendors (which includes weight measurements as well as income received),
- The amount of material that the company reuses (by volume [quantity or weight] – as well as what part of the company it went to), and
- The amount of material sent to landfill by weight (based on waste hauler invoices).

To round out *Sierra*'s waste measurements, greenhouse gas inventories are also kept. 'The amount of water produced and electricity consumed, as well as our natural gas and water consumption figures – and carbon emissions – are then compared to the number of beer barrels we produce every month,' Cheri says, 'all of which provides me with some great ratios to work with.'

As Ms. Chastain has discovered, it's difficult, if not impossible, to know how much waste a company produces, how much waste it has eliminated, or how much money it has saved without accurate, ongoing record-keeping. For many companies, this involves scrutinizing toxic or hazardous material purchases (as well as usage costs), examining the amount (and types) of waste different departments or processes produce (usually by recording what each one throws away), and investigating the fees, extraneous charges and taxes associated with current waste-handling practices.

The requirements of a good record-keeping system

Simplicity is the key to sound measurement. Additional suggestions include:

- The system should be easy to understand,
- Information and results should be expressed in real time,
- Collected data should be accurate, reliable and essential,
- The entire system should be easy to use (i.e. more time should be spent pursuing efficiency rather than keeping records), and
- All information should be easily transferable (i.e. easily shared and compared with other departments and employees).[2]

Transparency involves displaying the results of measurements. Accessibility involves making this information available and readable. Apart from providing informative feedback, regular monitoring shows that a business is serious about sustainability. Accessible, transparent measurement has also been known to create friendly competitions between employees or departments as teams try to outdo one another to reduce waste and resource use. For example, the *Intercontinental Hotel Group* acquired a new software system from *SolveIT-Labs*[3] that focuses on over 40 sustainability-based practices that its hotels can adopt – thereby enabling its 4,000 properties to clearly see ongoing electricity usage along with suggestions on how to reduce it by up to 25% (a savings of over $200 million annually). As a bonus, the system keeps a visual track of the energy savings at all *Intercontinental* hotels so managers can compare their results with others. Similarly, the waste-free *Subaru* plant in Lafayette, Indiana (USA), makes waste-reduction results an integral part of plant manager performance evaluations.

Environmental audits

Just as the process of mapping out a work system isn't called process-mapping by waste-minimization practitioners, when setting out to gather and/or check sustainability facts and figures, many practitioners don't refer to what they're doing as an *audit*. The word 'audit', however, is appropriate even though most accounting systems fall far short of what an understanding of sustainability requires (e.g. clean air has no financial value, but try living without it). Professional auditors go a step further, using the term *environmental audit* to describe the gathering, checking and analysis of material use – as well as the measuring of waste and emission levels. Make no mistake, despite the fact that the word 'environment' makes up the name, environmental audits are similar to financial audits in that they are very effective in reducing waste. Likewise, environmental audits can be performed by either trained employees or licensed professionals and they come in all shapes and sizes ranging from a simple checklist to a comprehensive investigation of a company's operations. Typical areas of examination include:

- Facility inspections,
- The collecting, analyzing and explaining of data,
- Communicating with contractors, customers, regulators and suppliers,
- The measurement of key environmental parameters,
- Going over internal records, policies, reports and objectives,
- Comparing audit results to industry standards (such as *ISO 14001* standards and guidelines), and
- Employee skills, thoughts and motivation levels.
- Additional services can include degrees of compliance with environmental laws and regulations, uncovering the expectations of customers, and liability obligations.[4]

Types of environmental audits

According to the American *Environmental Protection Agency*, the six most common audits performed by professional environmental auditors are the:

- *Acquisition audit.* An audit performed before or after a major purchase is made (the purchase can include another company, an area of land, and/or a major piece of equipment). The focus of an acquisition audit is usually on potential claims or liabilities – particularly regarding environmental damage – that can arise from a major purchase.

- *Compliance audit.* Usually part of an overall assessment with an emphasis placed on compliance with environmental legislation and comparisons with ISO 14004 environmental management systems.

- *Due diligence audit.* Similar to an acquisition audit in that an assessment is carried out to determine potential legal claims and liabilities (usually for potential investors). Health, safety and fire risk assessments are also included as well as site history analysis and legislative reviews.

- *Waste audit.* The emphasis here is on exploring waste creation and handling (i.e. ensuring that waste is handled safely and stored safely at a reasonable cost) as well as the origin and reason for the waste and its production. Hidden waste such as unused raw materials, wasted energy and water, and wasted time are also taken into consideration.

- *Waste disposal audit.* Often undertaken to comply, in part, with 'Duty of Care' regulations to investigate the transport and disposal of waste by contractors. During the first part of this audit, waste management documentation is usually the first thing that is checked (e.g. waste management licenses, waste carrier licenses, and duty of care reports).

- *Water audit.* Similar to a waste audit, however, the focus is on water wastage. Onsite water use is analyzed as well as wastewater production and treatment. Water intake is measured and compared with output. Discrepancies signify leakage or other problems.[5]

- *Peer review audit.* An audit conducted by colleagues from outside the plant or factory. For example, General Electric runs annual 'Green Factory' inspections performed by other GE factory managers.

Despite a growing acceptance of environmental auditing, it's not uncommon to hear practitioners say that the results they obtained from an outside environmental audit did little more than reaffirm what had already been discovered by their own efforts. As one practitioner put it, 'When we conduct a waste audit we not only measure the amount of waste produced we also know exactly where the waste came from. An outside auditor who does not have specific expertise in certain fields or equipment can only measure it.' That being said, some businesses that have been successfully reducing their waste levels for years sometimes feel the need to step back and ask an outside specialist to provide a second opinion, reveal a new way of thinking, or perhaps instigate a more serendipitous outcome.

Environmental audits don't hurt

According to companies that have undergone an environmental audit, the process is relatively painless. Particularly for first-timers, there is no shame in admitting a lack of knowledge regarding the full range of business operations in terms of regulatory compliance, energy and resource use, raw material sourcing, supply-side issues, the creation and delivery of products and services, the inputs and outputs of offices and/or production facilities, cost relationships with suppliers, and subjects related to environmental management. For example, the *Glasgow Housing Association* in Scotland (the largest social landlord in the UK) had a first-time environmental audit performed at its headquarters by the *British Safety Council*, which identified over $51,000 in savings. In the process several waste minimization plans were developed, a library of resources was created, recommendations were made to get employees involved in an efficiency drive, and waste reduction goals were set.[6]

Seen this way, an environmental audit can lead to cost savings that more than pay for the price of the audit. *Genzyme Diagnostics*, for example, a biotechnology company in the UK, had an environmental audit performed that uncovered over $80,000 in potential annual savings resulting from waste elimination suggestions, reuse and recycling tips, and lighting and water-use reduction measures.[7]

Getting started

- *Communicate the goals of the audit to everyone beforehand.* Inform employees in every department what will be done and why.
- *Identify the parameters of the audit.* Determine what will be studied: Waste? Water? Energy? One program? The entire facility?
- *Establish measurement metrics.* How will the audit's findings be recorded? How will waste be measured (in units, in monetary terms…)? Determine these issues before an audit begins.
- *Establish a 'no blame' policy.* Keep the emphasis on discovery rather than assigning blame.
- *Carry out the audit during normal, everyday operations* to ensure that the figures are accurate.
- *Verify and review the results.* Check finished work and measurements and review with all concerned.
- *Discuss the results.* Bring employees together, ask questions, identify areas that need improvement, gather improvement suggestions, and share successes when they've been achieved.
- *Repeat the process.* After agreeing on goals and objectives, set a date for the next audit and review the results. Audits should be conducted on a regular basis.[8] Just don't fall into the trap of placing more time and effort into creating measurement statistics than performance results.

For more information

Look for specialized private companies, government agencies and academic institutions with experienced staff (always conduct a thorough background check before hiring a professional service). For more information, contact:

- An *Environmental Protection Agency* (example: www.epa.gov).
- The *Global Reporting Initiative* (www.globalreporting.org)
- The *Institute of Social and Ethical Accountability* (www.accountability21. net)

12

Taxes and Legislation

When setting a tax, the idea is to match price with cost. Unfortunately, the cost of what's *heavily* taxed, what's *minimally* taxed, and what's *not* taxed sometimes doesn't square up. For example, a chemical that sells for $20 per kilo may be subject to minimal taxes to encourage sales on an industrial scale, but what is the chemical's true cost when it makes its way into water, food supplies and human bodies? (In a sustainability-based accounting system, health and medical damages resulting from improper disposal would be placed under 'disposal/future costs', which is one of the three major costs a business should strive to eliminate as depicted at the bottom of diagram A-2 on page 5 of the Introduction.) Of course, raising money isn't the only function taxes perform. Taxes also carry the potential to *discourage* the sale of the items or activities being taxed (which is why high taxes are often placed on alcohol and tobacco). Unfortunately, when taxes are placed on items or activities that people consider *valuable* they can have the same effect. Consider the duty placed on employees as a case in point. Most businesses are taxed, in part, on the number of individuals they employ (a practice that began in 19th-century Germany). Therefore, the more people a business hires the more taxes it has to pay. Equally as mind-boggling is the fact that the more a person works the more taxes he or she pays (in the USA alone, two-thirds of personal income tax – which constitutes 80% of the tax funds raised by the US government – is derived from the sale of labour). What effect does this have on consumer spending (the engine that drives a nation's economic growth)?

Making taxes pull double duty

For years, a growing number of independent thinkers have been proposing that current tax structures could be put to better use. The idea is simple: to tax what society wants *less* of (e.g. pollution and waste) and to reduce or eliminate taxes on what it wants *more* of (employment and income). A tax on carbon emissions, for example, could help reduce climate change and the costs and dangers associated with it. Unlike a cap-and-trade system, which allows markets to stipulate the amount of emissions that are tolerated (and which allows for the price of carbon to vary), a greenhouse gas tax would set a fixed price and let *it* determine the amount of emissions put forth. In other words, the higher the tax on greenhouse gases, the greater the incentive to reduce emissions. How much tax would have to be imposed? To achieve an adequate reduction in CO_2 emissions without unduly hurting the world economy, it has been estimated that the tax would probably have to amount to between $20 to $50 per ton of carbon emissions produced. In the United States, this would, in part, mean imposing a tax on gasoline, diesel fuel and motor oil of around 6% and a coal-produced electricity tax of about 14%.[1]

Since carbon emissions aren't the only harmful discharge the world wants less of, a similar duty would be placed on all dangerous discharges including chlorine, sulphur, tetrafluoromethane, hexafluoroethane, hydrofluorocarbons and nitrous oxides as well as hazardous materials such as chemical fertilizers, pesticides and phosphorous. Detrimental practices including topsoil depletion, non-renewable logging, and most mineral and metal extraction processes (including the mining of bauxite, chromium, coal, gold and silver) would provide additional taxation targets. Waste sent to a landfill site or tossed into an incinerator would be included as well.

No doubt many businesspeople will cringe at the prospect of a massive shift in taxation, but it's what would *not* be taxed that makes this proposition somewhat appealing. Corporate taxes could be reduced or eliminated, employment taxes could end, and personal income tax could be greatly lowered. People and businesses could then pocket most, if not all, of their earnings and no company would be penalized for employing more workers. Taxes on interest, savings plans, retirement accounts and college tuition accounts could also be eliminated. In addition:

- Businesses endeavouring to become more efficient would have more control over their tax burdens.
- Profits would increase as businesses became more sustainable.
- The quality of goods and services would improve (such is what happens when waste is eliminated).
- The costs and dangers associated with climate change would be mitigated.

Needless to say, a move of this magnitude would have to be gradual to allow businesses and industries to adapt. Furthermore, once a more sensible shift in taxation has been put into place, a common-sense approach to subsidies could also be adopted. Energy (including wind and solar power) could then trade at its true cost and billions of taxpayer dollars currently being directed toward problems that create waste and pollution could be redirected toward schools, social programs, job creation, and the promotion of cleaner and healthier working and living environments.

Legislative involvement

Redefining Progress is a leading sustainability think-tank located in the USA. For over 12 years it and several other organizations have been studying the effects of taxing waste. The conclusion is that a quarter or more of all American public revenues could be replaced if the government started taxing waste and natural resource consumption instead of revenues and income. A modest introductory tax placed on the burning of fossil fuels, for example, *coupled with a reduction in payroll taxes*, could boost America's GDP and create 1.4 million new jobs while cutting climate change pollutants by 50%.[2] The nation's economy would thus be put on a sounder footing because growth would be more sustainable, less costly, and less dependent on foreign commodities. The problem, of course, is that there are few people in government who have the vision (or backbone) to commence such a change. Equally as true is that most people don't want higher taxes placed on anything – particularly (and paradoxically) if they've already invested significant amounts of money in inefficient homes and businesses, wasteful heating systems, fuel-guzzling vehicles, and so on. Enter the need for legislation.

Historically, businesses have always fought against most forms of legislation, but the costs associated with climate change are causing many CEOs to think twice about how laws that promote higher taxes and carbon caps can be used to help industry. In early 2007, for example, the CEOs of several top American corporations called on President George W. Bush to enact mandatory reductions in carbon emissions to combat global climate change (their goal was to cut greenhouse gas emissions 60% by 2050). The group, calling itself the *U.S. Climate Action Partnership* (USCAP), consisted of chief executives from *Alcoa, BP America, Caterpillar, Duke Energy, DuPont, the FPL Group, General Electric, Lehman Brothers, PG&E* and *PNM Resources* – along with four leading non-governmental organizations including *Environmental Defense*, the *Natural Resources Defense Council*, the *Pew Center on Climate Change* and the *World Resources Institute*. By banding together to avoid a patchwork of potential costly and conflicting state or regional regulations, the group tried to work with lawmakers to set goals and targets that allow businesses time to make changes and implement solutions that will improve both the environment and energy efficiency, while protecting national trade and the economy.[3]

Investor involvement

Intelligent CEOs and shrewd, independent thinkers aren't the only ones hankering for sustainable change. In September of 2007, a prominent group of state officials, state pension fund managers, and environmental organizations filed a petition with the *Securities and Exchange Commission* asking it to adopt guidelines requiring all public companies to disclose the risks of climate change to their business as well as the actions they're taking to mitigate those risks. The 115-page petition, signed by state treasurers, attorney generals and state fund managers in California, Florida, Maine, New York, North Carolina, Oregon and Vermont, states that 'climate change has now become a significant factor bearing on a company's financial condition… Investors are [therefore] looking for companies that are best positioned to avoid the financial risks associated with climate change and to capitalize on the new opportunities that greenhouse gas regulation will provide.' The petition went on to claim that 'Interest in climate risk is not limited to investors with a specific moral or policy interest in climate change; climate change now covers an enormous range of investors whose interest is purely financial…'

The group claims that investors have the right to know:

- How seriously companies are taking climate change into account when making strategic business decisions (particularly the physical risks that climate change imposes on a company's operations and financial condition),
- The names of companies that are 'out front' in their response to climate risks and opportunities,
- The names of companies that are 'behind the curve' (so they can be avoided by investors), and
- Legal proceedings relating to climate change.[4]

Guidelines approved by the SEC in January of 2008 now require companies to weigh the impact of climate-change laws and regulations (including overseas regulations and accords) when assessing what information to include in corporate filings.

It's not just big business

Small businesses are also calling for increased legislation with the expectation that they'll soon reap its benefits. For example, an organization called *Small Business California* worked to support the state's *Global Warming Solutions Act* (AB 32), the passing of which imposes tough legislation to tackle global warming. The idea behind *AB 32* is simple: to balance the reduction of hazardous emissions with incentives for improvement. The program works like an interest-free loan: businesses are encouraged to exchange the profits they normally lose through wasted energy for energy-saving solutions (e.g. increased insulation, more efficient machinery, etc.) that quickly pay for themselves. The irony is that environmental groups have been lobbying for such changes for years – yet their efforts obtained fruition only after the local business community jumped on board.[5]

Additional examples

Taxes and legislation designed to reduce waste undoubtedly leaves some people fuming, yet a government report published in the United Kingdom states unequivocally that businesses and consumers want their government to do more to make it easier to be less wasteful.[6] The mandatory labelling and ranking of electrical goods and machinery in terms of efficiency (e.g. *Energy Star* labels) is just one example of how legislation can help inform consumers about cost and energy savings while increasing the demand for environmentally friendly goods. Other changes being considered in the UK would make it easier for companies to install green technologies like solar panels and wind turbines. At the time this was proposed, most businesses had to go through a lengthy planning application process (from 8 to 16 weeks) and pay the equivalent of $3,000 if they want to install a solar panel or small wind turbine. To encourage cleaner energy practices, however, the government has expressed an interest in placing renewable energy equipment under a 'permitted development' category, which would allow it to be installed without the need for planning permission. A 'route map' for improving the efficiency of new buildings with the aim of reducing carbon emissions is also being considered.

Meanwhile, in the USA, California officials discovered that most HVAC air ducts leak 20%–30% of the heated or cooled air they carry – so the government reduced leakage rate allowances to 6%. Further studies revealed that outdoor lights for parking lots and streets directed 15% of their beams up, not down. So outdoor lighting waste and leakage was set at 6%. Similarly, in 2009, a law was passed banning inefficient big-screen televisions from being sold in the state (the law went into effect in 2011). The irony is that although California's energy prices are the highest in the United States, its citizens pay the country's lowest energy bills thanks to increasing laws like these that outlaw inefficiencies. Interestingly, the state also 'de-coupled' utility profits from consumption rates (i.e. utility companies now base their profits on the number of customers serviced rather than the amount of electricity sold). So instead of selling more electricity to obtain more profit (which encourages waste), customers are encouraged to use less electricity so that more customers can be served by the limited amount of electricity that is produced by any given power company.[7] This move lowers the state's energy needs while contributing to higher power company profits and an increase in consumer savings.

Additional moves to reduce wasted energy include tax breaks for buyers of fuel-efficient vehicles, equipment, appliances and buildings. New York City is getting in on the act by declaring that all taxis must be fuel-efficient hybrids by 2012 – a move designed to save taxi drivers over $1,000 per month while eliminating tons of greenhouse gases. The moral of the story? Expect more such laws. The best advice on offer is to not wait for your government to tell you what you already know is true. Exceed the law by becoming as waste-free as possible. You can't go wrong that way.

13

The Perils of Greenwashing

The term used to describe the deliberate distortion of the truth in order to make false environmental claims is called 'greenwashing' and the legislation that covers this area is notoriously lax. For example, it's within the law of many countries for the 'recycled' symbol to be placed on any product or its packaging if either one (or both) contain just 1% recycled material. Similarly, a business can make its products (or production processes) *slightly* less harmful to the environment, yet still boast in its advertising that it's 'greener'. Major oil companies seem to be particularly keen on taking advantage of such loopholes. Under attack for reaping windfall profits from soaring fuel prices, many oil companies are trying to reposition themselves as part of the solution to the world's energy problems rather than the chief cause. Other manufacturers have recognized that they too can burnish their environmental image – without having to do much – as a way of promoting their products. Of course, there's nothing wrong with touting green credentials if the efforts behind such claims are valid. But problems can and do occur when happy-talk and unchecked promises turn out to be nothing more than greenwashing.

In the spring of 2007, *TerraChoice Environmental Marketing* (a green-certification organization) sent researchers into six national retail businesses to gather data about 'green' products. All in all, 1,018 products were looked at that covered a broad range of the consumer spectrum from air fresheners to appliances and televisions to toothpastes. Astonishingly, only one product turned out to be truly green – a paper product from Canada. All the others contained misleading claims that could not be proven. These claims included:

- *Not revealing hidden trade-offs.* 57% of the misleading claims made by manufacturers involved suggesting that the entire product was green when, in fact, the green aspect being promoted represented only a part of the product. The remainder of the product was both wasteful and destructive in terms of energy consumption, forestry destruction and water usage.

- *No proof to back up claims.* 26% of the products examined boasted green credentials, yet the manufacturer was not able to confirm the claims being made.

- *Vague labelling.* 11% of all misleading statements involved making a claim that was either poorly defined or meaningless, which made it likely to be misunderstood by consumers. For example, displaying a recycled symbol on the product without explaining what had been recycled.

- *Irrelevant claims.* 4% of the green claims turned out to be true, yet were of no real value. For example, boasting that a product is free of CFCs may sound good; however, since CFCs have been illegal for almost 20 years, making such a claim can be interpreted as a deliberate attempt to mislead the public into thinking that the manufacturer has gone the extra mile.

- *Promoting the green side of hazardous products.* Around 1% of manufacturers made claims that could be used to distract the consumer from the fact that the product is harmful to begin with (e.g. 'organically grown' tobacco).

- *Out-and-out lies.* Less than 1% of the products studied issued claims that were absolutely false, usually by using or misrepresenting a 'green' certification by an outside authority.[1]

Why do businesses greenwash?

Apart from the short-term financial benefits involved, the main reasons why organizations engage in greenwashing include:

- An attempt to divert the attention of regulators and reduce pressure for regulatory change,

- The desire to persuade critics that they're well intentioned and/or have changed their ways,

- A need to expand market share at the expense of rivals that are legitimately trying to become greener,

- An attempt to reduce the turnover of environmentally conscious staff (or to attract more staff), and

- A desire to make the company appear more attractive to investors.

Another twist: capitalizing on guilt

During the Middle Ages, professional pardoners sold 'indulgences' that allowed sinners to be forgiven for their sins. Similarly with greenwashing, the concept of paying a second party to atone for the sins of the first appears to still be alive and well.

The idea behind buying and selling carbon credits began in 1989 when global power firm *AES* invested $2 million in a forestry project in Guatemala. The company made its purchase under the belief that laws would soon be enacted that limited carbon emissions and that these same laws would probably give companies struggling to reduce their carbon emissions the option of offsetting them.[2] A growing number of businesses have since climbed onto the bandwagon by allowing customers to offset their carbon emissions by purchasing carbon credits. For example, some airlines will voluntarily add a few dollars to the price of their tickets and several power companies provide the option of paying a higher monthly fuel bill to help offset carbon emissions. In other examples, *Range Rover* automobiles offered an emissions offset for the first 45,000 miles (72,000 kilometres) which was factored into their purchase price and a ski resort in Vail, Colorado, once enticed skiers to buy energy credits to help buy a wind turbine so in the future the skiers will be carbon-neutral when they are lifted to the top of a nearby mountain.

Of course, the money raised for carbon credit programs is supposed to be used for building or promoting environmentally friendly projects such as the planting of trees, the protection of forests, the funding of alternative energy program or the instigation of a pollution clean-up campaign – and, according to the *World Bank*, approximately $100 million is given on behalf of customers every year for these purposes. Yet some of this money never reaches its intended destination. Brokers have been known to skim as much as 60% off of carbon-offsetting investments as they're passed from one middleman to another, tree-planting schemes have been found to be non-existent, and some solar energy projects have reportedly turned out to be little more than scams. Money invested in environmental clean-up campaigns has also been called into question (particularly campaigns that have already been paid for) and carbon credits have been repeatedly sold to scores of different buyers.

Separating the wheat from the chaff

With so much room for abuse, people and businesses wishing to partake in green or carbon offset programs are encouraged to investigate all claims before handing over any cash. Creators of greenwash campaigns are very good at fooling activists, customers, journalists and politicians alike. Protective suggestions include:

- *Use common sense.* If a company's claims seem too good to be true they probably are (particularly if the company is situated in a traditionally non-green industry or its product portfolio is filled with goods that aren't green). Don't be fooled by slogans, tear-jerking ads or safety claims designed to seduce.

- *Do your homework.* All products have a hidden history. Even bamboo, which is often billed as a green alternative to everything from building materials to textiles, uses hazardous chemicals in its processing (e.g. sodium hydroxide, a corrosive chemical used in drain cleaners and carbon disulphide – both chemicals are rarely recaptured and reused after processing). Do some research before buying into *any* green claim.

- *Ask questions and demand documentation.* If a company can't back up its claims with valid certifications, official audit reports or similar documentation it's probably not telling the truth. Some companies, for example, state in their advertising that they fund endangered forests, wetlands and species. What is not said, however, is that they were forced to do so by law because of their destructive practices.

- *Seek consistency over time.* It's quite common for companies to make announcements about changes in policy or the launching of new initiatives only to starve their plans of funds later on when the spotlight fades. To avoid falling victim to this practice, investigate the longevity and success of a company's previous green projects as a way to help predict the feasibility of new ones.

- *Confirm the validity of industry associations.* There's no shortage of questionable 'regulatory' industry associations that companies claim are watching over them and their industries. False third-party tactics makes it easy for companies to hide behind a façade of smoke and mirrors.

- *Look for trustworthy certifications.* These include the 'EPA' label, 'Energy Star' (for appliances and electronics), the 'EcoLogo' and 'Green Seal' (for cleaning products), and the 'Forest Stewardship Council' (for wood and paper products), and so on.

- *Follow the money.* Some businesses make private donations to groups or interests that don't square with their public statements. Examples include companies that claim to be doing everything possible to lessen waste and pollutants, but are secretly funding lawsuits, legislation and other measures to prevent them from having to do so.

- *Test for international consistency.* To determine if a company is truly turning green, see if it operates under different standards in different countries that have little or no regulation.

- *Examine how the company handles its critics.* Some companies will try almost anything to silence their critics. Tactics range from spouting legal threats to collaborating with police and military forces. Obviously, such practices are not a good indicator of environmental compliance.[3]

For additional suggestions on how greenwashing campaigns can be spotted, visit www.greenwashingindex.com.

Short-term gains, long-term pain

With a growing number of consumers and consumer groups on the lookout for disingenuous companies and their greenwashing campaigns, it's becoming increasingly difficult to get away with making deliberately false claims in order to obtain a short-term influx of revenue. For example, in July of 2007, *Royal Dutch Shell* was ordered by French authorities to withdraw several costly advertisements that showed flowers coming out of smokestacks. *Woolworths* in Australia was publicly named and shamed in August that same year for selling toilet paper that carried fake sustainable forest fibre labels. Other companies have had fines and/or experienced drops in sales for similar unethical or illegal behaviours. For example, *MacMillan Bloedel*, one of Canada's largest forest-product companies, was labelled a serial forest-clearer and a chronic chlorine user by environmental activists and subsequently lost 5% of its sales almost overnight when it was dropped as a UK supplier by *Scott Paper* and *Kimberley Clark*.[4] Simply put, neither *Scott Paper* nor *Kimberly Clark* wanted the negative publicity.

The bottom line

Companies that greenwash not only weaken brand image and invite further scrutiny, they also diminish the concept of becoming greener, which is something that doesn't rest easy with companies that make the effort. Recently, the American *Federal Trade Commission* called for a special meeting dedicated to the update of environmental guidelines, which will make greenwashing even more of a bad idea. The *European Union* is even more vociferous. Simply put, short-term duplicity designed to fool customers and the public can lead to long-term pain. All it takes is one dishonest practice to be exposed in the media or on the Internet and in a flash, weeks, months or perhaps even years of costly consumer retribution may have to be dealt with.

PEOPLE

Sustainability is not a technological issue. At its heart it's a behavioural issue and as such it is dependent upon teamwork, cooperation and motivation. For sustainable practices to take root and produce results, every employee – whether he or she is a cleaner, a production-line worker or an administrator – (as well as paying customers) must contribute to the process. No matter what level or experience a person has, everyone has the potential to discover a sustainable path that has been overlooked. Just as important, any employee has the ability to add that final jolt of effort that avoids failure and promotes success. Understanding the importance of people in all phases of the sustainability process is therefore necessary to ensure that a thorough and combined effort on all fronts is made

Simply put, people are a business's ultimate competitive advantage.

14

The Importance of Customers

To understand how important customers are to sustainability, it's first necessary to define the word 'customer'. In business, a customer *is everyone that an
organization serves*. Look carefully at this definition because it includes everyone involved in the business – not just the folks whose money is taken in
exchange for a product or service, but also the people who serve these individuals. Customer transactions are a two-way exchange. Every paying customer
wants something from the business that has a product or service that is wanted
and the business wants something from paying customers in return (money).
Similarly, every employee wants something from the business he or she serves
(wages, training, respect) and every business wants something back from its
employees (skill, labour, loyalty, honesty). This two-way, give-and-take service
scenario allows the word 'customer' to be classified into two categories:

- *External customers*: the people that exchange money for a product or
  service, and
- *Internal customers*: the individuals that are employed by, that use, or who
  rely on the work of others within an organization to perform responsibly
  (including employees, suppliers, contractors, shareholders, the community where the business is located, and other stakeholders). (If you don't
  believe that employees need to be serviced and don't fall under the category of 'internal customers', see pages 13-14 ['The acquisition, retention and motivation of astute employees'] and the reference to the Patagonia outdoor clothing company's achievements in attracting top-notch
  employees.)

Back to basics: the ten commandments of business success

One of the better ways to understand the importance of customers is the '10 Customer Commandments' list, which can be traced back to Mahatma Gandhi who reportedly taught them to his law clerks. Think of each in relation to internal and external customers and the importance of two-way service:

1. Customers are the most important people in our business
2. Customers are not dependent on us – we are dependent on them
3. Customers are not to argue or match wits with
4. Customers brings us their needs – it is our job to fill those needs
5. Customers are not an interruption of work – they are the purpose of it
6. Customers do us a favour when they call – we do not do them a favour by serving them
7. Customers are part of our business – they are not outsiders
8. Customers deserve the most courteous and attentive treatment we can give them
9. Customers are the individuals who make it possible to pay our wages
10. Customers are the lifeblood of this and every other business

Going green and people

The value of 'green' markets is estimated to be worth around $600 billion.[1] Indeed, *Wal-Mart* began introducing green versions of its products several years ago to test this market and gauge customer reactions. The conclusion? Consumers are indeed 'embracing products that help the environment'.[2] Note that this does not mean that going green is a guaranteed ride to success. Additional findings suggest that the following issues must also be addressed:[3]

- *Keep prices down.* The good news is that extra costs associated with going green (if there are any) can usually be offset by making production processes more efficient and sustainable.

- *Focus on quality.* Many successful green business practitioners suggest that the overall quality of a green product should be improved before announcing its green virtues. In other words, improve the reasons why customers purchase the product rather than hoping that 'greening' it will make it more appealing.

- *Incorporate new green products into a traditional product line.* By adding a green alternative alongside traditional product lines it becomes easier to enter the green market, learn the needs of consumers, overcome mistakes, and gather information and ideas for further improvements.

- *Make small changes first.* Many consumers still believe that environmentally safe products don't work as well as conventional products. This is largely a legacy of the 1970s when such charges were usually true. To offset this belief, some organizations advocate being modest when announcing a product's greenness and to refrain from announcing any green intentions until after an improvement in quality has been detected by consumers.

- *Be upbeat.* Avoid doom-and-gloom messages in green product advertising. Most consumers are turned off by negative messages and, as a rule, respond better to positive messages.

- *Seek out a bona fide green accreditation.* More government agencies, consumer organizations and environmental groups are issuing certifications to bolster the credentials of green products. Use them.

- *Green the place where your product is sold.* Eliminating waste not only reduces costs, it also leads to increased sales. For example, *Vic's Market,* a small grocery business in California, cut its annual energy bills by $48,000 (and therefore its carbon emissions) after adopting basic efficiency practices. An added bonus was an increase in sales due to brighter, energy-efficient lighting and the covering of food freezers with glass doors, which made interior temperatures more comfortable and resulted in customers shopping longer. Elsewhere, retail giant *Wal-Mart* fitted half of one of its stores in Lawrence, Kansas, with energy-efficient skylights and the other half with fluorescent lights – then watched with astonishment as sales rose substantially on the naturally lit side.[4]

Job security and people

No one wants to work for a company that's going to give them a pink slip through no fault of their own, but is job security something that can be expected in the long-term – particularly during a recession? Laying off workers is a time-honoured practice undertaken by many companies in order to survive difficult times, but making workers redundant costs money. A study conducted by *Bain & Company* (featured in an April 2002 issue of the *Harvard Business Review*) concluded that when a job is refilled within six to eighteen months of a layoff the business loses money on the deal[5] (see also, 'Lay Off the Layoff's' by Jeffrey Pfeffer, *Newsweek*, 5 February 2010). Expenses associated with layoffs include severance package costs, declines in productivity and quality, rehiring and retraining costs, and poor morale suffered by those left behind. Fortunately, there are better, more sustainable ways to treat people and get more out of them in the bargain. For example, nine companies featured in *Fortune* magazine's '100 Best Companies to Work For' list (2009) have never laid off an employee – ever.[6] These companies include:

- *Publix Supermarkets*. A strong balance sheet with no debt helped the *Publix* grocery chain acquire 49 stores and hire over 1,250 people in 2008. In its 79 years, *Publix* has never laid off a single employee – mostly because every employee owns a stake in the company.

- *The Container Store*, a storage retailer based in Coppell, Texas, froze salaries and watched its spending during 2008 to avoid layoffs. This strategy enabled it to expand operations in the midst of the recession by opening four stores and adding 70 employees to its roster.

- *Aflac*, based in Columbus, Georgia (USA), sells supplement insurance. Suggestions from employees that keep the business going (and save it millions of dollars) include telecommuting and flexible schedules. In return for their input, employees receive benefits that include onsite gym memberships, child care programs and job security.

- *Nugget Market* in Woodland, California, avoids layoffs with careful job placement and shrewd labour management. Instead of handing out redundancy notices during hard times, the 81-year-old grocery store refrains from replacing employees who leave. Since its worksites are fairly close to one another, positions are relatively easy to fill and employees are trained to perform a number of different duties. In 2009, despite a worldwide recession, the company filled 173 jobs, a 22% increase in job growth that year.

The bottom line? Engaging employees to find ways to cut costs and increase profits (instead of throwing them overboard when difficulties arise) can be both winning and sustainable.

Work environments and people

Over the past 10,000 years, sunlight, fresh air and natural settings have greatly influenced human evolution; so it should come as no surprise that artificial settings – combined with industrial noise – adversely affect human productivity and performance. Studies show that workers labouring in windowless factories experience more headaches, faintness and sickness compared with workers who toil under natural light. Additional studies have revealed that prolonged exposure to artificial light decreases antibody activity, increases infections and colds, and results in depression.[7] Creating workplaces that reduce these impediments is therefore an integral part of sustainable work practices. For example:

- *Lockheed Martin* reported saving half a million dollars on its energy bills *and* enjoyed a 15% reduction in absenteeism after moving its offices to a building lit by natural light. The company subsequently saved hundreds of thousands of dollars every year on energy costs and discovered, much to its surprise, that a 2% increase in productivity equates to $3 million extra per annum. The increase in productivity alone paid for the new building in less than one year.

- The *Boeing* aircraft company and *Prince Street Technologies* (PST) introduced natural light into their workplaces and watched as their quality control systems improved. Specifically, at *Boeing*, tool measurements could be read easier, previously unseen cracks in fuselages were detected, and subtle shades of colour were better differentiated. At PST, the introduction of natural light was so successful it reduced worker compensation cases by 90%.

- The *Diagnostics Products Corporation* in Flanders, New Jersey, saw employee productivity increase 19% after the installation of an efficient climate control system and the addition of skylights that 'let in lots of (free) natural light'.[8]

- By installing skylights and additional insulation to improve lighting and temperature control, *VeriFone*'s credit card verification facility in Costa Mesa, California, decreased energy consumption 59%, reduced absenteeism by 47% and boosted productivity 5%–7%.[9]

- At the headquarters of the *West Bend Mutual Insurance Company* in West Bend, Wisconsin, efficient workstation controls, which allow employees to alter temperature, airflow, lighting and noise based on their personal preferences, contributed to a 15% increase in claims processing *per employee*.[10]

(For more information about work environments and the effect they have on people, see the *Place* section.)

A word about 'bad people'

In November 2009, lean-thinking guru Jim Womack described in a newsletter an experience he had while touring a large service company. During the visit, his hosts complained about the people in another department and how they were dragging their feet in response to needed change. A short time later, in a different area, another team moaned about the resistance generated by the finance department over the same changes. At some point, Womack asked his hosts if the way changes were being made benefited the two departments where the 'bad people' were located. And the answer, after a bit of discussion, was obviously 'no'. Indeed, it quickly became clear that those offering resistance were, in fact, reacting quite rationally to protect their interests. Since the end result of the changes being requested would eventually end up benefiting everyone, Womack explained that the real problem was not the change itself, but rather a lack of discussion, inclusion and negotiation with those who saw themselves as losers in order to make everyone whole. Such is what all too often happens with internal and external customers when managers or teams choose to think by themselves and then broadcast edicts rather than work collaboratively with every stakeholder.

The people at the bottom of the pyramid

Eliminating the wasting of people is as much a part of sustainability as reducing physical waste. Consider then, that the world's largest consumer markets – upwards of two-thirds of humanity – are comprised of poor people that are either ignored or forgotten by most businesses because of tradition, ignorance, or prejudice (see FIGURE 14-1). However, an increasing number of companies have discovered that poor people, if given a chance, represent an economic force unto themselves. 'Inclusive business' is the term used to describe efforts that include 'bottom-of-the-pyramid' (BoP) customers in a company's business model – and the key to tapping into this powerful economic base is 'local partner selection'. Many BoP companies don't become successful by simply selling products to the poor. Successful inclusive business strategies rely heavily on embedded processes that include working with and/or helping to create intermediary businesses that bring local and outside companies into close personal relationships with BoP communities.

Three examples

In 1998, the *Cemex* cement manufacturing company in Mexico sent a team of managers into one of the poorest areas of the country to conduct a six-month study on how to increase sales. People with limited incomes accounted for around 40% of *Cemex*'s cement sales so the company wanted to learn how best to serve what they suspected was a virtually untapped market. After living amongst this customer base and learning its needs, the *Cemex* team discovered how poor people used cement, how they could pay for it, and a host of other profitable facts, which they then used to make their products more accessible. A savings organization named 'Patrimonio Hoy' was then set up to finance the selling of *Cemex* products to the company's new customer base. Sales subsequently grew 250% yearly.[11]

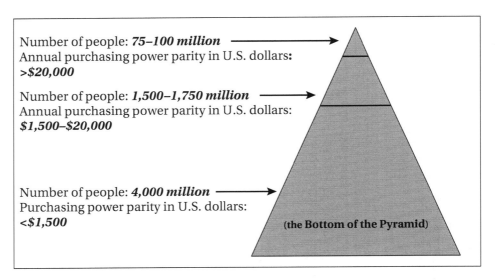

Number of people: *75–100 million*
Annual purchasing power parity in U.S. dollars: *>$20,000*

Number of people: *1,500–1,750 million*
Annual purchasing power parity in U.S. dollars: *$1,500–$20,000*

Number of people: *4,000 million*
Purchasing power parity in U.S. dollars: *<$1,500*

(the **Bottom of the Pyramid**)

FIGURE 14-1: The world economic pyramid
Adapted and reprinted with permission from "The Fortune at the Bottom of the Pyramid" by C. K. Prahalad and Stuart L. Hart from the First Quarter 2002 issue of *strategy+business* magazine, published by Booz & Company Inc. Copyright © 2002. All rights reserved. www. strategy-business.com

Cemex's story is not unique. In 2006, the Nobel Peace Prize was awarded to Mohammad Yunus, a former economics professor from Bangladesh, who invented the concept of micro-finance (giving small loans to poor people so they can start their own businesses). Although Yunus was repeatedly told by the establishment that poor people could not be trusted with money, his research (and his conscience) suggested otherwise. Yunus's solution was to help poor people help themselves by creating a new financial institution called the *Grameen Bank* (*grameen* means 'village'). Currently, the *Grameen Bank* provides over $445 million in small loans each year ($10 to $50 at a time) to those who need it most. It operates by visiting its customers rather than having them come to the bank. Far from being unable or unwilling to pay back their loans, those that borrow money from the *Grameen Bank* pay back their borrowings at a higher rate than any other group of borrowers in the world.

Realizing that he was on to a good thing, Yunus next helped a telecom company called *GrameenPhone* (from an idea conceived by former investment banker Iqbal Quadir) to adapt the selling of mobile phones to fit another wasted market. Basically, *GrameenPhone* sells mobile phones to villages rather than individuals. Selling phones to villages helps spread the cost of the phones, thereby enabling more people to receive information about crop prices, market conditions, and other vital statistics without wasting days walking back and forth to major communication hubs. The result? Profits from the

GrameenPhone project are expected to rise to over $100 million despite the fact that the company operates in a region of the world where the average yearly wage is only $286.

Meanwhile, in Central America, *Corporacion Dinant* is producing biodiesel from African Palm trees, which have low water needs and require intensive manpower – a situation that provides excellent opportunities for job creation (currently 2,000 small producers are involved in the project).[12]

The message of BoP economics is not about selling products to people who don't need them. Rather, the point is that companies – particularly global players – should not turn their backs on BoP opportunities in their search for new markets, new products, and new business partners. Businesses astute and creative enough to adapt to the needs of the world's largest collection of potential customers are currently reaping the benefit of increased profits, improved regional economic stability, and intense personal satisfaction – with little or no competition. For more information see *The New Age of Innovation: Driving Co-created Value through Global Networks* by C.K. Prahalad and M.S. Krishnan (McGraw-Hill, 2008) and *Capitalism at the Crossroads: Aligning Business, the Earth, and Humanity* by Stuart Hart (Wharton School Publishing, 2007, 2nd edition).

The final word on people

Nothing is as crucial to a business as customers – both internal and external. With few exceptions, the role of every business is to serve customers what they want, where they want it and the way they want it. No business should ever lose sight of the fact that every decision it makes and every action it takes must be customer-oriented. Anything else is a complete and utter waste of time, money and resources. Period.

15

Managing Change

Change is never easy. Just ask Amy Spatrisano, principal and co-founder of *Meeting Strategies Worldwide* (an international meeting and event organizer). Some time ago, Amy took a look at the number of everyday items used during a typical five-day conference and found that 2,500 attendees used and discarded over 62,500 plates, 85,000 napkins, 75,000 cups and glasses, and 90,000 cans and bottles. Determined to eliminate this (and other) waste, Amy did some research and discovered that using online registration could eliminate paper, printing and postage costs, thereby saving $3,900. Not providing conference bags could save $11,700. Avoiding presentation handouts saves $1,950 in printing and paper. Providing water in pitchers instead of plastic bottles saves $12,187. Serving condiments in bulk rather than in individual packages and eliminating the need for buses by choosing hotels close to the convention centre provided additional savings, all of which amounted to more than $60,000. Unfortunately, as Amy later lamented, many of the meeting planners, hotels, caterers and other businesses she works with remain unimpressed by these figures. 'Even if you show them they'll save money and even if you make it easy,' she says, 'it doesn't mean they'll do it.'[1]

This story is not uncommon. Many people and their organizations actively resist change even if the desired change guarantees the making of money creates additional job security. *Species that survive*, said Charles Darwin, *are usually not the smartest or the strongest, but the ones most responsive to change.*

Preparing for change

For any type of change to take hold within a business (particularly efficiency) *breadth* and *depth* is required. *Breadth* means that the change must take place across the entire organization (e.g. every department and/or person must be made aware of the need for change). *Depth* means that everyone becomes involved with, and brings their skills to, the change process. Having employees become part-owners in the change process by asking for their input is a powerful way to win them over. Involving employees also taps into a wider knowledge base, initiates motivation and reduces the chances of something being overlooked. Just as important, when a change process is shared the words, 'that's not my job' are heard less often. In 2003, for example, *Dow Chemical* achieved hundreds of millions of dollars in cost savings thanks to the pursuit of employee-led efficiency practices at its facilities in Texas and Louisiana. As part of the change process, employees worked alongside managers from the highest levels of the company. The solutions they came up with – on their own – included identifying and fixing steam leaks, reducing electricity consumption, super-insulating industrial furnaces and introducing real-time monitoring (*immediate* feedback from mechanical processes). By involving as many employees as possible from a wide range of departments, *Dow*'s ongoing efficiency drives ensure that: (1) breadth and depth is achieved, (2) there are fewer chances that something is missed, and (3) problems are attacked from many different angles.[2]

Probably the most important management theory ever developed

An adage often attributed to Albert Einstein states that 'insanity is the constant repetition of a behaviour with the expectation of a different result'. Consider, then, the following model developed by Kurt Lewin in 1951[3] (see FIGURE 15-1). Lewin's 'Force Field Theory'[4] states that two forces come into play when change is introduced into a work setting. The first force derives from those trying to instigate change (driving forces). The second force results from those who try to resist change (restraining forces).

Lewin's belief is that most managers use force to bring about change by exerting pressure on those who oppose them. In practice, however, the more management pushes, the more the other side pushes back. The result is that both sides get locked in an I'm-going-to-win-this power struggle hidden behind a thin veil of civility (e.g. the way most employees push back is not with violence or anger, but through inactivity, excuses and other forms of procrastination).

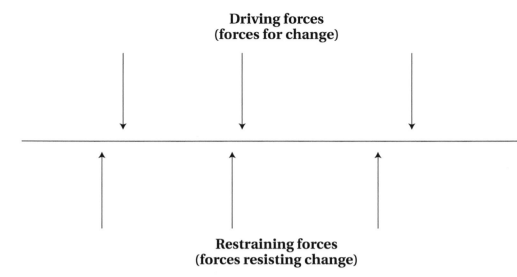

FIGURE 15-1: Lewin's Force Field Theory
Adapted from J. Scott, *The Concise Handbook of Management* (Haworth Press, 2005): 66.

The better way of overcoming resistance, says Lewin, is to get off the power-struggle merry-go-round and focus on why the opposition is resisting change. Almost always, the reason why people resist change is because they're afraid of something. Thus, the question management should be asking isn't, 'How can we persuade these people of our arguments for change?' (i.e. 'How can we force change upon them?') but rather, 'What are their fears and objections and how can we remove them?'

Why employees fear change

Initiating change in a business can be a gut-wrenching experience. This is because in many instances change removes comfortable habits and protective barriers and leaves people feeling stranded and defensive. The following text, adapted from *Creating Value for Customers*[5] by William Band, describes the typical concerns associated with workplace change.

Job loss   Mention 'efficiency' or 'change' in a workplace and many employees immediately assume that jobs are on the line. That's why many change initiatives should begin with a promise that job losses are a last resort.

Fear of loss of control	Feeling that things are being done *to* employees rather than *by* them.
Too much uncertainty	The future is not obvious and every day feels like the beginning of the end. This can lead to employees wanting excessive details and other procrastination techniques (i.e. paralysis by analysis).
Too many surprises	People like novelty, but hate surprises. Early warnings are therefore necessary to avoid unwanted shocks.
The changing of habits	Habits are easy and mindless. Change is uncomfortable.
Need for familiarity	Everybody likes what is familiar. Most people feel comfortable going to places and doing things they know are risk-free.
New things mean more work	This usually happens when introducing change. But the initial workload often subsides when new tasks become easier (which is often the reason for change).
Concern for competence	Whenever something new is introduced, people question their ability to master new skills, particularly if training and ongoing support are not provided.
No time to adjust	Saying 'let's do things differently' is not enough. It takes time for new skills to develop. Rushing through the change process can lead to disruption, sabotage, foot-dragging and/or poor performance.

Change from another angle

Kurt Lewin later developed his Force Field Theory further (with input from Edgar Schein) by introducing a 'Three Stage Approach to Change Behavior'.[6] Since good habits are recognized as being just as difficult to break as bad habits, the analogy the two men make is to unfreeze bad habits and freeze improved habits once they've been established. Here's how it works:

1. *Unfreeze existing behaviours.* Gain acceptance for change by *getting employees to admit that a change is needed*. This doesn't mean that a decision must be made or a solution must be found just yet. At this stage, only a general consensus is required in which everyone agrees that something new has to be done. Examples of how some businesses get their employees to admit that waste reduction is needed is to involve them in estimating the amount (and cost) of the waste the business produces, analyzing

energy and fuel consumption, offering carbon emission estimates, and/or pointing out garbage levels and costs. Studying the cost savings achieved by sustainable businesses (particularly competitors) is another tactic that has produced results.

2. *Change existing behaviours.* Get employees involved in the change process by asking for their advice and input (breadth and depth). This can be accomplished by putting together a team (or teams) whose job is to collect ideas. Once again, the more employees that contribute the more likely change will be accepted because, in effect, change will be seen as the employees' idea rather than management's.

3. *Freeze new behaviours.* Reinforce new work practices with rewards. If this isn't done, people will stop making progress and will revert to the safety of their old habits.

Building the commitment for change (a summation)

George Bernard Shaw once said that *to learn something at first feels like losing something.* To eliminate the feeling of loss (and the sense of fear that loss creates), try the following:

- Involve as many people as possible. Participation leads to ownership, enthusiasm and motivation.

- Emphasize that job loss is not part of the change process. Explain *and show* that every redundant employee will be reassigned and retrained.

- Communicate clearly and often. Make the change message unmistakable and provide as much information as possible about every change.

- Divide changes into manageable, comprehensive steps. Make these steps as familiar as possible and make them small and easy. Ensure each step is deemed a success before moving on to the next.

- Never surprise anyone with change.

- Let commitment grow. Don't ask for allegiance to new and untried ways (you won't get it).

- Make clear what will be expected of people during and after changes are made. Communicate these standards and requirements often (i.e. provide feedback).

- Provide as much continuous training as needed.

- Bear in mind that new work habits often require three to four weeks (or longer) to make or break.

Learn as you go

Lack of experience in a change situation is not an excuse for inactivity. Indeed, most successful efficiency initiatives begin with a handful of individuals stepping into the unknown with little more than common sense, a healthy understanding of their business (and its customers) and an overwhelming desire to succeed. Ken Tannenbaum, a technology associate at *Dow Chemical* who has successfully led several efficiency projects, explains this concept as follows: 'Most of the work on efficiency [at Dow Chemical] is done by Dow employees. We have utilized consultants from time to time to validate our assumptions or to give us an opportunity to ensure we did not miss anything, but in most of our plants, [because] the processes are very specific, external experts cannot bring much additional help.'[7]

Ken went on to say that the same techniques used every day to change, improve and maintain *Dow Chemical*'s numerous plants are the same techniques *Dow* uses to foment sustainability initiatives because when it comes to change there is no sense reinventing the wheel every time.

Just do it

In some businesses employees will refuse to undertake new tasks and responsibilities no matter what is tried. Managing change in the face of strong opposition may therefore require stern procedures that include disciplinary action, reassignment or perhaps termination. Most practitioners agree, however, that managers should first try to stimulate change by encouraging employees to lead their own way through the change process. To be sure, stepping into the unknown is intimidating and frightening to many, but just as with life, sometimes one simply has to do what needs to be done while afraid. The alternative, as the saying goes, is that if you continue to do what you've always done, you're likely to end up with what you always got. Equally as true are the words of George Addair: 'Everything you want is on the other side of fear.'

16

Putting a Team Together

The following team-creation recommendations have been compiled from a number of successful waste elimination schemes:

1. *Before putting a team together, state the company's goals.* What is the current situation and what does the business want to achieve? Zero per cent waste? The replacement of toxic substances with safe alternatives? A reduction in production times? A revised budgeting system that charges the cost of waste to the department that creates it? Examine the difference between what exists and what is wanted. Assume that everything being examined is broken and must be improved.

2. *Keep team sizes at a manageable level.* Research shows that team sizes should be limited to less that 10 or 12 individuals for maximum effect. Larger groupings are usually more difficult to handle.

3. *Involve individuals who are knowledgeable about what is being examined.* Input will probably be needed from front-line workers, suppliers, maintenance crews, health and safety personnel, the purchasing department, engineers, the legal department, research and development staff, paying customers, the community where you're located, environmental specialists, etc. Bring these folks on board. For example, *Procter & Gamble* has set a goal of sourcing 50% of its innovation ideas from outside the company in a bid to shake things up and create new ways of thinking.

4. *Don't turn away volunteers.* Enthusiasm should not be curtailed and no one should be made to feel left out. For example, the *Scandic* hotel chain involved its employees in reducing unnecessary costs and discovered that most ideas came from the maids that cleaned the rooms (proving yet again that workers on the front lines often know more than most).

5. *Start off small.* If energy saving is the goal, take a look at the company's electricity meter then go around and switch off all unneeded lights and equipment. Read the meter again and determine the savings. Multiply the daily savings by the days of the year the business is in operation and you'll end up with a rough estimate of how much money can be saved in a year just be turning off the lights and equipment you don't use. That should provide enough motivation to keep going.

6. *Provide continuous communication, results verification and training.* Consolidate training and information distributions to allow different groups to meet and communicate. Ensure that every employee (including shift workers) is aware of what needs to be done, what is being done, what has been done, and why.

7. *Agree on motivational tools.* Determine how employees will be motivated. Recognition, extra holiday time, cash bonuses, or award ceremonies are all valid motivators. In one business, employees wanted to be rewarded with a carrot cake baked by the wife of their foreman. Another business displayed team achievements on giant scoreboards (thereby satisfying the 'nudges' concept explained in Chapter 3: 'What the Reformer is Up Against'). Points were generated for reducing kilowatt-hours of electricity, saving amounts of raw materials, reducing production minutes, and so on. Other companies tie annual bonuses to the waste minimization performance of employees.

8. *Maintain links between your teams and the rest of the organization.* Learn the fears and needs of the individuals involved. Be aware and share what every team is attempting and accomplishing.

9. *Update goals as they are achieved.* Emphasize the notion of ongoing, no-finish-line improvement, build on previous successes, and measure and track all progress no matter how small. Fifteen or twenty ideas that can each save 1% of costs will quickly add up. Let them.[1]

Organizing team meetings

The following issues should be discussed, agreed upon and written down *before* a team can be expected to perform:

- *The purpose of the group posted for all to see.* For example, in a waste reduction scenario, typical questions that should be presented can include: What is the waste? Where is the waste created? When is the waste created? How much waste is created? What can be done to eliminate and prevent the waste?

- *Attendance expectations.* Some practitioners suggest that efficiency teams should meet at least two to four times a month. Whatever is decided, put it in writing and enforce it.

- *Behaviour rules.* Examples include: no interruptions, no eye-rolling, no name calling, and no criticism focused on personality rather than the task.

- *Work performance expectations.* Set the standards that determine if members are pulling their own weight and what will be done if they are not.

- *Methods of agreement* (or dissent). Will votes be cast? Will objections be listened to?

- *Clearly defined tasks and responsibilities* (both general and specific). For example, inform every department that energy use must be cut by 10% in one month. Then let it be known that more such improvements will be expected.

- *Explanations that articulate how deadlock will be handled.* Will lots be cast or will a coin be flipped?

Ideas and suggestions should be recorded on a large display board where they can be clearly seen and referred to. Concentrating on positives is essential. Staying upbeat is a good way to build morale and reinforce individual cooperation and participation. Those who work with teams on a regular basis suggest countering every negative criticism with a positive suggestion for improvement. Negative outcomes can also be corrected with measures designed to overcome defeatist attitudes. These include:

- Hold second-chance meetings after a consensus has supposedly been achieved,

- Avoid being partial to only one course of action (perhaps make it a rule to always come up with two or three alternatives),

- Go around the table with team members and insist on feedback (this helps prevent quiet people's opinions from being withheld and big-mouths from dominating discussions),

- Encourage team members to do their own research and collect their own facts,

- Remember that the point of formulating a group is to *produce results* (i.e. assigning teams is not a solution in itself),

- Understand that every group is unique and requires a different start-up, functional style and form of leadership,

- Assign team members to question suggestions and obtain better solutions.[2]

What to do when efforts slow

Not every team project story has a happy ending. Sometimes the enthusiasm and work of even the best teams can slow or falter. Typical comments associated with stalled efforts include: 'We don't have time for this', 'This isn't working', 'This stuff isn't relevant' or 'We're just treading water'. Additional examples include the development of a 'committee mentality' where 'too much analysis leads to paralysis' and nothing gets done. Further problems can develop when the smug air of superiority creeps into a team or when the team refuses to consider what it feels are weird or different viewpoints from outsiders. As a result, contradictory data is ignored or shelved, other alternatives are not considered, and a jumping to conclusions or inactivity dominates. More often than not, this usually results from a lack of clear goals and leadership. Suggestions include:

- *Make sure that everyone knows what is expected of him or her and what needs to be done.* This may involve establishing another form of readable compass that helps explain where the business wants to go and what it wants to do (and why) *before* numerical targets are set.

- *Make a 'to do' list.* Although it may seem a bit basic, a simple list filled with clear, itemized tasks that can be checked off after they've been completed could be just what's needed to help employees focus on one goal at time and affirm that progress is being made.

- *Delegate tasks.* Reward good people with additional responsibility and recognition by letting them come up with their own solutions.

- *Display results.* Provide feedback. Let employees know that you're taking this seriously and that they're being watched. Allow civil competitions to spring up with other departments and/or coworkers.

- *Analyze and reflect.* Divide every workday into time blocks and record what was done in each. Compare what was accomplished to what was expected. Do the two compare? If not, why not?

- *Avoid procrastination.* If a task seems too daunting or elusive stop thinking about it and move on to the next item on the 'to do' list. This can help maintain momentum.

WASTE ELIMINATION: IMPLEMENTATION ESSENTIALS
1. Assign responsibility (keep in mind that 'everyone is responsible' is often interpreted as no one is responsible).
2. Display appropriate measurements for all to see.
3. Educate and involve all employees and departments.
4. Gather ideas and put them into action.
5. Make improvements, tabulate and display the results, keep going...

PLACE

Whether in an office, a factory, a store or a home, most work is conducted in buildings – and the vast majority of the world's buildings are problematic. In the United States alone, buildings consume more than 68% of all electricity produced. Buildings also account for over 39% of America's energy demands and are responsible for contributing 38% to the country's total carbon dioxide emissions. Equally as unsettling, it's not uncommon for indoor pollution levels to be two to five times higher (occasionally 100 times higher) than outdoor levels due to dust and fumes from interior building materials, cleaning solutions, production processes, central heating and cooling systems, radon gas, pesticides, paint, glue, carpets, and so on. In fact, building-related productivity losses and illnesses resulting from toxins are estimated to cost businesses $60 billion annually. Eliminating these obstacles is therefore fundamental to the sustainability process.

17

Building Better Buildings

The *Rocky Mountain Institute* (RMI) is an entrepreneurial, non-profit, environmental think-tank located in Old Snowmass, Colorado. Within its 372 m^2 headquarters is a fishpond where turtles, frogs, carp and catfish swim year-round. Bougainvillea blossom under insulated skylights that cast a warm glow upon a profusion of grapevines and mango trees. Papayas, passion fruit and bananas are also harvested inside the RMI building despite the fact that the entire structure is situated at an elevation of 2,164 m, the outdoor growing season amounts to 52 days a year, midwinter cloudy spells last as long as a month and a half, and temperatures occasionally drop to –44°C. Yet the RMI has no central heating system and its monthly energy bill amounts to around five dollars. Layers of super-efficient insulation, heat-recovering ventilators and insulated windows help keep the building and its occupants warm all winter long. Most astonishing, however, is the fact that this building actually cost *less* to construct than a conventional structure its size and that the efficiencies that make it so cost-effective came from 1983 technologies that paid for themselves within ten months.[1]

Further north, in Minnesota, stands the *Phillips Eco-Enterprise Center* (PEEC), a $5.3 million commercial and industrial facility. Currently, PEEC, which is a pilot project for the *Green Building Council*, is home to 20 manufacturing companies and office tenants. Features built into the 5,946 m^2 building include salvaged and recycled construction materials, wind and solar power sourcing, geo-exchange heating and cooling (heat pumps), active day lighting, a green roof, non-toxic low-emission wall coatings, and exterior storm water retention and treatment systems. Because of these efficiencies PEEC has won two design awards – including one from the *American Institute of Architects*. Interestingly, however, that's not why the building is in such high demand on the rental market. What draws clients to PEEC is the fact that it's less expensive to operate a business under its roof. According to the *Building Owners and Managers Association* (BOMA), normal utility costs for a 5,946 m² building add up to around 20% of its annual operating budget. PEEC's annual utility bills amount to only $25,000 or about 5% of its annual operating budget. Furthermore, PEEC spends only 17% of its operating budget on repairs, security and ground maintenance, compared with the 23% that BOMA says is typical.[2]

Additional examples of efficient buildings

Commercial buildings that pay for their costs and, in some cases, produce more energy than they use, are not a fantasy. Low-cost technologies combined with common sense have been producing efficient structures for years. For example, *VeriFone* (a division of *Hewlett-Packard*) renovated its California headquarters and subsequently saw its energy consumption drop by 59%. Soon thereafter, employee absenteeism decreased by 47% and employee productivity increased by 5%. Elsewhere, the *California State Automobile Association* office in Antioch, (the cheapest CSAA building ever built), decided to flood its 1,459 m² interior with lighting from energy-efficient light bulbs and (free) daylight that streams in through super-insulated windows. The resulting 63% reduction in energy bills covered the cost of improvements in six months. One of the most written about case studies in commercial building efficiency, however, concerns the *ING Bank* in Amsterdam (The Netherlands), which was built in 1987. The *ING Bank* building requires 92% less energy to operate compared with standard structures its size. Moreover, the $3 million in annual reduced energy costs paid for the building's efficiency upgrade in three months. Today, the building is so aesthetically pleasant to work in that absenteeism is down 15%, productivity is up, and employees sometimes don't leave after work hours.[3]

Take another look at these examples. What makes them particularly compelling is the fact that efficient buildings not only save money, they also help the businesses that reside in them make more money by providing increases in productivity and decreases in employee absenteeism.

Overcoming wasteful building practices

Slowly, architects and builders are waking up to the fact that buildings – where most people spend over 90% of their time – do not need to be a major cause of waste or inefficiency. So why are most of the world's buildings either inefficient or built inefficiently? The main reasons include:

- Compensation paid to architects and engineers is usually based either directly or indirectly on a percentage of the cost of the building or the equipment specified for it (i.e. fees are based on how much the building costs rather than how much it saves), and

- Most property developers do not expect to pay the energy bills of the structures they build so they have little or no interest in energy-saving or waste-reduction solutions.

Fortunately, progress is being made remunerating contractors for long-term savings rather than how much money can be saved in building expenses in the short term. This is good news when one takes into account that efficient buildings typically sell or lease faster and retain tenants better than their inefficient counterparts. In addition, green buildings have greater visual, thermal and acoustic comforts that yield valuable financial gains in terms of productivity, retail sales and manufacturing output. In a 2004 survey of 719 building owners, developers, architects, engineers and consultants, 91% believed that green buildings improve the health and well-being of their occupants.[4]

Efficient buildings increase profits

Financial savings in terms of lower energy needs are not the only benefit provided by energy-efficient buildings. Following is a list of documented improvements obtained after natural light (derived from windows or tubular skylight systems) was introduced into workplaces:[5]

- Dramatic staff-turnover reductions,

- A doubling of customer numbers,

- Customers shop for longer periods of time,

- An increase of up to 40% in retail sales,

- Productivity increases of up to 18%,

- A drop in accident rates by as much as 50%,

- Improvements in task performance times,

- Employees able to identify items (including defects) better and faster,

- An increase in patient recovery rates and reduced hospital staff stress,

- Improvements in the vision abilities of the elderly,

- Students enjoy increased health benefits and, strangely enough, fewer dental cavities.

These types of improvements have not just been recorded in the United States. The *Canada Green Business Council* drew similar conclusions when it discovered that the introduction of natural daylight raised productivity 13% in

Canadian businesses, increased retail sales by up to 40%, and helped improve school test scores by as much as 5%. Improved ventilation added to these enhancements by increasing productivity an additional 17% and decreasing sickness by up to 50%.[6]

Getting over the hurdles

Without question, the greatest misconception about energy-efficient buildings is that they always cost more – which many architects insist is not true. Any building can be made either more expensive or less expensive depending on how it's designed and constructed. Yes, adding more insulation, installing rainwater collectors, fitting higher-quality windows, placing solar panels on roofs and putting passive shading structures over windows can incur extra expenses, but when these improvements eliminate the need for a heating and cooling system the extra costs can be negated.

High-rise tower buildings can also enjoy the benefits of efficient construction even though, on average, they require 30% more energy and materials to build and operate. Just as with small buildings, extra costs can be neutralized through efficient design and materials. For example, several years ago the *Rocky Mountain Institute* showed how a six-storey building can fit into a five-storey structure (five storeys is usually the limit for building code heights in many towns and small cities) by making a few structural changes and virtually eliminating ducts and suspended ceilings. Under-floor ventilation and wiring and super-efficient windows and daylighting are also incorporated. Construction expenses remain virtually unchanged (mostly because of a reduction in heating, ventilation and air-conditioning needs) with subsequent energy costs reduced by one-half to three-fourths. Natural light and ventilation, the building's low energy and maintenance costs, a propensity to produce more income, and natural good looks and interior comfort means that everybody wins: the owners of the building, the occupants of the building, and the neighbourhood where the structure is located.

Fix an existing building first

Efficient buildings do not have to be built from scratch. A business looking to build a new factory, office building or retail operation should first consider upgrading an existing building before constructing a new one. It's relatively easy (and often more cost-effective) to refit an old building – even historical buildings – than to build new. For example, the American *National Audubon Society* upgraded a 100-year-old 9,104 m^2 building in 1992 at a cost roughly

27% below that of building from scratch (all costs were recouped within five years). The resulting retrofit cut two-thirds off the building's energy requirements, improved ventilation, eliminated indoor toxins and introduced an office recycling program that reduced waste by 70%.

Maximizing building interiors

One of the more intriguing aspects of waste is that the costs it creates don't just add up, they tend to multiply. Take, for example, a parametric analysis of an office building in Florida, which revealed that:

- 30% of the building's annual cooling load was used to fight the heat produced by its lighting system,
- 20% was used to combat solar heat that streamed in from the windows,
- 15% was used to offset heat build-up from the roof, and
- 13% was used to neutralize the heat generated by internal office equipment (i.e. photocopiers, computers, printers, coffee makers, etc.).[7]

In other words, 78% of the building's cooling needs were needed to offset wasteful inefficiencies (basically, one poorly designed system was fighting against that of another and the bill-payer was funding both sides). For either a small or big business, these costs create significant money loss, but can they always be offset? To be sure, firms that lease or rent their premises or share building space with other companies may not be able to perform renovations or improvements that optimize their workplaces. That being said, it may be feasible to negotiate new lease terms if envisioned improvements are seen to reduce operating costs.

Suggestions for improving the efficiency of building interiors

How can a business reduce the unseen, unfelt and silent pile-up of compounding inefficiencies? An effective first step is to turn off all office equipment and machinery *at its source* when the items are not in use, which can cut 5% to 40% off energy bills (even the battery charger for a mobile phone draws electricity when the phone is not hooked up to it). Additional suggestions include:

- *Replace all light bulbs with energy-efficient light bulbs.* Energy-efficient light bulbs save money by: using less electricity, emitting less heat (which reduces a building's cooling needs) and lasting longer than standard bulbs (a recent study showed that 70% of energy-efficient bulbs last significantly longer than their manufacturers claim).

- *Install intelligent lighting systems.* Instead of lighting up entire rooms or work areas, use 'task lighting' that produces light only where it is needed.

- *Replace old exit signs with* Energy Star *rated alternatives.* For every sign changed, $10 can be eliminated from the energy bills and the bulb will last ten times longer than a standard bulb.

- *Put lighting systems on a timer and hook up exterior lights – as well as bathroom, closet and storage area lighting – to motion detectors.* The city of Eindhoven, in The Netherlands, for example, is considering attaching motion detectors to its outside lighting – including its billboards – which is predicted to reduce the city's energy bills by 30%.

- *Insulate interior walls, ceilings and wall spaces.* Extra insulation is usually worth the cost.

- *Replace all office equipment with energy-efficient alternatives.* Doing so not only reduces energy costs, it also reduces the heat these devices emit. Electrical equipment always carries two price tags: the purchase price and operating cost. Look for accredited energy-saving labels to ensure that the electricity requirements of the equipment you need will be reduced by as much as 30% (or more). The *A-OK Auto Body Shop* in Philadelphia, Pennsylvania, for example, replaced its interior lighting system with efficient substitutes, installed motion detectors on exterior and bathroom lighting, placed timers on water heaters and coffee pots, and added programmable thermostats to its climate control system. As a result, its energy bills declined $5,577 in one year.[8]

- *Remove paper towel dispensers from restrooms and replace them with* low-energy *blow dryers.* Making one ton of paper towels from recycled paper requires 26,498 litres of water, 1,363 litres of oil, and 158 million BTUs of energy. During this process 39 kilos of pollutants are released into the atmosphere. Noting this waste, the university student union at *California State Northridge* removed its paper towel dispensers and replaced them with wall-mounted, low-energy hand-dryers that eliminated $21,000 worth of annual paper towel costs.

- *Seal all leaks in ducts and ventilation systems as well as around plumbing and wiring.* Duct system leakage can account for up to 30% or more of wasted energy. Proper duct sealing also keeps dust, mould and mildew at bay.

- *Take advantage of under-floor heating.* Heat rises so an under-floor heating system is usually more efficient than one that uses wall-mounted radiators or ceiling vents.

- *Take extra care to select non-toxic carpets (and carpet glue), paint, varnish and other safe interior decorations.* Fumes and particles from these materials debilitate human health and performance.

- *Consider purchasing an evaporative cooler (or 'swamp cooler') for cooling needs.* Evaporative coolers pull air over pads soaked in water, which uses a quarter of the energy of refrigerated air.

- *Install low-energy ceiling fans.* By gradually circulating air through a building, slow-speed ceiling fans make the most of a heating and cooling system and can drastically reduce energy costs. A *Subway Sandwiches* shop in Norman, Oklahoma, for example, cut its annual energy costs by $20,000, in part by installing ceiling fans in its kitchen. The shop also replaced its lighting with energy-efficient bulbs (reducing the number of bulbs, yet doubling the store's brightness), replaced old ice makers and water heaters with efficient models, and tinted the building's windows.[9]

- *Use a programmable thermostat.* For every degree a thermostat is lowered, up to 5% can be saved on the heating portion of an energy bill. Another good tip is to keep electrical equipment and lamps away from thermostats where they can adversely affect temperature readings.

- *Wrap hot water heaters in an insulated blanket.* This not only saves money the electricity it saves can prevent hundreds of pounds of carbon emissions from entering the atmosphere.

- *Where possible, fill workplaces with indoor plants and trees.* Indoor gardens have a remarkable effect in reducing employee fatigue and can be instrumental in increasing productivity.

- *Consolidate offices and work areas located in several buildings into one.* This practice, along with sealing off and shutting down unused work areas, can save huge amounts of money.

- *Check to see if your business is eligible for energy-efficient tax incentives.* Some governments offer tax breaks or tax credits for businesses that strive to increase the efficiency of the building in which they operate. Typically, tax credits are awarded for installing energy-saving technology and equipment, using hybrid vehicles, adopting efficient heating and cooling systems, switching to solar (or wind) energy systems – and/or for making efficient constructions or renovations.

- *Keep in mind that these suggestions are just a fraction of the energy-saving practices available to building operators and owners.* Involve your employees in finding more.

- For more information on how the overall energy efficiency of a workplace can be improved along with a reduction in energy bills, visit the *Energy Star* website (www.energystar.gov) – a no-cost program run by the *U.S. Environmental Protection Agency*. In Europe, visit *Energy Star* at www.eu-energystar.org. Alternatively, in the UK, seek out the *Energy Saving Recommended* (ESR) logo when buying electronics. The ESR endorses products considered to be the most energy-efficient available (the ESR program is managed by the *Energy Saving Trust*: www.energysavingtrust.org.uk).

A third European label is the *TCO Certification* (*Tjanstemannens Centralorganisation*) established by the *TCO Development* (www.tcodevelopment. com) and run by the *Swedish Confederation of Professional Employees*.

When building new, think before doing

If upgrading an existing building is not an option and the decision to construct a new structure has been made, planning should begin well in advance (see Chapter 9). Most buildings can cut 20%–50% (or more) off their annual heating and cooling costs – with no additional expense – by maximizing location, positioning and shape before construction starts. This includes placing the building close to major transportation routes, locating next to hills or trees for protection from wind and sun, aligning the building with the sun's trajectory to maximize or minimize solar heat gain, and using the structural mass and shape of the building to the utmost benefit. Additional examples include:

- *Cover parking areas with light-coloured cement or other light-coloured surfacing rather than asphalt.* This can reduce exterior air temperatures around a building by as much as 5°C.

- *Install a porous parking lot.* Chunky, light-coloured gravel that has had its finer particles removed allows rain and snow to be absorbed into the ground. This simple idea was once presented to administrators at the *Ford Motor Company* who refused to consider it. Eventually, however, they were persuaded to gravel a small test zone. Soon managers and employees from all over the *Ford* complex were going out of their way to park their cars on the test area because it contained no standing water or ice (or road salt), which kept the cars cleaner.[10]

- *Carefully choose the colour and texture of the building's exterior.* Dark colours absorb sunlight (and heat) and textured surfaces tend to be more heat-absorbing. To prevent solar heat build-up, paint buildings a light colour and make sure the finish is shiny and smooth.

- *Utilize natural storm water treatment.* Channelling rainwater runoff from a building into tanks (for later use) or swales lined with indigenous vegetation is not only eco-friendly it's also cost-effective when compared to an expensive network of underground pipes and treatment plants.

- *Avoid unshaded rock, cement or asphalt landscaping on the south or west sides of a building,* which increase ambient temperatures and radiate heat long after the sun has set.

- *Surround buildings with as much indigenous vegetation as possible.* Not only does this decrease surrounding air temperatures and reduce landscaping water needs, it also reduces labour costs, fertilizer expenses and landscaping waste (non-native plant species are often more labour-, water- and cost-intensive). Trees are not only valuable 'carbon sucking tools', they're an excellent source of shade and a great way to increase property values.

- *Ivy or grapevines grown in window boxes or on trellises* can shade and beautify entire sides of a building (this is called a 'green wall').

Building efficiently

If the following suggestions were used to build the over 170,000 commercial buildings constructed across the USA every year, it has been estimated that these structures would not only pay for themselves very quickly (and be cheaper to operate), they would substantially reduce the country's dependence on foreign oil and drastically reduce its carbon emissions:

- *Reuse, reclaim and recycle from demolition sites.* Nearly 44,000 commercial buildings in the USA are demolished every year – and the construction, renovation and demolition debris from these work sites accounts for nearly 60% of the country's total non-industrial waste. Recoverable materials include concrete, asphalt, metal (including wiring), bricks, plumbing material and wood.

- *Use local materials.* The further afield materials are sourced, the more energy, labour and money it may take to harvest, package and transport them.

- *Reduce the use of concrete.* Cement production accounts for almost 10% of global carbon emissions. If concrete must be used, consider a mixture of 55% concrete and 45% slag (a waste product from blast furnaces) which saves energy and produces an alternative that is stronger than concrete alone. When bricklaying, use reclaimed bricks with a carbon-neutral lime mortar.

- *Use sustainable engineered wood products in place of standard wood products.* Also called *composite wood*, engineered wood is manufactured by binding fibres from young trees, sawmill scraps and wood particles. Engineered woods produce more open living and working space by reduces the amount of wood needed for load-bearing interior walls.

- *Ensure that all wood products are approved by the* Forest Stewardship Council *or a similar recognized environmental organization to ensure that they come from a sustainable source.*

- *When wiring a building, use the next higher size diameter of electrical wire than that recommended by building code requirements.* Thicker copper wire costs more, but because it reduces electrical resistance it costs less to operate. In a typical office lighting circuit, using a larger wire size yields about a 193%-per-year (after tax) return on investment.[11] A student of mine in France lowered his monthly electricity bill more than two-thirds by rewiring his house with fatter wire and replacing all the light bulbs with energy-efficient bulbs.

- *Use water-based paints and wood treatments* that are less toxic and emit fewer harmful fumes.

- *Insulate, insulate, insulate.* By insulating a building both *inside* and *outside*, it's possible to dramatically reduce or eliminate a heating and cooling system. For example, around 10,000 structures (called *passive houses*) without furnaces or air conditioners have been built in Germany, Sweden and Switzerland. Within these structures, everyday appliances (such as a television or hot water heater) emit enough heat to keep the occupants warm and snug in winter.

- *Use energy-efficient windows.* Energy-efficient windows are fundamental to the overall reduction of a building's energy requirements. It has been estimated that a routine renovation of all big office towers in the USA with insulated windows would probably save the country $45 billion in energy costs. Standard glass windows have an efficiency *R-value* of 1, which means that more heat is lost through a window than an entire exterior wall (a reasonable R-value of an efficient wall is around 25 or 30). Super-insulated windows have an R-value of up to nine (or more) and can be 'programmed' to reflect unwanted heat and/or ultraviolet light while letting in more ambient light.

- *Ensure the heating and cooling system is both efficient and not too big for the building.* Far too many buildings are constructed with HVAC systems that are more powerful than what is actually needed. In addition, many HVAC systems leak up to 30% of their heating and cooling.

- *Solar shading is essential for all glass exteriors that face the sun.* Although super-efficient windows and skylights do a good job of letting in light while keeping out heat, 'light shelves' (a type of indoor awning) offer additional protection from solar heat and are much cheaper than buying and running an air-conditioning system to offset solar heat. Adjustable window glazing allows a building to either deflect unwanted light and heat or capture it like a greenhouse during cooler months.

- *Look into drilling geothermal wells that use ground temperature to both heat and cool.* Just a few metres down from sea level, the Earth's crust remains relatively constant at 14°C. Low-cost interior environmental control systems can use this consistency to either warm or cool a building.

- *Consider installing a green roof on your building.* Roofs are huge accumulators of heat that usually require massive amounts of air conditioning to offset. A green roof is an inexpensive and lightweight roofing system planted with heat-loving foliage. The benefits of a green roof include a reduction in ultraviolet radiation (which helps prolong the life of the roof), increased energy efficiency for the building (green roofs provide excellent insulation properties), a decrease in rainwater runoff, and excellent noise reduction properties. Wider, regional benefits include increased air quality, lower electricity demands (particularly in the summer), reductions in local air temperatures, and an improvement in the aesthetics of the area where the building is located. When used in conjunction with a system that collects and stores excess rainwater, green roofs can also reduce maintenance costs associated with standard roofs.

- *If installing a green roof is not possible, cover your roof with reflective material or solar panels.*

- *Incorporate good cross-ventilation in the building.* Take advantage of side vents, wind scoops, skycourts, balconies, atriums and low-power ceiling fans. Good air movement promotes temperature balance (which reduces the need for heating and cooling) and provides greater comfort. Tower buildings should allow occupants to open their windows, if just a few inches, to promote ventilation.

- *Avoid the use of PVC and other energy-intensive, non-ecological construction materials.* Replace them with sustainable alternatives. For example, sewer pipes can be made of clay rather than plastic.

Building a better future

As one developer put it, once you learn a better way to build you don't go back. For more information about the planning and construction of efficient, energy-saving buildings, visit the *Advanced Buildings* website at www.advancedbuildings.org. Another option is to contact the *U.S. Green Building Council* (USGBC; www.usgbc.org). The USGBC is a network of 10,000 construction leaders from every sector of the building industry who have made it their mission to transform the building industry. The USGBC has developed a rating and certification system titled *Leadership in Energy and Environmental Design* (LEED) to recognize the efficiency performance of buildings (as well as healthcare systems and labs) in five key areas: sustainable site development, water savings, energy efficiency, materials selection, and indoor environmental quality. The purpose is 'to transform the way buildings and communities are designed, built, and operated, enabling an environmentally and socially responsible, healthy, and prosperous environment to improve the quality of life'.

The average LEED-certified building uses 32% less electricity, consumes 30%–50% less energy, draws 40% less potable water, enjoys a 70% savings on waste output, and saves 350 metric tons of carbon emissions every year.

(Note: thanks are due to the staff at the *Rocky Mountain Institute* who reviewed this chapter prior to it being published in *Managing the New Frontiers*.)

18

Saving Water

The amount of water in the world is finite, yet between 1900 and 1995 global water consumption rose sixfold – more than double the rate of population growth.[1] Interestingly, although our planet is mostly covered by water, more than 97% of it contains salt, making it unsuitable for drinking or irrigation (desalinating salt water produces one-third potable water and two-thirds poisonous, intensely salted waste that cannot be reintroduced into the environment without repercussions). The less than 3% of what remains is either frozen at the poles, crystallized in glaciers, or is locked in underground aquifers and is too deep to retrieve. Less than half of one per cent can be used by humans, but this amount increasingly poses a potential hazard because it's rapidly becoming more polluted. Currently, around 50% of the world's diseases are caused by contaminated water, and water rights have been – and continue to be – a worldwide source of conflict because water shortages often translate into food shortages and manufacturing difficulties. The bottom line is that minimizing water consumption in business not only lowers operating costs, reduces water disposal expenses and promotes regional, national and international stability, it's also the right thing to do.

How businesses waste water

According to the Australian government (keep in mind that Australia is a chronically drought-stricken country), most businesses waste water in the same ways they waste energy and other materials. Among these practices are:

- Installing wasteful production systems that require more input than is needed,
- Acting as if supplies are ubiquitous and renewable and don't need to be managed,
- Using pristine supplies for purposes that don't require pristine inputs,
- Not thinking in the long term, and
- In general, not making better use of what little is available.

How a business can save water

Saving water is always worth the effort. For example, the *Frito Lay* factory in Casa Grande, Arizona, is working to recycle 85%–90% of the water used in its plant combined with an intense energy-efficiency program. Faced with regional droughts and potential water use restrictions, the company decided to act fast and expects to save $60 million annually.[2] 'When water becomes scarce our ability to produce products comes into play,' says Al Halvoreson, *Frito Lay*'s director of environmental sustainability. 'We want to have technology developed and scaled so we don't need to move production to follow the water.' Suggestions used by *Frito Lay* and other companies to conserve water include:

- *Educate employees and involve them in all water conservation practices.* It's everyone's job to save water so *make it* everyone's job to save water. *Kraft Foods* set an objective of reducing its water consumption by 15% before 2011 and surpassed that goal by obtaining a 21% reduction. 'We're changing behaviour and getting results,' says Steve Yucknut, vice president of sustainability.

- *Designate a water efficiency coordinator,* support him or her, and, as with other sustainable practices, constantly remind employees what your company is trying to achieve.

- *Locate the sources where water is used at your place of work* (washrooms, sinks, climate control systems, hoses, etc.) *and discuss and identify ways that water can be saved at each.*

- *Get employees in the habit of reporting all leaks and water losses immediately.* Train security guards and cleaning crew to identify, handle, or report water wastage when they're making their rounds.

- *Install motion detectors under taps, which operate when a hand is placed beneath them and immediately turn off afterwards.* Alternatively, install taps that automatically shut off after running a few seconds.

- *Install water flow fixtures* (aerators) *on all faucets, toilets, urinals and showerheads.* This alone can reduce water requirements by 60% or more.

Screw-on water flow reducers (also called aerators) are inexpensive, yet can cut the amount of water that flows from a faucet by one-half or more. The remaining water is mixed with air and the result feels as though the tap is full on. Additional water saving devices can be installed in toilets (which are widely considered to be the greatest wasters of water in any building) and urinals. Toilet technology has advanced to such a degree that some toilets require no water for flushing. A university in California, for example, replaced its 13 male restrooms with waterless urinals and saved $15,000 on its annual water bill. Further east, an office building in Denver, Colorado, switched its toilets, urinals, faucets and showers with water-saving replacements and saw its water bills plunge 80%.[3]

- *Fix all leaks and repair or replace inefficient control valves, pumps and pipes.* 10%–20% of a business's water loss usually comes from ignored leaks – which is tantamount to pouring money down the drain. A single tap left trickling in a washroom, for example, can cost up to $80 in water charges per year. In the UK, a 25 mm hose, left running at 66 litres per minute, wastes 4,000 litres per hour and could add over £45,000 to the annual water services bill.[4]

- *Install a closed-loop water system to reclaim and reuse industrial waste-water.* High-efficiency reverse osmosis (HERO) systems, for example, reclaim wastewater. Similar techniques to filter and reuse water from industrial processes or air-conditioning cooling towers can cut water bills by 90%.

- *Recycle 'grey water' and rainwater.* Most industrial systems use tap water (e.g. drinking water) for most, if not all, of their production needs. The irony is that recycled water from sinks, showers, production processes, washing machines and drinking fountains (also known as 'grey water') can often be used in place of tap water. Even rainwater is of sufficient purity for most industrial processes and has the added benefit of being free. Harvested rainwater (from collection tanks on rooftops or building sides) can be used for irrigation, landscaping, toilet flushing and other purposes.

- *Use pressurized air to perform functions previously done with water.* Pressurized air can be used to clean equipment, products and packaging (e.g. bottles and cans).

- *Don't use toilets as a garbage disposal.*

- *Shut off all cooling units when they're not needed.*

- *Optimize the blowdown or bleed-off controls* on boilers and cooling towers.

- *Minimize water used in cooling equipment* in accordance with the manufacturer's directions.

- *Turn hoses off at the faucet* rather than the nozzle.

- *Use drip irrigation methods for landscaping needs.* Drip irrigation involves laying a perforated water hose a few centimetres below the ground.

When turned on, the holes emit water – one drop at a time – which is sufficient to keep plants hydrated. This system was used at a business I ran in the Middle East. The business was located in the middle of a scorching desert, yet the grounds were surrounded year in and year out with flowers, fruit trees and shrubbery. Potable bottled water cost twice as much as petrol, so we used grey water (from a sewage treatment plant) in our drip irrigation system.

- *Never place watering or irrigation systems on a timer.* If you recall the last time you passed through a neighbourhood in the rain and saw the water sprinklers on you'll understand why.

Efficient wastewater treatment

All workplaces produce sewage, and sewage is a disposal expense. There is, however, a way to eliminate sewage costs: treat the sewage where it's produced instead of paying to have it transported and treated elsewhere. *Ecological engineering* (also known as *ecological sanitation* or *living machines*) is an emerging industry that treats raw sewage, including effluent, heavy metals and other chemicals, economically and safely by pumping them through a series of open tanks filled with organic plant and animal life. Based on the science of estuaries – nature's own filtration system – each tank, which averages about 4 m, contains a unique ecosystem designed to break down select toxins before passing them on to others further down the line. The result is odour-free and can resemble a pristine garden complete with waterfalls, lily pads and fishponds. Indeed, one ecological engineering company (*Living Technologies* in Burlington, Vermont) held a wine and cheese party at one of its 'living machine' locations and had to keep reminding the guests to keep their hands out of the water.[5]

Typically, it takes one to three days for sewage to pass through all the required tanks in a living machine system. The first tank is covered with a layer of soil and living grass. Odours and gases filter through the layer and are broken down into carbon dioxide and oxygen. Bacteria and plants work their magic in the remaining tanks. The only waste created is that from the plants, which feed off the system and have to be pruned regularly. In regions that experience harsh winters, tank systems can be positioned in a passive greenhouse-type structure or they can be built into, and complement, the building they service. Conversely, a system can be arranged outside. Every system can be uniquely tailored to suit the volume and make-up of its waste. The end result is water of such high purity that it only requires a small amount of additional treatment to make it drinkable. Some companies even harvest and sell the methane gas their living systems produce, as well as the flowers, fish, tomatoes and lettuce that grow within them – which means that 'living machine' systems can be money-spinners.

Like many efficient processes, the cost of a living machine not only pays for itself, it is also a huge source of pride and admiration for employees. For example, *M&M Mars* in Brazil and Australia, the *Vermont Welcome Center* on U.S. Interstate 91, the *Sonora Mountain Brewery* in California, the *Body Shop* factory in Ontario, Canada, and the *National Audubon Society* in Florida have all boasted at one time or another about the beauty and efficiency of their wastewater treatment 'living machines'.

For more information on how to save water...

Many regional and national governments (particularly those in dry parts of the world) are keen to help fund water saving and water treatment business projects. Contact them. Additional organizations that can help minimize water use (many of which come from regions where droughts force inhabitants to treat water respectfully) can be found at www.bewaterwise.com; www.epa.gov/watersense; www.savewater.com.au; www.savingwater.org; www.sydneywater.com.au; and www.waterwise.org.uk

19

The Macro Advantages of Micro-power

Oil, coal, natural gas... business communities will continue to need them all. However, there is a way to reduce, in whole or in part, the many current and future expenses that are seen as inseparable from non-renewable energy sources. For example, although oil has traded at $147 a barrel, and may soon climb to $200, many analysts insist that the worst is yet to come. Here are the numbers. In 2009, the world consumed 86 million barrels of oil a day (up from 78 million barrels in 2002) and every year consumption increases. Between 1995 and 2004, for example, demand grew by 3.9 million barrels per year in the USA alone (currently, America consumes 25% of the world's oil production). China's demand grew by 2.8 million barrels annually during the same period) but there's no doubt that it (as well as India) needs to secure additional amounts every year to ensure economic growth. The problem, as Jeroen van der Veer, CEO of *Royal Dutch Shell*, stated in a recent email to his staff, is that '... after [the year] 2015, supplies of easy-to-access oil and gas will no longer keep up with demand'.

John Hess, Chairman of the *Hess Corporation*, agrees. 'An oil crisis is coming in the next 10 years,' he says, 'it's not a matter of supply. It's not a matter of demand. It's both.' James Mulva, CEO of *ConocoPhillips*, is also worried. In November of 2007, he told a Wall Street conference, 'I don't think we're going to see the supply [of oil] going over 100 million barrels a day... Where is it going to come from?' Earlier, in October of 2007, Cristophe de Margerie, CEO of French oil company *Total S.A.*, relayed that the production of even 100 million barrels of oil a day by the year 2030 'will be difficult'.[1]

When the CEOs of the world's oil companies start issuing warnings – and with climate change resulting from the burning of fossil fuels posing an ever-increasing threat – there's no better time than now for astute businesses to consider alternative sources of energy. Micro-power involves equipping a building or group of buildings with an independent power source that either wholly or partially supplies needed energy. For example, the *Mauna Lani Bay Hotel* on the Kona-Kohala coast of Hawaii turned its premises into a 100 kilowatt power station by retiling its roof with solar cells. In Aberdeen, Scotland, the *Cults Primary School* set up a 5 kilowatt wind turbine in May of 2007 that not only reduced its electricity bill, but also cut its annual carbon emissions by 5,633 kilos. And across the American state of Iowa, wind turbines now power ten schools either partially or completely. The 4,924 m² elementary school in Spirit Lake, Iowa, for example, installed a 250 kilowatt wind turbine that provides an average of 350,000 kilowatt-hours of electricity per year. Excess electricity, which can be fed into the local utility system, earned the school $25,000 in its first five years of operation.[2]

Payback, ROI and renewable energy

The long-term financial rewards of renewable energy cannot be understood without comprehending 'payback' or return-on-investment (ROI), both of which measure profitability in relation to capital expenses. Costs for non-renewable energy sources, such as coal and oil, include extraction from the ground and refinement (both of which are expensive). This is not the case with wind, sunlight and many other renewable energy sources. All energy sources, however, must be converted or transformed into electricity or heat before they can be used. With renewable energy (e.g. wind and sunlight), however, after the expense of conversion machinery is paid for, the electricity or heat obtained is free of charge (minus the cost of maintenance and disposal) while non-renewables maintain the constant expenses associated with: continuous extraction and refinement, waste treatment, maintenance and disposal, and related environmental disasters and healthcare costs.

   To determine payback or ROI… Imagine that a factory pays €10,000 annually to purchase electricity from a coal-burning power plant – and that the cost of equipment (wind turbines or solar voltaics) that can transform sunlight or wind into the same amount of electricity is €50,000. The payback period of the €50,000 investment, which is based on the annual market cost of electricity if the switch to renewable energy had not been made (€10,000) is therefore 5 years (€10,000 x 5 years = €50,000). 'Return-on-investment' is usually expressed as a percentage, so it is 20% (of the original investment) per year. Note that accountants typically like to see financial investment estimates in terms of ROI, while almost everyone else prefers to see the 'payback' period of an investment in terms of months or years. **Again, the ultimate payoff is that at the end of the payback period, the business receives free electricity**

(minus maintenance and disposal costs) which is why renewable energy can be a smart investment.

Wind power

Whether for sailing or rolling a grindstone in a flourmill, wind power has been around for centuries. Today, Denmark derives over 20% of its electricity needs from wind turbines; Germany gets over 10% of its electricity from the wind; and every year Spain installs over 2,000 megawatts of wind turbine generators. Even the United States is getting in on the act. In 2012, American wind turbines pumped out 50 gigawatts of energy (enough to power 15 million homes) and every year the number grows (as do the total number of jobs wind turbines create).

Wind turbines come in a variety of shapes, sizes and configurations, and usually last around 20 years or longer if they're maintained correctly. The traditional variety look like windmills, but some designs look like spires, others can be imbedded into walls horizontally like rolling pins, and it's common to see those that resemble the whisks of a giant egg-beater. Size-wise, wind turbines can range from huge multi-megawatt, 11-storey towers (which power thousands of homes), to modest 1 megawatt turbines that can power 350 homes, or smaller 1–10 kilowatt roof-mounted turbines which are purchased from specialized retailers and can power a house or business.

Is wind power affordable? Dr. David Toke of *Birmingham University* (UK) estimated as far back as 2007 that onshore wind power produced electricity at the equivalent oil price of $50–$60 a barrel (before payback) – and offshore wind power is pumping out energy at the equivalent of $70–$80 per barrel (before payback). Keep in mind that Toke's estimates assume a guaranteed income flow of 15–20 years and do not take into account government subsidies associated with coal and oil.[3]

Is wind power practical? Most users of wind power seem to agree that the benefits outweigh the disadvantages. A model created by the *National Renewable Energy Laboratory* (USA), for example, found that several locally owned wind turbine projects in Iowa generated significantly higher economic impact levels than projects of equal capacity owned by other investors. Additionally, the use of wind power was found to positively influence the entire local region where it was located, which led to increased community pride and cohesiveness.

Is wind power right for your business?

The single most important factor in deciding whether or not a wind turbine will provide an adequate energy source for a business is to measure the force and duration of wind that is available. Some turbines are designed to operate at low wind speeds while others can withstand powerful gusts. A good site must have a minimum annual average wind speed of around 18–21 kilometres per hour. To determine the average wind speed in your area, contact a local airport or meteorological station. Installing a wind turbine also involves learning about a variety of factors including costs versus productivity, ice throw, net metering, rotor radius (the length and size of a turbine's blades is directly proportionate to the amount of energy it can produce) as well as the programs, laws and incentives of local, state and federal authorities. For example, some regions actively discourage the use of sustainable energy by insisting that electricity production must come from local nuclear or coal-fired utility plants. Additional considerations that should be researched before buying into wind power include:

1. *Determine whether or not a favourable agreement can be reached with the local utility company.* Some electrical producers do not tolerate competition and may refuse to buy the additional electricity a wind turbine produces or may force all your micro-power to be fed directly into the nation's grid.

2. *Project feasibility concerns.* Will the noise, movement and aesthetics of the proposed wind turbine be an issue for the local community? Is the site's geology suitable? Will the turbulence (which is created by every wind turbine) effect nearby structures? Can zoning permits be obtained? These questions will need answers.

3. *Availability and maintenance concerns.* The availability of wind turbine parts, the reliability of the manufacturer, and the services of a professional who is familiar with their operation and maintenance is exceptionally valuable. Will a qualified professional be available to maintain and repair your wind turbine when it needs servicing?

Keep in mind that not all wind turbine stories have happy endings. Years ago a student of mine relayed the story of a village that invested in a huge wind turbine which produced hundreds of kilowatts of power. Unfortunately, the regional power company would not buy the additional electricity and residents discovered that the cost of their purchase would end up taking years to recoup. If the locals had done their homework, they would have discovered that a smaller, less expensive wind turbine would have been more suitable. For more information on turbines, visit the *American Wind Energy Association* website at www.awea.org.

Solar power

Before payback occurs, solar power is often considered one of the more expensive sustainable energy options available. And that's because, generally speaking, it does cost three to four times more to produce power from solar cells than it does from conventional sources. The good news, however, is that the cost of solar power drops almost every year because prices decrease about 18% every time production doubles. Power from the first solar cells, for example, cost about $200 per watt. In 2007, the price was $2.70 per watt (before payback) and in 2012, in Germany, the cost (minus installation fees) was $1.34 per watt (before payback). Electricity produced from solar power is now so competitive that in some cases it's actually cheaper to use solar cells than conventionally produced electricity (isolated street lamps, emergency phones on highways, and electrical systems in remote communities are cheaper to operate with solar power when one takes into account the cost of installing long-distance electrical transmission lines). Also, once again, after payback occurs, electricity from solar power is virtually free.

Indeed, in situations where solar power costs are greater than conventionally produced electricity, solar voltaics can pay for themselves in a relatively short period of time. Take the Times Square headquarters of *Conde Nast*, for example. Situated in a 48-storey building in New York City, 14 of the building's floors are covered with solar panels that added an additional 5%–10% to the overall construction price tag. The half million dollars in annual energy savings, however, paid for their cost within five years.[4] Meanwhile, in Madrid, Spain, telecom company *Telefonica* installed Europe's largest solar power plant on its roof. The 16,000 solar panels generate 3 megawatts of power, which means that the building is energy-self-sufficient and also makes money by selling excess power.

Solar cell facts

- Solar cells do not require direct sunlight to operate. They function quite well under cloudy or rainy conditions. For maximum effect, however, they should be placed where direct sunlight will hit them.

- Solar energy offers a one-time capital expense. Virtually no other costs accrue.

- Solar cells last a long time. Many solar cells produced in the 1970s still function to this day. Lab testing has shown that under the right conditions solar cells can last up to 40 years or more (although the energy output of solar voltaics usually decreases over time).

- Most solar cells are made from silicon, which is plentiful and does not have to be mined.

- Some solar cell applications are so thin they can be 'painted' onto foil or other materials. SVs can also be sewn into clothing, backpacks and briefcases to provide power for portable electrical devices.

- Solar panels can be used on new and old buildings as roofing, or mounted vertically on exterior building walls, or used as sunshades or covers over windows, walkways and carports.
- Solar cells reduce a business's impact on the environment, cut its electricity costs, and send a positive message to the public about the business's commitment to clean and sustainable practices.
- Most solar voltaics have efficiency variables of between 5% and 17%. Specialized solar cells produced in the laboratory – as well as those used in space – can reach efficiency levels of 25%–40%. The reason why solar voltaics are so inefficient is because about 30% of the energy they collect is converted into heat. Moreover, most solar cells cannot convert a broad spectrum of the sun's wavelengths into electricity. Improvements in technology, however, are making up for these shortcomings. Since sunlight is plentiful (and free), 'waste' is not much of a concern.

Are solar voltaics right for your business?

If your organization can afford to buy several years of its power in advance while awaiting payback, and if your business is situated in a location that receives adequate sunlight then, yes, solar power may be right for business. Note that energy from the sun can also heat water (and buildings) as well as drive steam turbines. For example, calculations for concentrated solar power, which uses mirrors to concentrate sunlight onto a fluid-filled container to produce steam that drives a turbine, is cost-equivalent to oil priced at $50 per barrel (before payback) – or as low as $20 per barrel (before payback) when the technology is scaled up.[5] For more information about solar power visit www.solarserver.de and click on the English translation icon at the top of the home page.

Fuel cells

Without question, of all the clean-energy-producing alternatives currently being talked about, fuel cells elicit the most excitement. Fuel cells require no combustion, have no moving parts, are silent, and are virtually pollution-free. Most important, since hydrogen is almost always found combined with other elements, its supply is cheap and plentiful. Some fuel cells run on the hydrogen found in sugar. Others use the hydrogen in the water produced by the cell itself. Hydrogen derived from traditional hydrocarbon sources (i.e. coal, gasoline, methane, methanol, natural gas or propane) can also be used as a fuel, although a small amount of carbon dioxide, sulphur, and other bits of matter from these sources is emitted as a result. Just as important, fuels cells can be made in all sizes, which makes them as versatile as they are clean. For example, a fuel cell can be reduced to fit inside a portable music player – or be increased to the size of a refrigerator to power a house, office or apartment. Fuels cells are also reliable. Manned spacecraft and submarines have been using them for decades because they don't produce toxic emissions and thirsty crews can drink the pure water emitted as a waste product.

Advantages of fuel cells

- 70%–85% of the energy obtained from the fuel in a fuel cell can be converted into power and heat compared to coal or oil, which is around 35%.
- Fuel cells are inherently reliable, rugged, quiet and versatile and they can be used to power almost anything from a hearing aid to an office building. Currently, fuel cells are being developed to power cars (every major automotive manufacturer in the world now has a fuel cell vehicle in development), buses, boats, trains, planes, consumer electronics, portable power units and wastewater treatment plants (where the methane produced by the wastewater is used as a fuel source).
- Since fuel cells are smaller than coal-fired furnaces, less land is required to set them up as compared to traditional power plants.
- The pure water emitted as a waste product from a fuel cell can always be put to good use.
- Recent breakthroughs in fuel cell technology have produced electricity from carbon and bacterial enzymes, which eliminates the need for precious metals (such as platinum).

Disadvantages of fuel cells

- The price of electricity produced by fuel cells makes the technology somewhat prohibitive. Fuel cells large enough to power a home can cost thousands of dollars (resulting in a payback period of up to 15 years), which means that the electricity they produce costs around $1,500–$6,000 per kW (before payback). However, prices are expected to fall dramatically as the ability to mass produce increases. Depending on the cost of the hydrogen source (such as natural gas), electricity from a 2 kW fuel cell system could, in theory, provide power at eight to ten cents per kWh within the next decade or so.

- Long-term performance estimates for fuel cells have not yet been determined – although, to date, most fuel cells require maintenance overhauls every five years or so.

- For more information visit www.fuelcells.org or the *U.S. Fuel Cell Council* website at www.usfcc.com.

Micro-hydro power stations

Micro-hydro stations use natural water flows from rivers and streams to produce hydroelectricity. The turbines they house are small so they blend into natural settings while producing enough electricity to power several hundred homes or businesses. Micro-hydro stations are particularly viable in areas where industrialists during the 18th and 19th centuries built now-unused weirs to turn water wheels that powered looms and other industrial machinery. To read more about micro-hydro stations visit www.energysavingtrust.org. uk/Generate-your-own-energy/Hydroelectricity or www.absak.com/library/ micro-hydro-power-systems.

For more information about micro-power...

Payback is always better than pay more. With the rising cost of fossil fuels showing no signs of abatement, and carbon emissions placing increasing levels of stress on the environment (and the purse strings of governments), micro-power, in part or in whole, is an appealing option when used in appropriate settings. Likewise, the more efficient and energy-independent a nation's businesses become, the less the government has to spend on expanding or building more electrical power plants. For these and other reasons, a rising number of building owners, business managers and governments are wondering why they didn't consider micro-power sooner. For more information about sustainable micro-energy sources check out: www.clean-energy-ideas.com, www. alternative-energy-news.info and www.eere.energy.gov/greenpower.

You can also download the free booklet, *The Lean and Energy Toolkit* at www. gov/lean/toolkit/LeanEnergyToolkit.pdf. This highly recommended publication is specifically designed to help businesses of all sizes to reduce their energy needs.

PRODUCT

Because of the vast quantities of materials and energy that many products and services require, not to mention the huge amounts of waste they produce while they're being manufactured, making products and services more efficient (and more efficiently) is crucial to reducing the costs of running a sustainable business. To be sure, redesigning products and the methods used to make them is time-consuming and arduous; however, many practitioners attest that it is also one of the most financially rewarding.

20

The Hidden History of Products

Ever wondered what's involved in the making of a Styrofoam cup or a pair of blue jeans or even one serving of a hamburger, fries and a soda? How about the costs that are involved? (purchase costs, operating costs, and disposal costs) What are the true costs of raw materials before they're made into products and how much do the products cost after being sold? Most of us are blissfully unaware of the genealogy of the products we use as well as the trail of waste and inefficiency they leave behind. Consider, for example, the making of a typical aluminium can for the UK soft-drinks industry (provided below courtesy of the *Lean Enterprise Institute*).

To make aluminium, bauxite is needed. This reddish, clay-like ore is usually mined in Australia, Jamaica or Guinea and is then transported to a local chemical reduction plant (or a smelter). One ton of bauxite is needed to produce a half-ton of aluminium oxide. When a sufficient amount of aluminium oxide has been collected it's taken from the smelter, loaded onto a ship, and sent to Sweden or Norway (a journey of one month across two oceans). Next, the aluminium oxide is dissolved in a salt solution and zapped with powerful electric currents that purify it (electricity is cheap in these countries, which is why the process is done there). Making about half a kilogram of aluminium from aluminium oxide (which is enough to make 34 beverage cans) requires 7.5 kilowatt-hours of electricity – equivalent to the amount of energy needed to power a home or small business for a single day. As the electrical process unfolds, it reduces the aluminium oxide by half before what's left is shaped into ingots and trucked to a different part of Sweden (or Germany). The ingots are then heated in ovens and pressed into thin sheets. Afterwards, the sheets are rolled and trucked to another country where they're rolled and pressed again. When the sheets are thin enough, they are then shipped to the UK where they're punched and formed into cans.

Next, the cans are washed, dried, primed and painted. After a thin lacquer has been applied, the empty cans are flanged and sprayed with a protective film that prevents them from corroding. They are then sent to a bottler where they're washed again before being filled with a beverage. The beverage contains sugar harvested from beet fields in France (or cane fields in the tropics) as well as phosphorus from mines in Idaho (in Idaho, the 24-hour phosphorus mining process consumes, in one day, an amount of electricity equal to that required for the daily needs of a city of 100,000 people). After the beverage has been made it's squirted into the aluminium cans, and the cans are then sealed at a rate of 1,500 per minute. The soda-filled cans are next inserted into cardboard packaging (derived from trees cut down in Canada, Sweden or Siberia) and loaded onto pallets. More shipping ensues as the cartons are transported to supermarkets and vendors across the UK. On average, the finished product is purchased within three or four days and consumed within a week. Drinking the beverage takes a few minutes and throwing the can away takes a few seconds.

All in all, the entire process takes about 319 days. So perhaps it's not surprising that just a one per cent reduction in the aluminium needed to make beverage cans could save can manufacturers $20 million a year. This story also helps explain why recycling just one aluminium can is equivalent to saving the same amount of energy needed to power a television set for three hours.

Plastic is another material used to package soft drinks, and bottles made from plastic (like their aluminium counterparts) create their own unique waste trail. The total mass of a typical one-litre plastic container, for example, can contain 25 grams of non-recycled polyethylene teraphthalate (PET). And making half a kilogram of PET from scratch requires over 6.5 kilograms of oil and 294 kilograms of water resulting in 3.7 kilograms of greenhouse gas emissions being emitted during the production process. This means that every one-litre PET bottle needs 162 grams of oil and over 7 litres of water to produce – while emitting around 100 grams of greenhouse gas emissions (which is equal to the amount an average car produces driving half a kilometre). Keep these figures in mind when taking into account that Americans throw away approximately 2.5 million plastic bottles an *hour*.

As with aluminium cans, shipping and distribution merely increases the trail of waste that plastic bottles leave behind. Transportation emissions are measured in grams (in units of CO_2 equivalencies) per metric ton, per kilometre. Container ships emit about 17 grams of CO_2 per ton, per kilometre. Trains release 56 grams per ton, per kilometre; trucks spew out 102 grams per ton, per kilometre; and jet aircraft emit 570 grams per ton, per kilometre. When the costs of packaging and marketing (and a profit margin) are factored in, a one-litre container of bottled water can cost two to five times more than the same amount of petrol – or

50,000% more than tap water (which is ironic when one considers that about a third of the bottled water brands get their product straight from municipal taps).[1]

Ecological rucksack

The term for the amount of waste a product leaves behind as it winds its way from raw material harvesting through production and afterwards is called *ecological rucksack* – and almost every product carries a greater load than meets the eye. For example, according to Friedrich Schmidt-Bleek, formerly of the German *Umweltbundesamt* and the *Wuppertal Institute*, an ordinary cotton T-shirt carries an ecological rucksack of approximately 4,584 kilos.[2] How is this possible? First, the processes behind the growing of the cotton must be taken into account including the manufacture, transportation and distribution of fertilizers, herbicides and pesticides. Irrigation equipment (and water usage), farm machinery and petrol – as well as the processes behind these items – must also be factored in. Next come the steps involved in turning the cotton fibres into thread. Weaving, dyeing, packaging the completed product, and transporting it to retail outlets results in the creation of even more waste. Additional factors to consider include after-sale practices such as the efficiency of the washing machine the customer uses, the use of hot or cold water (hot water uses more energy), whether the shirt is air dried or put in a tumble-dryer, and so on. Every process creates and leaves behind some form of waste.

Of course, the waste estimation of a product is dependent upon how far back its materials can be traced, which makes any waste study highly subjective; however, reasonable estimates claim that a semiconductor chip can leave behind 100,000 times its weight in waste during the manufacturing process and the making of a laptop computer produces 4,000 times its weight in waste. The production of platinum creates 250,000 units of waste for every unit of precious metal created and a gold ring leaves behind approximately 400,000 times its weight in waste. The manufacture of one ton of paper requires the destruction of 20 trees and enough electricity to power the average home for six months. Two quarts of petrol are needed to produce one quart of orange juice – and one serving of a hamburger, fries and a soft drink requires 7,000 litres of water. Such is how raw material use in the United States multiplied 17 times between 1900 and 1989 while the country's population multiplied only three times.

Why is waste (and its costs) so difficult to see?

Mention the amounts of waste most products leave behind and many people roll their eyes under the assumption that the numbers are being exaggerated to prove a point. 'How can a quart of orange juice require two quarts of petrol to produce?' a student once asked me, 'that means orange juice should cost twice as much as petrol.'

The answer is that mass production, bulk raw material costs, mass transportation and externalized costs don't just lower the expense of making a product they also hide the cost of waste – and a common city public transport ticket can be used to illustrate this point. A $1 or $2 ticket, for example, enables a passenger to board a bus or a light rail service and either get off at the first stop or stay on until the vehicle reaches the last stop. Although the lengthier journey requires more energy and produces more waste, these extra costs are not reflected in the fixed price of the ticket – and it is this mistaken logic that sceptics use to debunk product waste costs (the reasoning is that since the price of the ticket remains the same, the bus or train can't be using more fuel or be producing more waste during the longer journey). Understanding mass production economics is the key to rectifying this misconception. The general rule is that when production volume doubles, the price of the product or service being produced tends to drop 10%–30%. And with waste outputs, many of the costs are externalized – which is why so many waste costs seemingly disappear. Put another way, by selling more, the costs of raw materials are spread out; meanwhile, the cost of waste is paid for by the general public in the form of pollution, industrial disasters, health costs, job layoffs, climate change and so on.

Hidden poisons

Just as worrisome as a product's trail of waste is the amount of toxins that are found in – or are used to make – everyday products. The average television, for example, contains 4,000 toxic chemicals (200 of which emit hazardous fumes when the TV is turned on) and many buildings are insulated with formaldehyde-laden particleboard that heavily pollutes indoor air. Moreover, the average PC consumes ten times its weight in hazardous chemicals *and* fossil fuels to complete its production (in India and China alone, about 70% of arsenic, lead, cadmium, chromium, cobalt, mercury and other heavy-metal pollutants come from electronic waste created just by computer manufacturers). If that isn't enough, of the over 8,000 chemicals used to dye clothes and fabric, less than 0.004% are actually considered *non-toxic*. Even glues and paints contain solvents that steadily pollute the air long after they dry.

Ten ways to minimize product waste

The key to reducing ecological rucksack is innovative thinking in the form of *product waste elimination*, a design process that goes beyond the examples of a carpenter examining a piece of wood before it's cut to ensure that all its pieces will be useable afterwards – or a dressmaker arranging pattern pieces on a length of fabric to reduce wasted cloth. True waste elimination takes into account the waste created during the production of a product while also eliminating the product's potential to create waste during and after its use (see Chapter 9). For example, when designers at *Nike Inc.* tried to manufacture shoes more sustainably, many of the problems the company encountered resulted from the fact that traditional materials and specifications were being used in production. So the company began developing new product engineering concepts called "considered design" principles with the aim of reducing environmental impact, eliminating waste, using environmentally sustainable materials, and eliminating toxins in manufacturing processes and the shoes themselves. *Nike* estimates that designing products beforehand using optimized resources that can be reused in a closed-loop system reduces supply chain waste by 17% and increases the company's use of sustainable materials by 20%.

Of course, 'considered design' thinking is only a first step. Following is a complete list of generic guidelines[3] that are widely considered to help eliminate product waste:

1. *Carefully design the product beforehand so that its resources can be optimized and reused in a closed-loop system.* In the past, product design was based on appearance, function and financial profit. Today's goods need to add 'material recovery' and 'reduced complexity' to the list in order to eliminate waste. Two types of raw materials usually constitute most products: technical and biological. Technical materials are synthetic or mineral and can remain in a closed-loop system of recovery and reuse. Biological materials are biodegradable and should be returned to the environment where they can be broken down safely and organically. For example, the '*gDiaper*' came into existence after its inventors learned that approximately 38,000 'disposable' diapers go into landfill sites in the USA every minute and each one can take 500 years to decompose. *gDiapers* are made from biodegradable materials that are put together using environmentally friendly production methods. This means that unlike their wasteful counterparts, *gDiapers* contain no elemental chlorine, no oil-based plastics, no perfumes and no smell. They're so benign that they can be flushed down a toilet or composted in a garden after use.

   Reducing the complexity and/or number of components in a product also helps eliminate waste and manufacturing costs. For example, a toilet valve was redesigned by its manufacturer and ended up weighing seven times less, went from 14 parts to one moulded part, and had its production costs reduced by 80%. Elsewhere, a windshield wiper was re-engineered and went from 49 parts to one part, which was therefore manufactured at a lower cost despite the fact that the new product was made from more expensive carbon fibre.[4]

2. *Design products so they can be easily disassembled after use.* One of the more important aspects of product waste elimination is called 'designing for disassembly',[5] which allows a product to be quickly taken apart at the end of its life for recycling or remanufacture. This involves:

- Enabling the removal of the product's parts without damaging them (including the quick removal of all fasteners and connectors),
- Clarifying and simplifying the parts classification process (thereby making it easier to determine which parts can be reused, remanufactured or recycled),
- Maximizing all reuse, remanufacturing or recycling processes, and
- Ensuring the processes that sort, separate and purify disassembled parts do not create waste.

3. *Reduce the hazardous makeup of the product.* Lower or eliminate the toxicity of a product's raw materials or parts by replacing them with non-toxic alternatives. Reducing toxin use helps eliminate the often unconsidered expenses induced by hazardous materials. These costs include: (a) special handling and packaging requirements, (b) specialized transport needs, (c) basic health and safety costs, (d) specialized equipment expenses, (e) employee training expenses, and (f) specialized disposal costs.

Examples for reducing these expenses include: In Poland, a street-light manufacturer discovered a way to replace the methylene chloride used to make its products with an environmentally safe alternative and saw its costs plummet. Elsewhere, the *Hollywood Memorial Hospital* in Hollywood, Florida, replaced the hazardous mercury-based batteries in its portable cardiac monitoring equipment with environmentally friendly zinc-air batteries. Although the new batteries cost 15 cents more, they reduce costs by more than 25% because they last longer and they lower the hospital's mercury waste by 155 kilograms annually. In Sweden, chemist Mats Nilsson discovered a flame-retardant chemical that's both harmless to humans and safe for the environment. Currently, the most widely used flame retardant in the world (bromide) is lethal, yet the danger is seen as a price worth paying for reducing the flammability of clothing. Derived from grapes and citrus fruits, Nilsson's alternative can be used in applications from mattresses to high-tech goods to kids' clothes while reducing bromide levels around the world.[6] Note: Nilsson's work is a good example of *biomimicry*, which involves replacing toxic or hazardous production processes with safe, sustainable and biodegradable alternatives. Carpets, chemicals, clothing, medicines, motor oils and plastics are just some of the products that can now be created by biological organisms in a safe and environmentally sustainable manner[7] by recreating what nature does.

4. *Switch to non-hazardous manufacturing methods.* Manufacturing processes that rely on hazardous chemicals, heavy metals, refrigeration or combustion are usually more expensive than they appear. For example, the *GlaxoSmithKline* pharmaceutical company in Verona, Italy, reduced the environmental impact of manufacturing a chemical being tested to treat chemotherapy-induced nausea and vomiting. Originally, the method for making the chemical relied upon subfreezing temperatures during production which required huge amounts of energy and produced significant amounts of waste. The improved process removed a number of hazardous substances from the production of the chemical, reduced the need for extremely low temperatures (which saved energy), reduced waste by 75%, and lowered the cost of raw materials by 50%.[8] Meanwhile, in the USA, a company that manufactures biological slides used a toxic solution made from mercury to prepare its specimens because it could not find a safe alternative for the mercury solution. Then one day a lab worker jokingly suggested using the soft drink he had just purchased as an alternative. Incredibly, it worked. Since *the alternative* is safer and cheaper than mercury, it reduced the lab's expenses.

5. *Reduce the amount of energy required to make the product, and use sustainable energy sources.* Examples include:

   • Using energy-efficient equipment in production processes,

   • Using remanufactured material in the product's makeup, and

   • Using sustainable energy supplies (i.e. wind or solar energy) from major energy producers or using micro-energy sources to supplement the powering of production equipment.

6. *Use newer and cleaner technologies whenever possible.* Many older products can be made more efficient by teaming them with new technologies. Examples include: containers that safely and effectively store liquids yet are still biodegradable; tubular skylighting, which captures outside light and redirects it into buildings; transmitting subscriber-based news and information over the Internet instead of printing it (a growing number of university courses benefit from this practice, which eliminates the need for students to travel to a classroom); and the *eCube*, a device the size of a hockey puck that attaches to a refrigerator's temperature sensor (the *eCube* prevents the wasteful turning on of the cooling unit every time the refrigerator door is opened, thereby reducing energy requirements by up to 30%). An additional example includes *Procter & Gamble*'s super-concentrated detergents that fit into smaller containers, thereby eliminating 40,000 truck deliveries annually. (In 2007, *Wal-Mart* announced that

it would begin selling similarly concentrated laundry detergents, which use less water and therefore require less packaging and space for storage. Every major supplier in the detergent industry has now become involved.)

7. *Use sustainable re-manufactured, recycled or scrap materials to manufacture products.* Closed-loop practices allow the original raw materials, energy and manpower of a product to be recaptured and used again. For example, in 2004, the *3M* company reformulated a brand of carrier tape that could be manufactured entirely from the waste materials of other products. The new product, which is made of 100% recycled material, not only costs less to make, it also reduced the plant's waste by 120 tons in the first year of production. Similar examples include efficient-minded paper companies that reincorporate damaged rolls back into production lines and plastics manufacturers that take off-cuts and place them back into machining processes.

8. *Improve quality control and process monitoring in all production processes.* By increasing production inspections (and inspection points) *and* displaying real-time production information, most production problems can be identified, stopped and corrected at an early stage before waste becomes a problem. For example, American retail giant *JCPenney*'s installed a computer program that shows ongoing electricity use in its stores every 15 minutes. Any spike in power usage is immediately investigated by employees who are specifically assigned to reduce energy costs.

9. *Find ways to have products returned to their place of manufacture so they can be disassembled, harvested and used to make new products.* By rewarding customers for returning used products back to their place of purchase or manufacture, a steady supply of (free) raw materials is maintained and relationships with customers are strengthened.

10. *Reduce packaging requirements, use recyclable packaging material, or find ways to eliminate packaging altogether.* Less packaging saves money in two ways: it reduces production expenses and it reduces waste disposal costs. A *Pollution Prevention Pays* team at *3M*, for example, redesigned the packaging of *Post-It* notes by eliminating cardboard back cards and blister covers from every package – thereby saving the company over $350,000 annually and eliminating 35 tons of waste every year.

Additional examples of companies that use product waste elimination concepts to reduce costs include:

- *Clorox*, which unveiled its first new brand in 20 years (*Green Works*) and includes five cleaning products that are at least 99% natural. The company subsequently won a rare endorsement from the *Sierra Club* for its efforts.

- Floor cleaning machine manufacturer *Tennant* designed a new technology that uses electrically charged tap water in its machines to produce a result that is superior to anything else on the market.

- The *Nitech* company (a battery manufacturer) developed a new product line of rechargeable batteries.

- The *Hoover* washing machine company created a new range of washing machines that reduce energy, water and detergent consumption. The designs won several awards and have dramatically increased profits.

- *Frigidaire* improved its refrigerators by reducing chemical levels, improving the efficiency of its motors, improving compressor design, developing better seals and gaskets, and designing smaller refrigerator doors (which helps keep cold air in). Increased profits followed.

- *Stelrad Ideal* (*Caradon Heating*) improved its line of domestic boilers by using flue heat to supplement the heat produced by the boiler's gas burner – thereby boosting the efficiency of its product to over 95%.

- *SC Johnson Wax* made a pledge to develop product packaging from 100% recycled materials. The change not only saves the company money, it generated lots of welcome attention in the press.

- The *Trannon* furniture company developed a whole new range of sustainable products from locally grown forestry thinnings and coppiced wood – and won several awards for doing so.

- *Pax* designed a new line of air gun pellets (under the brand name *Prometheus*) which are lead-free. Since 80% of *Prometheus* pellets are sold to farmers in Indonesia for pest control, this move greatly reduced the amount of lead detected in the region's paddy fields. What's more, *Pax* now uses the waste plastic from the production of its new pellets to make its packaging.[9]

The bottom line

With public expectations about sustainability continually increasing, 'future-proofing products' is a safe bet. Future-proofing products involves working to insulate products and services from risk and uncertainty by eliminating waste in all phases of a product's life-cycle to: (1) avoid rises in raw material costs, (2) reduce the chances of bad publicity, and (3) prepare for coming changes in environmental legislation.

Forewarned is forearmed.

21

Minimizing Packaging

Packaging comes in many shapes and forms: boxes, bags, cans, foam pellets, shrink wrap, tubes, paper, etc. The purpose of packaging is to protect a product and keep it fresh. Additional benefits include enhanced attractiveness and protection from tampering. The three most common types of packaging are:

- *Primary* packaging: the wrapping or container handled by the consumer.
- *Secondary* packaging: larger cases, boxes, or bags used to group goods for distribution, ease of carrying, or display in shops.
- *Transit* packaging: pallets, boards, plastic wrap, and containers used to collate products into larger loads for shipping.

Despite the benefits that packaging provides, many products are ridiculously over-packaged, which is annoying to those who have to pay to throw it away. *Wal-Mart*, for example, received quite a bit of favourable publicity when it unveiled a packaging 'scorecard' to its suppliers demanding that they reduce their packaging by at least 5% (*Wal-Mart* discovered that up to 20% of its garbage was directly attributed to packaging waste). By issuing this edict to its 60,000 suppliers, it reduced solid waste by 25% and shaved $3.4 billion off its annual operation costs.

The improved milk jug is another good packaging improvement example embraced by *Wal-Mart*. The new package is more cube-shaped, which lowers packaging expenses by 10–20 cents per container. Square jugs also store 50% more milk per square metre so more milk can be put on trucks, which reduces trips and fuel costs (by over 11,000 truck journeys annually). *Sam's Club* (a division of *Wal-Mart*) says that the new jug also enables almost three times more milk to be placed in coolers.

Reducing the costs and waste of extraneous packaging

Since packaging produces a substantial amount of waste, and waste is always a sign of wasted money, reducing packaging material is a good way for a business to decrease its expenses. For example, the British government's waste advisor (WRAP) states that food and drink packaging waste in UK supply streams amounts to 6.6 million tons of material and costs £5 billion annually. To combat this waste, food retailer giant *Tesco* introduced trayless bags for chickens that reduced packaging by 68% resulting in 540 fewer *Tesco* delivery vehicles on the road. Also at *Tesco*, tomato purée tubes no longer come in cartons, which reduces packaging by 45%. The company also decreased the thickness of the caps on 2 litre bottles of carbonated drinks, which saves 603 tons of plastic a year. And lightweight wine bottles now reduce glass usage by 560 tons (even double-concentrated drink mixes have resulted in smaller and lighter packaging – which further decreases delivery numbers). There is little doubt that knowing how much packaging delivers true customer satisfaction often leads to substantial reductions in costs as well as the elimination of unnecessary materials that nobody wants or needs.

Tried and tested suggestions for reducing packaging waste

- *Use the least amount of packaging possible (or, better yet, none at all)*. It is said that up to 98% of secondary packing (i.e. a box within a box, a bag within a bag…) and a significant amount of primary packaging can be reduced without any perceived decrease in the quality of the product or its package. In Australia, for example, several small business manufacturers have been able to save up to $30,000 a year by reducing the packaging surrounding their products.[1] In the USA, the *State Farm Insurance Company* in Bloomington, Illinois, saves $23,100 in annual packaging costs by eliminating unnecessary shrink-wrap from the booklets it distributes.[2]

- *Redesign packaging to reduce material use*. Sometimes a small change in the design of a package can significantly reduce the cost of raw materials. For example, *Anheuser-Busch* reduced its aluminium usage by 9.5 million kilos per year by shaving a third of a centimetre off the rims of its beer cans. In 1989, the *Digital Equipment Corporation* in Maynard, Massachusetts, made it a priority to reduce packaging materials and subsequently redesigned the amount of packaging used to ship metal computer cabinets – which saves the company $300,000 every year. Furthermore, by using bakery racks on wheels in place of disposable packaging to transport sheet metal parts from one area of a plant to another, the company saves an additional $200,000 annually.[3]

- *Reuse packaging materials and containers whenever possible.* Extending the life of packaging materials saves money. The *3M* corporation's plant in Valley, Nebraska, for example, worked with a supplier to produce returnable packaging that reduced shipping waste by eight tons and saved over $1,500 per shipment in packaging and disposal costs. Other companies have begun similar policies by asking customers if they mind having their purchases placed in used packaging (apparently, most customers don't mind a bit). Some CEOs consider this practice to be so financially advantageous, they believe that reusable packaging is the same as being given money by suppliers.

- *Repair and reuse heavy-duty shipping materials.* This is particularly true with pallet shipments. For example, *Wilton Industries* used to pay over $100,000 every year for approximately 14,000 new pallets. Now the company saves $64,400 annually by repairing and reusing damaged pallets and avoiding unnecessary pallet disposal costs.

- *Use recycled materials from sustainable, renewable sources or alternative materials* (such as wheat straw) *whenever possible for packaging.* The pulp and paper industry is the third largest emitter of global pollution in the world. The benefits of recycling paper therefore cannot be overstated.

- *Maximize the amount of material shipped on pallets and in vehicles.* This practice alone has saved many companies millions of dollars a year in shipping costs. For example, *3M Inc.*'s St. Ouen L'Aumone facility in France developed a new stacking system that allowed more materials to be packed onto transport vehicles. The new system has doubled load capacity, reduces the number of daily truckloads by 40%, saves 47,316 litres of fuel, and cut transportation costs $110,000 per year.

- *Use cardboard edges on the corners of large items (or those shipped in bulk) and shrink-wrap what remains rather than boxing each item separately.* This practice saves furniture maker *Herman Miller, Inc.* (in Zeeland, Michigan) $250,000 every year in packaging costs with just one of its products.

- *Use thinner, stronger and more opaque paper for paper packaging needs.*

- *Replace cardboard boxes with more durable, reusable containers.* This is especially advantageous for warehouses or interdepartmental shipments. In Cottage Grove, Minnesota, a *3M* facility designed collapsible, reusable steel crates robust enough to stack on top of one another. As a result, the company avoided producing 315 tons of solid waste and saved $101,800 in the first year alone.

- *Ask suppliers to accept returnable containers and packaging materials.* Automotive giant *General Motors* did this and slashed over $400 million from its supply chain costs.

- *Sell unused packaging waste to a recycler.* Contact a local waste disposal company or public works department for details.
- *Work out a shipping system that reduces the time it takes to package and send items.* Generally speaking, the more time it takes to package and ship products the more it costs.

It's not just good business, it's the law

Don't ignore the obvious. As you read this, local, state and federal governments around the world are passing more laws making it mandatory to return products and their packaging to their point of origin after use. Recyclable materials such as paper and plastic are being banned from landfill sites because these sites are rapidly filling up and any available space cannot be used for materials that can (and should) easily be recycled. Indeed, the day may soon come when products – and their packaging – will be tagged with a toll-free telephone number or a bar code so that they can be identified and picked up at the end of their useful life for reuse, remanufacturing or recycling purposes.

The bottom line: Reusing packaging materials is among the easiest of sustainability targets. Stay ahead of the curve.

22

Reuse, Repair, Remanufacturing and Recycling

Of all the sustainable options available, the simplest and most cost-effective is to reuse a product (or its components) as many times as possible. *Stewart's Shops* in the northeastern United States, for example, has been using refillable glass soda bottles and plastic milk bottle containers in its over 200 stores for more than 40 years. *Stewart's* milk bottles are reused around 50 times before they're replaced (which saves the company five cents per bottle). The company's soda bottles are reused about 20 times, thereby saving 14 cents per bottle. With sales of more than 12 million bottles annually, these savings add up. One program in particular that *Stewart*'s is involved with sells milk in refillable bottles to a local school. Since the bottles are reused 100 times before being replaced, the school's waste has been reduced by 700,000 milk cartons per year, which dramatically lowered the school's disposal and purchasing costs.

In a similar product reuse story, the *Ashbury Park Press* in Neptune, New Jersey, changed its machine-cleaning procedures by switching from disposable rags to reusable cloth rags. Even though the reusable cloth rags must be laundered, the company still enjoys an annual cost savings of $36,400. Further west, in Minnesota, the *Itasca County Road and Bridge Department* replaced the disposable air filters in its garages with reusable filters. The switchover means that a bit of extra labour is needed to clean the reusable filters, but fewer filter purchases and reduced disposal expenses amount to thousands of dollars in savings every year.[1]

When extending the life of a product, quality counts

The ability to extend the life of a product is reliant upon quality – and, as most people are aware, quality usually costs more. The good news with sustainability, however, is that the extra costs associated with quality almost always results in the ability of a product or its materials to be used longer – and the longer a product or its materials are used, as we learned in Chapters 5 and 6, the less expensive it becomes to produce the finished product. Take, for example, the decision made by local authorities in Itasca County, Minnesota. County buyers came to a decision to purchase only one brand of high-quality chainsaw instead of a multitude of cheaper chainsaws. The more expensive purchases were approved after officials factored in the savings from the longer product life associated with higher quality combined with the ease with which quality chainsaws could be repaired. Furthermore, when it came time to make repairs, the county saved even more money because parts from the higher-quality saws could be used as repair replacements (something that couldn't be done with the cheaper saws). This practice not only helped extend the life of the remaining saws (thereby reducing the number of new saws needed) it also reduced the disposal costs associated with throwing away a used chainsaw – and, as the old adage says, 'if you buy cheap, you buy twice'.

Product life extension

Reusing products and their materials is a win–win situation for all involved. From a customer's standpoint, reusing a product decreases waste, reduces disposal costs, and lowers the expense of purchasing replacements. From a manufacturer's viewpoint, similar savings occur. At some point, however, a product or its parts may undergo too much wear and tear and be deemed unsuitable in a reuse application. This does not mean that the product or its parts have reached the end of their useful life. In many cases, products can be broken down into base materials or components in order to be used again for the same or other applications.

Remanufacturing (to as-good-as-new condition)

Remanufacturing to as-good-as-new condition is a three-step process whereby: (1) a used product is disassembled, (2) its parts are cleaned and repaired, and (3) the parts are reassembled to a sound working condition. The term 'sound working condition' is key because in some areas of the world, reassembled products made from used parts are considered new and come with the same guarantee and warranty as products made from virgin raw materials. Conversely, in other regions, remanufactured (or *refurbished*) products must be labelled as such by law even if they carry the same warranty.

A case study

In 1972, *Caterpillar Inc*, a manufacturer of heavy earth-moving and construction equipment, was chosen by the *Ford Motor Company* to supply diesel engines for a new *Ford* delivery van. *Ford's* decision surprised a number of people. At the time, the *Cummins Diesel Company* was expected to win the *Ford* contract because it dominated the diesel engine business partially by keeping its costs down through the remanufacturing of used engines. *Caterpillar* knew that to remain competitive and retain its relationship with *Ford*, it too had would have to keep its costs down and increase its knowledge base. So after careful analysis *Caterpillar* decided to open up a remanufacturing plant in Bettendorf, Iowa, close to its Peoria headquarters. The idea was to test this new venture and see where remanufacturing would lead.

Ten years later, convinced that it was moving in the right direction, *Caterpillar* relocated its growing remanufacturing activities to Corinth, Mississippi and set up shop in an abandoned factory building. Land was cheaper in this part of the country and the location was more central to the majority of *Caterpillar's* customers as well as a proliferation of road networks. Three years passed before a second *Caterpillar* remanufacturing operation was opened up across town.[2] Success met with success and soon thereafter the company began operating a third facility in nearby Prentiss, Mississippi. Today, *Caterpillar's* Sawyer plant in Corinth receives worn engines and assemblies from all over the country – mostly from dealers who send the company around 160 tons of used equipment (about 17 truckloads) every day. The items *Caterpillar* finds suitable for remanufacturing include engines, fuel pumps, injectors, oil coolers, cylinder packs and hydraulic assemblies – each of which must be exhaustively taken apart by hand. On average it takes two workers a half-day of hard work to reduce one engine to its components. Every piece, including the tiniest screw, is saved because employees have been taught that anything placed in the trash is money thrown away.[3]

Almost every part that *Caterpillar* tries to salvage is embedded with grease, oil, carbon build-up, paint or rust. A mixture of baking soda with 10% alumina grit is needed to remove these contaminants. Afterwards, the scrubbed parts are sent away for inspection and sorting. The waste used to clean the parts is collected and used as a reagent in the neutralization of acidic liquid waste – a process that renders both liquids non-hazardous and has reduced the company's annual liquid waste from over 4 million kilos to just over 2 million kilos.[4] Of course, not everything is recoverable. Parts and materials that aren't suitable for remanufacturing are passed on to the company's foundry in Mapleton, Illinois, where they're melted and recast. In 1999, *Caterpillar*'s foundry recycled 106,835 kilos of aluminium alloy; 7,650,312 kilos of cast iron; and 2,576,679 kilos of steel.

It isn't all smooth sailing. One of the difficulties inherent in remanufacturing is maintaining a steady stream of used equipment. Without prior preparation it's quite possible to receive several truckloads of used products one week and then nothing for several weeks afterwards. *Caterpillar* eliminates this problem by offering its customers incentives that make them unwitting suppliers in the remanufacturing process. For example, when a customer needs a new part or a new piece of equipment, he or she is first asked to submit the old one. The customer is rewarded with a new part at up to half its full price. If the customer does not hand in the old part, the full price is charged.

Additional lessons have also been learned. By designing and producing higher-quality parts in advance, *Caterpillar* has discovered that it can get two or three lives out of its products. Manufacturing a component with another millimetre layer of metal on it may cost more, but the company knows that this investment will ultimately yield more profits because the improved product can be remanufactured. For example, *Caterpillar* estimates that it can remanufacture a good engine three times before it simply can't be used again – a practice that produces such substantial profit margins that more than $1 billion worth of sales were reported in 2005 at *Caterpillar*'s Corinth operation alone.[5] Before the recession of 2009, this number grew at least 15% annually.

Further savings are derived at *Caterpillar* from the company's commitment to reuse and recycle common work materials to add to its remanufacturing processes. For example, the wood pallets on which most equipment arrives are regularly inspected, repaired and reused. When they can no longer be repaired they're sold to a packaging company as boiler fuel. Similar waste reduction systems are in place to reduce office paper, aluminium cans, computer equipment and cardboard packaging. Today, 96% of the waste stream at *Caterpillar*'s Corinth plant is either reused or recycled – making the program so successful that it's sparked off similar programs in local schools, government offices and 15 nearby industries.[6]

Remanufacturing: the basics

For all the dirty work involved, the costs of revitalizing a previously manufactured product are often 60%–70% less than creating the product from scratch. This is because remanufacturing conserves the original energy, materials, labour and manufacturing effort that exist in every product.

Generally speaking, in most manufacturing processes 70% of the cost of producing a product from scratch is needed for materials and 30% pays for labour. Remanufacturing tries to recover the 70% of material costs invested in the original product. By recapturing pre-existing value, remanufactured products cost about half as much to make as new products made from scratch.

How much energy and materials can be exhumed from a remanufactured product? According to studies undertaken by Dr. Rolf Steinhilper formerly of the *Fraunhofer Institute* in Stuttgart, Germany (he is currently at the *University of Bayreuth*), the energy savings derived from remanufacturing worldwide equal the electricity generated by five nuclear plants or 10,744,000 barrels of crude oil carried by a fleet of 233 oil tankers. In addition, the amount of raw materials saved would fill 155,000 railroad cars and form a train 1,770 kilometres long. By avoiding these expenses, remanufacturing allows companies the choice of offering lower-cost product ranges to customers while enticing new buyers into markets where the price of introducing new products is seen as prohibitively high.[7] Refurbished (i.e. remanufactured) computers, for example, particularly laptops and PCs, are renowned for offering good value-for-money.

The economic advantages of remanufacturing

Over 70,000 firms in the United States, most of which employ 20 people or fewer, are involved in remanufacturing. Because these firms are virtually unknown, remanufacturing is often called the 'invisible industry'. Together, these businesses accumulate over $50 billion in annual sales and directly employ hundreds of thousands of workers. If all the people *indirectly* employed by remanufacturing were added to the latter figure (e.g. suppliers, distributors, retailers, installers, service providers, etc.) it has been estimated that the total number of people involved would be in the millions.[8] Evidence has shown that most remanufacturing firms also do well during times of recession and that no end to the industry's growth is in sight. According to researchers Robert Lund and William Hauser, the total financial value of products that could be remanufactured is around $1.4 trillion. With only $50 billion worth of goods currently being remanufactured, this suggests that the potential of the remanufacturing industry has yet to be fully tapped.

Despite the positive outlook, however, remanufacturing is virtually ignored by many businesspeople, which is why it's called the stealth business model. Those who study the remanufacturing industry say this invisibility is due to the wide dispersion of remanufacturers, the diversity of products they breathe new life into, and the small size of the majority of players. With the profit margins of remanufactured goods as high as 40%, however, one can only wonder why more businesses aren't taking advantage of this practice.

The challenges involved with remanufacturing

As with any product process, remanufacturing is not a panacea nor is it suitable for every product, market or business operation. Traditionally, it has proven difficult to remanufacture the following:

- Products that regularly undergo rapid technological changes.
- Products that take advantage of current or fleeting trends ('Industrial design is a field that was specifically invented to convince people that the washing machine, the car, or the refrigerator they had was out of fashion,' says Walter Stahel, 'and fashion is something that can't be remanufactured.').
- Products specifically designed to thwart attempts to disassemble and rebuild them (an act of protectionism to prevent firms from remanufacturing another business's products).
- Products that are sold at such a low cost that it's cheaper to buy a new version.
- Markets where consumers consider the terms 'remanufactured' or 'refurbished' to be synonymous with low quality.

Getting started in remanufacturing

Despite the gains that can be obtained from remanufacturing, the commitment to establish a remanufacturing setup should not be taken lightly. First and foremost a study should be taken of the market potential for the proposed remanufactured product and the company involved should be certain that it will not be competing against itself and its other products. A sound marketing plan must also be established to inform new and current customers that remanufactured products are just as durable as new products made from virgin raw materials. Additionally, employees will need to be educated and trained so they firmly believe that what many of them used to call garbage is seen as 'assets in transition'. Equally as important is that the company must have the means to locate, recover and transport its used products and have the resources and ability to disassemble, clean, sort, and inspect them for remanufacturing (a.k.a. reverse logistics). For this reason many companies partaking in remanufacturing practices find it advantageous to have their disassembly-process employees communicate openly and often with their product designers. This allows for a wealth of information to be accumulated as to how long-life improvements can be made in original products. In addition, tools and equipment may have to be purchased or developed to quality-test remanufactured parts before they're used again. Lastly, a plan for properly disposing unusable parts (as well as any chemical agents or materials used in the remanufacturing process) must also be developed and implemented.[9]

Recycling

Cascade Engineering, a Grand Rapids, Michigan, plastics manufacturer that makes parts for cars and various plastic containers – including trash cans – has cut the amount of trash it sends to landfills from 2,475 tons in 2003 to just over 700 tons this year. 'We've gone from every-other-day pickups to once every couple of weeks,' says Kelley Losey, an environmental services manager at the company. The secret to this success is recycling.[10]

Although the word 'recycling' is a generic term that often includes the reuse or remanufacture of a product or material, for the most part it refers to a process in which used products or packaging are collected, cleaned, shredded, melted down or otherwise reduced to recover their base materials. What remains is used as a total or partial replacement to create anew. Virtually anything from building materials to metals to chemicals to paper to plastic to fabrics or food and cloth – and, in some cases, unused medicine – can be recycled. Even substances at a molecular level can be tagged with nanotech markers for later reclamation and recycling. That being said, as we learned in Chapter 9, recycling should always be considered *after* a successful waste elimination program has been implemented.

Recycling is more expensive than reuse, repair and remanufacturing because more labour and energy is required to reduce materials back to their original form and then once again reconvert them into a specified intent. That being said, it still makes financial sense to recycle because recycling recaptures the value of raw materials as well as the energy and manpower that went into converting them into products. In some cases as much as 70% or more of this value can be reclaimed. For example:

- Making paper from recycled materials uses 70% less energy and produces 73% less air pollution compared with making paper from virgin raw materials.

- Recycling a plastic bottle saves enough energy to power a 60 watt light bulb for three hours.

- 25–30 plastic 1 litre plastic bottles can be recycled into one fleece jacket.

- A recycled glass bottle saves the amount of energy needed to power a computer for 25 minutes.

- Manufacturing aluminium from scrap requires up to 95% less energy than producing it from scratch.

- In Britain, it's been estimated that if all the aluminium beverage cans in the UK were recycled instead of thrown away, the country would need 14 million fewer garbage cans.[11]

Recycling and job growth

Recycling statistics go back a long way. According to a *White House Task Force* study, recycling activities prior to 1998 employed more than 2.5% of the USA's manufacturing workers – which amounted to 1 million jobs and more than $100 billion in revenues. Two years after this study was published, recycling was credited with producing 1.1 million jobs and grossing over $236 billion in revenues. Indirectly, it has been estimated that recycling creates an additional 1.4 million jobs and over $173 billion in receipts. According to the *Institute for Local Self-Reliance*, the United States grew 2.1% per year between 1967 and 2000 while the recycling industry enjoyed, on average, an 8.3% increase in employment and a 12.7% increase in sales per year.[12] This means that for every 10,000 tons of waste that's recycled, around 36 new jobs are created. Compare that to the incineration of the same amount of waste, which creates one job.

The complexities of recycling

Recycling is not without its costs and complexities. Many materials cannot be endlessly recycled because they weaken or degrade during the recycling process, which means that part (or all) of the original value of the material, energy, labour and other manufacturing inputs that went into making the product is lost or destroyed (a process called 'downcycling'). Additional labour, energy and manufacturing capital may therefore be needed to bring the desired material up to scratch. In terms of strength and mass, for example, aluminium is reduced by around half after being melted down during the recycling process thereby requiring the addition of pristine inputs to meet basic quality standards. Some common forms of glass, however, can be recycled dozens of times – a fact that can open up new cost-saving opportunities in terms of packaging and building materials (e.g. liquids that are traditionally shipped in aluminium cans or glass bottles can instead be shipped in giant plastic vats and be poured into bottles at their destination, which reduces transport costs and carries the potential to create local jobs). Still other materials (such as those used to make carpets), actually *improve* after recycling for reasons that continue to puzzle scientists. Welcome to the world of material science!

A good way to illustrate the versatility, strength and weakness of recycling is with plastic. Some plastics, such as those made from *high-density polyethylene*

(HDPE), can be recycled several times. Others either aren't recyclable or require a percentage of non-recycled material added to them so as to maintain an acceptable level of quality. Also, keep in mind that mixing different plastics together in different quantities forms hybrids that are unknown and untested and therefore can't be used for industrial purposes (this is why plastics are separated at recycling centres).

Following are the seven most common forms of plastic:

1. Type one plastics, *polyethylene teraphthalate* (PET or PETE), are clear and tough and resistant to heat. PET plastics are commonly used to make food and drink containers. When recycled, PET plastic shreds can be endlessly converted into recyclable fibres (also known as *polyester*) for clothing, carpeting, fibrefill and geo-textiles.

2. Type two plastics are stiff and tough and are made from *high-density polyethylene* (HDPE). Because HDPE plastics have good chemical resistance, they make excellent opaque containers for household and industrial chemicals. When recycled, HDPE plastics are reduced to landfill liners, fencing material, flower pots, plastic lumber, recycling bins, buckets, oil containers and benches.

3. Category three plastic (*polyvinyl chloride* or *vinyl*) is commonly referred to as PVC and is used to make food containers, medical tubing, wire and cable insulation, clear packaging (cling film), plastic pipes (for plumbing and construction), gutters, floor tiles, carpet backing and window frames. When recycled, PVC is often reduced to traffic cones, flooring, garden hoses and mobile home skirting.

4. Category four plastics, *low-density polyethylenes* (LDPE), are used to make garbage bags, dry-cleaning bags, shopping bags, squeezable bottles, food storage containers and flexible lids. After recycling, LDPEs are downgraded to floor tiles, shipping envelopes and furniture.

5. Type five plastic, *polypropylene* (PP), is resistant to heat, chemicals, grease and oil and is therefore used to make food containers such as margarine tubs, microwaveable trays, packaging material, medicine bottles, aerosol caps and drinking straws. Recycled PP is reduced to ice scrapers, rakes, sheeting, traffic signal lights, automobile battery cases, brooms and oil funnels.

6. *Polystyrene* (PS) is quite versatile and can be made into a hard, brittle plastic for compact disc jackets, combs, pens, plastic tableware, aspirin bottles, etc. Polystyrene can also be injected with air (foamed) and moulded into Styrofoam packing, grocery store meat trays, clamshell containers (used in fast-food restaurants) and egg cartons. When recycled, polystyrene can be converted into foam packaging, foam plates, thermometer casings, light switch plates, vents and desk trays.

7. The seventh category of plastic includes plastics that do not fall into the previous six categories. One example is *malamine*, a plastic used to make

plastic cups and plates. Category seven plastics are often mixed with resins and used in multi-layer configurations. Applications include large reusable water bottles, citrus juice bottles, food containers and *Tupperware*. When recycled, category-seven plastics can be used to make plastic lumber and plastic bottles.

Recycling and industrial waste

Almost any substance, no matter how toxic or filthy, can be recycled in some way. This is particularly true with hazardous, concentrated substances found in industrial waste (many of which require expensive, specialized disposal methods). The good news is that many of these substances can be reused in applications that require a great deal of material strength. Foundry sand used in metal casting, for example, can be recycled into sub-base filling for road construction, road embankments and structural fill. Coal waste (ash, boiler slag, fly ash, flue deposits and desulphurised material) can improve the strength and durability of concrete and manufactured wallboard. Material from construction and demolition sites (including shingles, scrap wood and drywall) can be recycled into asphalt paving, remilled lumber, wallboard and concrete.[13] Even paint and old tyres can be made into high-quality caulks and flooring. The point is that recycling carries almost endless possibilities. In India, for example, discarded plastic bottles and bags are being shredded, melted and added to roadway asphalt to improve the integrity, water resistance and durability of paved roads. Apparently, roads embedded with melted plastic last three times longer than conventional roads (although keep in mind that the environmental impact of this practice is unknown).

If recycling has so many advantages, why do so many businesses ignore it?

'So let me get this straight,' a student once remarked, 'reuse, repair, remanufacturing and recycling the products and materials we throw away [he held up a finger to emphasize each point]: (1) drastically cut a company's energy needs, (2) lower raw material costs, (3) reduce climate-change problems, (4) employ more people and (5) can lower production costs up to 70% or more, and yet most of the world's businesses don't take part in any of them?'

This wry observation helps explain why pressure is mounting to increase recycling legislation. Economists claim that if the possibilities of cutting costs and increasing profits exist, companies operating in a free market will eventually find these savings whether or not government intervenes. Yet for countries stricken with rising unemployment and rising waste and pollution levels, the question being asked is 'exactly when will the majority of businesses take note?'

Is everything recyclable?

Unfortunately, no. Substances used in the medical and livestock industries, for example, can be unsuitable (some scientists believe that the mad cow disease outbreaks in the UK began when infected sheep carcasses were ground up and recycled as cattle feed). Clearly, there is no substitute for research, common sense, and basic safety that errs on the side of caution when it comes to recycling.

For more information

For additional facts about recycling and its financial benefits, the book, *WASTEnomics: Turning Waste Liabilities into Assets* by Ken Tang and Jacob Yeoh (Middlesex University Press, 2008) is recommended. Contacting a local waste disposal company or public works department for the names of nearby recycling centres is also a good idea. In addition, you can visit www.euwid.de (click on the appropriate language translation icon). *Euwid* is a German-based organization that publishes newsletters and trade journals in German, English and French. Many waste specialists keep abreast of the latest recycling developments using information posted on this site.

Alternatively, visit the *Recycled Products Purchasing Cooperative* website at www.recycledproducts.org or try www.nfib.com/object/IO_28768.html (an American recycling site for small businesses). In the UK, visit www.defra.gov. uk/environmental/waste/business/regulation/index.htm.

Reuse, remanufacturing and recycling: an overview

FIGURE 22-1 illustrates the costs and time involved in reuse, recycling and remanufacturing. The further away from the original product the reclamation process lies, the more the investment in raw materials and other inputs is lost and the greater the costs are to the manufacturer (who has to purchase replacements). Similarly, the wider the base of each closed-loop practice, the more time, effort and expense is involved in collecting and reprocessing reclaimed material:

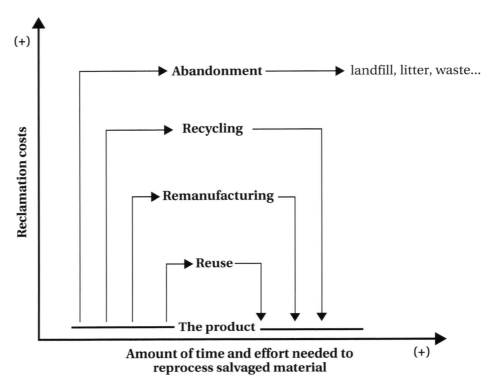

FIGURE 22-1: Costs and time associated with reuse, recycling and remanufacturing

PRODUCTION

... The mechanical, biological, or chemical processes used to transform materials or information into products or services and deliver them to where they need to be. Offices, factories, farms and restaurants all rely upon equipment and machinery in one form or another to turn information and resources into goods and services and since many of these tools (and processes) can waste as much or more than they produce, they present a prime target for efficient, sustainable practices.

23

Sustainable Production Locations

The term 'industrial ecology' was coined in 1989 by Robert Frosch and Nicolas Gallopoulus to describe the practice of bringing manufacturing and service facilities together in a symbiotic manner. In layman's terms, industrial ecology (also known in a more limited manner as 'industrial symbiosis') involves arranging businesses in a way so that wastewater, emissions, wastes and other outputs from one or more of the participating businesses can be used as raw materials by one or more of the others. For example, in a process called 'energy cascading', excess energy from one company (usually in the form of residual heat or steam) can be used to provide heating, cooling or system pressure for another. The advantages include a reduction in raw material costs, low waste disposal expenses and reduced energy requirements. Additional benefits associated with symbiotic setups involve a reduction in pollutants, a decrease in company regulatory burdens and lower demands on municipal infrastructures. Nearby cities and towns benefit too, thanks to enhanced business and job development, increased tax revenues and reduced environmental concerns and health costs. The city of Londonderry, New Hampshire, for example, became interested in eco-industrial parks after spending ten years and $13 million of taxpayer money cleaning up three toxic waste sites. In Canada, Burnside Park (Halifax, Nova Scotia) is perhaps the best-known example of an eco-industrial park with an estimated 1,500 businesses involved.

Building a closed-loop eco-industrial park

Most eco-industrial park projects start by estimating the material, water and energy needs of interested businesses. A network flow strategy is then devised to examine synergistic links between existing or interested companies (see FIGURE 23-1). Afterwards, active recruiting takes place to entice businesses whose production processes will help fill any gaps. According to industrial ecology planners, the most common characteristics of a successful eco-industrial park include:

1. Establishing material, water and energy flows that can be used as raw materials to build sustainable or semi-sustainable closed-loop systems (material flows can include heat, steam, fly ash, sulphur, sludge, gypsum, steam, paper and plastic packaging, metal scrap, wood pallets, machine oil, and so on).

2. Placing companies in close proximity to minimize transportation and material transfer costs.

3. Establishing strong informal ties between plant managers and promoting free exchanges of information (which helps participating companies work toward a more collaborative work environment).

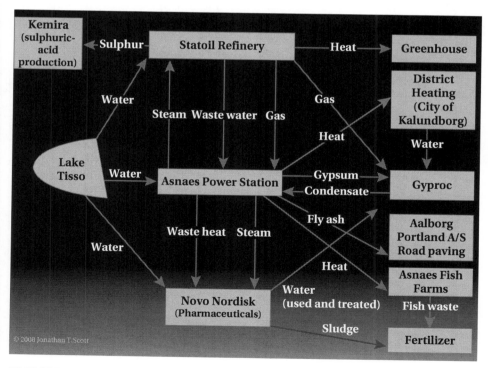

FIGURE 23-1: Waste exchange at the Kalundborg Eco-industrial Park (Denmark)[1]

4. Helping with the minor retrofitting of existing infrastructure (carrying out modifications to the involved companies so their outputs can be more easily shared).

5. Maintaining 'anchor tenants' (usually in the form of a wastewater treatment facility or an energy producer) whose continued presence and outputs make industrial symbiosis practical.[2]

How successful are eco-industrial parks?

A study of eco-industrial parks in Denmark (Kalundborg), Texas (Brownsville and Pasadena), New Hampshire (Londonderry) and Mexico (Matamaros), revealed that the annual economic benefit enjoyed by participating companies in an industrial ecology arrangement is as high as $8 million, with an annual return on investment reaching 59%. In addition, reductions in millions of kilos' worth of materials, waste and emissions were also identified as well as significant decreases in the need for natural resources such as water.[3] The longevity of the Harjavalta industrial area in Finland, however, best demonstrates the amount of success an eco-industrial park can enjoy. After World War II, Finland suffered from severe energy shortages that forced Finish copper company *Outokumpu* to resort to 'autogenous smelting' (or 'flash' smelting) in which the heat produced by oxidizing metal is used to maintain smelting processes. *Outokumpu*'s flash smelter, which was the world's first, started operations in Harjavalta in 1949. Over the years, the Harjavalta site has expanded to include over a dozen major firms that rely on each other to compliment various production processes. Sulphur, sulphuric acid, slag, heavy metals and wastewater are just a few of the waste outputs used as resources. Today, almost 60 years after it began, the Harjavalta site employs over 1,000 people and incorporates the services of more than 100 subcontractors on a regular basis.[4] Eco-industrial parks, it seems, have staying power.

For more information, visit www.indigodev.com. For over 20 years, *Indigo Development* (headed by Ernest Lowe) has worked to cultivate, and provide information about, industrial symbiosis and eco-industrial parks. A free handbook containing the lessons learned can be downloaded from the site.

24

Clean Production

Banskia Food Products Pty Ltd. is a multi-million-dollar company in the Sydney, Australia, suburb of Moorebank. Its 30 employees process and package apples for the baking and catering industry. Not long ago, at the beginning of each production cycle, the company used a substantial amount of fresh water for washing the company's main raw material (apples). Afterward, the floors of the production areas became littered with apple cores and peelings that were then washed into drains using the excess juice derived from apple parts blanched in heated tanks. Recognizing that a sizeable amount of money was literally being washed away due to wastage and other inefficiencies, the company asked an independent environmental management team to come in and investigate its efficiency options. As *Banskia* saw it, it was time to transform waste into profits.

A thorough investigation revealed that a significant portion of the company's raw materials was indeed being wasted at every stage of operation due to a poorly designed plant layout, the inability of certain production stages to cope with the smooth flow of production, and inefficient conveyors and dicing machines. In addition, far too much juice, rich in sugar and fine apple particles, was being flushed away. Steps were subsequently taken to collect and concentrate the excess juice, together with waste peelings and cores, for use as a sugar supplement in sauces and jams. Annual revenues from this practice alone amount to between $6,000 and $10,000. Next, a new conveyer and a more efficient dicer were obtained that reduced product loss (and cleaning requirements) and helped to generate a 3% increase in product yield. Further measures the company adopted included collecting and bailing cardboard and other waste packaging for recycling (a practice that eliminated between $3,000 and $4,000 in rubbish disposal costs) and the conversion of recovered apple peels into powder for use in baking, confectionery, and as a pectin replacement (this project was the result of a waste stream analysis done in conjunction with the *University of Western Sydney*). *Banskia* has since used the knowledge and impetus gained from its efficiency successes to further clean up its production processes by identifying additional profit-making and cost-cutting practices including: lagging steam pipes to save energy, seeking better electricity and gas rates, and utilizing cleaner, more efficient labelling and purchasing processes.[1]

Clean production defined

'Clean production' or 'cleaner production' is often defined as an integrated preventive strategy used in the production of products and services to increase efficiency and reduce risks to humans and the environment. According to the *United Nations Environment Programme,* clean production is neither a legal nor a scientific definition to be dissected, analyzed or subjected to theoretical disputes. Rather, it is a broad term that encompasses what many different people, countries and organizations refer to as 'eco-efficiency', 'waste elimination, 'pollution prevention' or 'green productivity'.[2]

In many countries, at organizations both large and small, clean production methods encouraged by national environmental agencies, regional conservation groups and university departments are reducing business operating costs, improving profitability, increasing worker safety and reducing negative environmental impacts. Far from being expensive, most companies are surprised at the cost reductions achievable through the adoption of clean production techniques and the minimal capital expenditure required to obtain worthwhile gains. Fast capital payback periods are also common. Furthermore, by adopting clean production methods, waste handling charges are being cut, raw material use is being lowered and business insurance premiums are being slashed.[3] For example, the *Cleaner Production Challenge* (CPC) conservation program, a voluntary resource program that helps the metal-finishing and printed-circuit-board manufacturing industries in the American state of Washington, has helped 40 businesses reduce wastewater by 67% and sludge by 40%. In the process, *CPC* helped its clients gain more control over their production, produce less waste, and greatly improve compliance with local environmental laws. A key to the success of the program has been the willingness of industry leaders to share their techniques with other agencies and companies.[4] Good news, it seems, is contagious.

Production lines come in all shapes and sizes

If you think that the word 'production' only refers to factory assembly lines, think again. Food service setups, service provider procedures, delivery routines, office systems, even agriculture are all good examples of 'production' in that commodities (e.g. raw materials) flow from one area (or machine or department) to another whereupon a set of procedures, labour skills or other processes are performed so as to end up with a finished product (or service). With office systems, the 'raw material' is usually information that passes from one person (or department or computer) to another before the converted end result is made ready for distribution and sale. With agriculture, the 'product' usually stays in one place while all sorts of materials and processes are brought to it. The point here is not to think of production as pertaining only to manufacturers, but rather to assume that every system is a production line in one form or another.

Putting together a clean production line

For the most part, cleaner production starts with lean production systems. The term *Chaku-Chaku* (Japanese for *Load-Load*), for example, is used to describe a single-piece production system that eliminates waste, improves product quality, reduces production setup times, lowers inventory costs and reduces floor space requirements. Central to its success is the creation of a *dedicated* production line consisting of *dedicated* machines or tools that perform only one or two steps in the sequence of making a part or product. As Peter Zelinski, editor of *Modern Machine Shop Magazine* explains, usually there are two ways to produce a machine part or product. The first is to purchase an expensive machine tool capable of multiple functions. The second is to identify every step involved in transforming a raw material into a finished component and to create a separate, simplified machine or workstation for each transformational step. The steps must then be arranged in a close-knit series of workstations so operators can move unfinished parts or products from one station to another as they're being produced.

Although the first method sounds faster (and less complicated) than the second, it's not always the case. Big, multi-function machines can cost much more when compared to a series of smaller machines that perform the same function. In addition, big machines all too often waste the time of workers because they usually have to be programmed and calibrated for each function they perform. Production bottlenecks are also a concern with large multi-functional machines, especially if the numerous operations they perform have to be scheduled or performed in a single cycle (most multi-functional machines can only perform one function at a time). Moreover, an entire production operation can grind to a halt when a large, multi-functional machine tool is shut down for repairs (in addition, maintenance costs for large machines are also higher than those of smaller machines). These factors are what the *Boeing Corporation* took into consideration when it replaced several giant, multi-function machine tools at a number of its production sites with a series of smaller, simplified machines that performed the same functions of big machines for a fraction of the cost. For example, a contoured composite part used on 777 aircraft was previously machined on a $1 million grinder capable of performing five different functions (four of which could not be used when the machine was in operation). *Boeing* replaced this machine tool with a one-function grinder specifically designed to do only what was required. The cost of the smaller machine? $50,000. Elsewhere, *Boeing* engineers discovered that one of its landing gear support assemblies involved a 1.6 km-long production process. Determined to eliminate this waste, the engineers consolidated assembly operations into a series of close-knit procedures, thereby reducing the part's travel distance by 80%. In the process, a large machine costing more than $1 million was replaced with a $15,000 alternative and a large 'oven' used for curing was replaced with a smaller one that matched the part's size and shape and cost one per cent that of the larger oven's price tag (the smaller oven also uses less than one per cent of the electricity of the larger oven). Further production achievements from the improved setup at *Boeing* included reducing the various stages required to manufacture metal parts from five days to 25 minutes.

Before Chaku-Chaku principles were adopted, employees used to have to travel to separate locations around the production shop to drill and grind components to a desirable shape. Now *Boeing*'s production procedures are performed on smaller, more numerous, but dedicated machines placed in close proximity – thereby saving much time and money.[5]

Putting Chaku-Chaku into practice

The first rule in setting up a lean and efficient production line is 'don't overbuy'. Overbuying includes: (1) purchasing equipment that will only be used once or twice (in this case, leasing may be a better option), (2) buying machinery that produces or performs far more than what is needed, and (3) taking on board anything that requires more investment in time, input and money (i.e. energy) than what is obtained in return. To help avoid these pitfalls, the following questions[6] should be asked before purchasing any piece of machinery or equipment:

- Is this machine or item really necessary? Big isn't always better. Big machines can cost a lot more in terms of time, money and energy – and result in extra capacity that will never be needed. Before buying large machinery, find out if smaller, more efficient machinery is more economically feasible.

- Is the full life-cycle cost of the machine being considered rather than its purchase price? Buying a cheaper piece of equipment is not always the bargain it seems. Inefficient, energy-hungry machines can consume their initial purchasing cost in energy per week. When buying equipment or machinery, remember that there are always two price tags. The first reveals the machine's purchase cost. The second includes how much the machine costs to operate in the long-term.

- Make certain that it's possible to accurately measure – in real time – what the machine produces and consumes in terms of materials and energy. Deficient (or zero) measurement makes it difficult, if not impossible, to determine how much a machine costs. Additionally, too many production systems contain monitoring procedures that measure what occurs after the manufacturing process has been completed. This means that a mistake or malfunction can repeat itself countless times before someone realizes what has happened. Real-time monitoring avoids this scenario because it provides instant feedback. Yes, real-time monitoring usually requires an initial investment in equipment – as well as the subsequent training of employees – but the results are worth it. For example, in 1897, Sakichi Toyoda innovated his company's power-driven weaving looms with a unique device that automatically shut the machines off when a thread broke, thereby preventing the wasting of good thread and the making of defective cloth. The money this idea saved was enough to create the Tomen Corporation (a large Japanese general trading company) and the Toyota Motor Corporation.

Additional suggestions for eliminating production waste

- Establish and support an in-house employee training and sharing program. The more people that are involved in a waste-reduction program, the more cost savings will be enjoyed. More often than not, employees hold the answers to most waste reduction and efficiency questions. Coax these answers out of them with motivational management and teamwork techniques.

- Seek outside help when needed. If answers from inside the business aren't forthcoming, seek assistance from a local environmental agency, a dedicated government program, or an interested university. Many times the services these institutions offer are either free or minimally priced. The School of Chemical Engineering at the South China University of Technology in Guangzhou, China, for example, developed a cleaner production process for producing sodium chlorite by reducing sodium chlorate with hydrogen peroxide. The result? Waste acids were dramatically reduced and the byproduct (sodium sulphate) can now be minimized and reclaimed.[7] This discovery saved several companies in the chemical industry the time and expense of figuring it out on their own. (Note: many government agencies gladly provide funding for production improvements if the improvements reduce water or energy needs and/or eliminate waste.)

- Replace toxic or hazardous substances with non-toxic raw materials. Using safe and sustainable raw materials reduces raw materials costs, lowers the training expenses and danger of handling toxic substances and reduces waste disposal costs while avoiding resource depletion and environment destruction. For example, in the USA, a 3M plant saved $120,000 in capital investment – and $15,000 annually – by replacing the toxic solvents it used with water-based alternatives.

- Reduce the energy requirements of machines and equipment. Clean production requires that every piece of equipment and machinery be inherently efficient before production starts. Whether production requires a photocopier, a million-dollar machine tool, a coffee maker, or a vast configuration of motors and pumps, everything should run on as little energy as possible. Before buying any piece of equipment or machinery read the label to determine the amount of power it consumes and compare its efficiency rating with other models.

- Keep equipment and machinery running at optimal levels. Good maintenance not only involves operating most equipment and machinery at peak levels (anything less and the full potential of the machine is being wasted), it also requires keeping these items in optimal condition with scheduled inspections and maintenance. Regular, scheduled machine maintenance may not be glamorous or exciting; however, it saves money in four ways:

  - It prevents possible breakdowns,
  - It reduces additional costs resulting from broken equipment,
  - It extends the life of the machine, and
  - It lowers energy costs (well-maintained machines almost always use less power). To ensure that equipment and machinery is operating at optimal levels:
    - Conduct (and record) frequent inspections,
    - Ensure that all moving machine parts are properly lubricated,
    - Clean equipment and machinery on a regular basis,
    - Replace worn or damaged parts as soon as they are discovered,
    - Ensure that drive belts, couplings, chains and bearings are adjusted and in good condition,
    - Keep equipment or machinery well ventilated, and
    - Replace old and/or outdated equipment with more efficient models.

- Mix only the volume of materials needed to fill an order. This guideline is a classic building block of lean thinking. Knowing how much of a product is needed before it's produced can greatly reduce raw material costs, energy expenses and the costs of labour and storage. A good example of this is seen in the publishing industry with 'print-on-demand' technology. The number of books a publisher prints is often based on guesswork, which can result in piles of unsold books that have to be collected and pulped. Today, specialized printing machines can print the electronically stored text of almost any book in less than a minute, which means that only the number of books ordered is printed – and that publishers can keep titles 'in print' indefinitely at little or no cost.

- Collect all recoverable materials and outputs for reuse. This includes steam and water as well as oil, solvents, chemicals, cleaning liquids and material scraps. If you can't find another business that needs these materials, figure out how your organization can use them at a profit. 3M's Traffic Safety Systems Division, for example, used its scraps and outputs to devise a new reflective product for signs that uses less energy, reduces process and design waste by 65%, and emits fewer toxins during production. As 3M sees it, anything not built into a product is waste – and therefore a cost – and is thus a sign of poor quality. In another example, a small modification to the production process of a Polish metalworking plant allowed scrap metal to be incorporated straight back into the system, which led to a 30% reduction of raw materials and annual cost savings amounting to $70,500. In Germany, a paper manufacturer virtually eliminated its massive water needs by filtering its base supply and reusing it in a closed-loop system. Across the Atlantic, an American jewellery-making business saved nearly $300,000 in capital costs and more than $115,000 in operating costs per year by introducing a closed-loop system that recycles and reuses its jewellery-plating outputs.

- Recover waste heat from kilns, ovens and other high-temperature machines. Waste heat from furnaces and boilers, exhaust, compressors and hot-liquid blowdowns can be collected and used in other processes. In the USA, for example, most power stations convert 34% of their fuel into electricity. The remainder, 66%, escapes as waste heat. Denmark, on the other hand, converts 61% or more of its electrical-plant fuel into power by, in part, recapturing heat with efficient furnace design.

- Insulate boilers and furnaces with ceramic fibres or other super-efficient materials. Even with efficient flue technology, more than 23% of the heat a furnace generates can go up its smokestack while 40% or more can dissipate through the furnace's walls. To minimize heat loss, focus on where most of the loss occurs. As one factory worker told me, 'If you can't place your hand on the exterior wall of a furnace because it's too hot, you're burning money.'

- Explore and discuss alternative practices to reduce energy requirements. A Kraft Foods plant in Campbell, New York, for example, reduced its natural gas needs by over 13% per year by improving boiler efficiency, reducing steam demand via the installation of direct-contact water heaters, and using lower-grade fuel oil for backup purposes to obtain a more favourable utility rates.[8]

Clean production and water reduction

Water often carries two costs. First, the water itself has to be paid for. Second, discarded water accrues expenses because most municipalities compute their sewage fees as a percentage of metered water use. Examples of water-saving practices used in clean industrial production systems include:

- Install closed-loop compressor cooling systems. Using fresh municipal water (tap water) once, then flushing it away, is both costly and a waste of good water. Close your company's wastewater loop by reusing what was previously discarded (e.g. filter what has been used and re-route it back into the production system). For example, Simon Fraser University in Burnaby, British Columbia, installed a closed system to reduce domestic water use and saw its water bills fall by $35,000 in one year.[9]

- Consider waterless alternatives in production lines. In Australia, the owners of Spectrum Printing invested in a waterless printing process rarely used by other printers. Apart from saving water, the process also saves 40% of waste paper and eliminates the need for isopropyl alcohol, which halts the discharge of volatile organic compounds as well as the costs associated with their disposal.[10]

- Consider using grey water (or rainwater) in production processes. If high-grade tap water is not needed for production purposes (and in many processes it's not), consider substituting it with collected rainwater or water gathered from other sources. Vam Organic Chemicals Ltd. in Gajraula, India, for example, uses spent water for dust control and incorporates the effluent into its distilling operation. Combined with a system that recycles sealed water in a vacuum pump, the net savings amounted to $33,330 per year in fresh water costs.

- Invest in water-saving practices and technologies. The Godfrey Hirst carpet manufacturing plant in Geelong, Australia, has been saving the equivalent of 38 Olympic-sized swimming pools of water annually after it modified its production system to include in-line drying practices, which eliminated an entire washing and vacuuming stage. In addition, the company upgraded a fluoro-chemical application process and invested in the production of solution-dyed nylon products that do not require dyeing or drying. Two textile-dyeing companies in Korea (Colorland and WS Dyetech Ltd.) substituted water-intensive alkaline fabric scouring with more efficient enzymatic scouring and saved 8–10 tons of water per ton of fabric production (while eliminating the need for caustic soda). If 200 other dyeing companies across Korea adopted the same practice, it's been estimated that the industry's total annual water use rate would fall by 3,200,000 tons – a cost saving of $2,133,333.[11]

It doesn't add up, it multiplies

Controlling production waste is all too often an after-the-fact endeavour that asks 'How can we deal with our waste?' Instead, the question should be 'What alternatives are there?' Seen in this light, cleaner, more efficient production does not create obstacles to production and growth. On the contrary, sustainable, closed-loop production practices reduce costs, conserve raw materials, help eliminate toxins and hazardous materials (and their expense), and reduce negative impacts on the environment. For more information about cleaner production, visit www.cleanproduction.org.

25

Motors and Pumps

Motors are ubiquitous. Virtually every business or office contains at least one. Some have thousands. Motors are used to drive almost everything from pumps, conveyers, refrigeration equipment, air compressors and fans to a host of other operations too numerous to mention. In the process, they can consume up to 60% (or more) of a company's fuel costs, which translates to around 40% of the world's electricity or roughly 75% of all industrial electricity. In fact, motors use up so much electricity that the amount they consume over their lifetime *always* costs more than the price of the motors themselves (some motors actually consume, in electricity costs, the amount of their purchase price every few *weeks*).[1] A new electric motor purchased for $1,500, for example, can cost as much as $13,000 a year to run and a typical 100 horsepower AC induction motor purchased for $5,000 will use as much as $35,000 worth of electricity in a year. Compare these figures to an older model 100 horsepower motor running continuously at full load (as many motors are designed to do), which can cost $70,000 a year to operate – or an older 20 horsepower motor, which can consume up to $14,000 worth of electricity annually.

Even with electricity rates as low as four cents per kilowatt-hour, most 20 horsepower motors (running continuously) use up to $6,000 worth of electricity annually. That's about six times the purchase price of the motor. Diesel or gasoline motors can be even more costly. Even if diesel prices were to fall to $0.85 for 3.78 litres, a 75 horsepower motor would still cost $6,400 a year to operate.

Determining the true costs of a motor

A general assumption held by engineers and mechanics in many industries is that efficient motors are more expensive than their inefficient counterparts because heavier copper wire, thinner core laminations, higher-grade steel and higher-grade bearings cost more. In the long run, however, motors designed to be more efficient always end up costing less. Equally as important is that contrary to what many people believe, most motors do not become more efficient when they are given less of a load to perform. Most motors need to run at or near their designed power rating (usually 75%–100% of their full load rating) in order for them to operate at optimal efficiency.

No matter how it's looked at, the overall financial impact a motor will have on a business's revenues should be considered long before a purchase is made. To calculate the amount of money a motor will consume (in electricity) over its lifetime, it is first necessary to find out the local cost of electricity per kilowatt-hour. The efficiency rating and amount of time the motor will be in operation are also needed. For example, the normal lifespan of a typical 100 horsepower motor is around 40,000 hours or about five years of continuous operation (although a well-maintained motor can last much longer). Let's assume that electricity costs are $0.05 per kilowatt-hour, the motor in question will run 24 hours a day, seven days a week at full load, and that it's rated as 94% efficient. The formula for determining the amount of electricity that the motor will consume over five years of operation is:

$$\textbf{(100 horsepower} \times \textbf{.746 kW/hp} \times \textbf{40,000 hours} \times \textbf{\$.05 kW-hour)} \\ \textbf{/ .94 efficiency} = \textit{\$158,723 electricity costs}$$

Another way to compare the amount of money a motor can cost to operate is to take the difference in efficiency points (expressed as a percentage) from the efficiency rating of two similar-horsepower motors and to multiply the difference by the amount of horsepower. If electricity costs $0.05 per kilowatt-hour, multiply the first sum by $50 to obtain the overall electricity costs of the motor in question.

For example, the difference between a 96%-efficient 100 horsepower motor and a 92%-efficient 100 horsepower motor is four percentage points. Four times 100 horsepower is 400. Assuming that electricity cost five cents per kilowatt-hour, multiply 400 by $50. The total ($20,000) shows how much extra will have to be paid in electricity over the life of the motor (assuming the motor is in continuous operation).

Reducing the costs of operating electric motors

The golden rule in reducing the cost of running a motor is to ensure that it's the right-size motor for the job. Many businesses run motors that are too big for the task under the assumption that the additional horsepower may be needed in the future. More often than not, this is expensive, costly and unnecessary. Over-sized (and therefore under-loaded) motors waste energy and cost more to run. In many cases running two smaller energy-efficient motors can actually cost less than operating one over-sized motor.

Reducing the cost of pumps and pumping

Up to 20% of the world's motors are used for pumping purposes and most of what they pump is water. Water and wastewater pumps consume over 50 billion kilowatt-hours of electricity in the USA every year (about $4 billion worth of power) and most of the energy they consume is used to fight against the friction created when water is forced through narrow pipes, around bends and up steep inclines.

Just as with motors, most pumps are bigger and more powerful than they need to be because in many cases production designers did not know what the exact pumping requirements were when the pumping system was being planned. The result is that valves and other devices are later installed to create intentional friction to reduce output to manageable levels. Obviously, this is not an efficient practice – particularly when the annual expense of running an over-sized pump can cost several times more than the price of the pump itself. In some cases, over-sized pumps can be balanced by trimming the impeller or replacing it with one of a smaller diameter (an impeller, which is similar to a propeller, transfers energy from a motor to the fluid being pumped inside a tube or pipe by directing, increasing and pressurizing the flow of liquid inside). For a pump operating at less than 10% of its designated flow rate, trimming an impeller can reduce electrical consumption by as much as 25%.

Improving pump efficiency

Thinking ahead is probably the best way to avoid the costs associated with buying an over-sized pump. Try to envision the entire pumping system beforehand with an eye toward maximizing efficiency – then seek a pump that is compatible with its operation while thinking about how the entire system can be made more efficient. The authors of the book *Natural Capitalism*[2] (Amory Lovins is widely seen as a pioneer in exposing motors as major energy wasters) describe how several years ago the *Interface* carpet company in Shanghai built a factory where the production process required 14 pumps totaling 95 horsepower. By redesigning the layout of the entire system, however, the main engineer, a man named Jan Schilham, was able to cut costs, improve efficiency and reduce the overall pumping power needed by 92%. Schilham's design incorporated two simple changes from which almost any pumping system can benefit. First, fatter pipes were used. By using fatter pipes less friction is created when fluid moves through them. By increasing the diameter of a pipe by 50%, friction can be reduced by 86%. The result is that less pumping energy is needed, which means that smaller, more economical pumps can be used. Traditionally, engineering students are taught that the extra cost of fatter pipes does not justify the cost of the pumping energy saved. Unfortunately, this argument that does not take into account the savings that are made from the lower cost of a smaller pump, the lower costs of operating a smaller motor, and the reduced costs involved with fewer motor controls and fewer electrical components.

Schilham's second money-saving idea was to lay out the pipes first and install the pumps afterward – which is exactly the reverse of how most people construct a pumping system. Most engineers install pumps and motors in a convenient or arbitrary spot and then attach pipes to them. The pipes then have to be bent, turned, raised and twisted so their contents can be directed from one point to another. Unfortunately, each bend and turn, as well as the number of valves added, increases friction, which requires a larger pump and increases the amount of pipe needed. Conversely, the straighter the pipe, the fewer pipes are needed and the less friction is created. When fewer pipes are needed less insulating material is required to cover them, which also lowers costs. Furthermore, by using plastic or epoxy-coated steel pipes, friction can be reduced by another 40%, resulting in a proportionate savings in pumping expenses that can eliminate up to 95% of the costs of pumping.

Additional cost and energy saving suggestions for pumps

Pumps don't just push fluids, they can also direct pressurized air from one spot to another. Whatever substance is being pumped, the following suggestions can reduce the costs involved:

- Eliminate leaks in compressed air lines and valves. Up to 20% of the work output of a compressor is sometimes needed to make up for losses from air leaks. A General Motors assembly plant in Flint, Michigan, for example, reduced its energy needs by around 8% after, in part, decommissioning unused air supply systems and ensuring that those that remained worked properly.[3]

- Eliminate leaks in steam pipes and fittings. A leak in a steam line can result in higher steam production requirements to compensate for what is lost. In addition, leaking condensate return lines bring back less condensate to their boiler, thereby forcing the boiler to use more energy to heat up replacement water. In 2006, an Eastman Kodak manufacturing plant in Rochester, New York, reduced its annual natural gas needs by 11% after improving and modifying its feed-water heat recovery system – a move that was accomplished at virtually no cost.[4]

- Insulate pipes and heating equipment to reduce heat loss. All pipes that transfer heated fluids or gases from one process to another should be well insulated.

- Consider using industrial heat pumps (IHPs). IHPs use heat from heat-producing processes to supplement other industrial heating processes or in preheating procedures.

For more information about getting the most from pumps and pumping, visit www.plantservices.com. Alternatively, browse the pump section of the *Industrial Efficiency Alliance* website at www.industrialefficiencyalliance.org.

26

Eliminating Waste at Work: Getting Started

Whether you represent a business that desires to become sustainable or a business school that wants to add sustainability to your curriculum, you'll need to practise what you preach before trying to convince others. To get started, gather your employees together, explain what needs to be done (and why) and begin with what is commonly called 'the low-hanging fruit' (the easiest tasks). Creating and displaying a process map that illustrates the inputs and outputs that flow around and through the organization is a good first step. Along with the map, the amount of electricity every workstation or department consumes should be mentioned (perhaps with facts and figures relaying their CO_2 emissions), as well as the amount and cost of materials the business swallows up (e.g. office supplies, raw materials, water), how much waste (garbage) is created, and the *types* of waste being generated. This is necessary to ensure that the organization is seen as serious in its attempts and to highlight the fact that the efforts employees make (or don't make) will be monitored.

Some businesses start their sustainability programs by suggesting that staff transport themselves to work more efficiently. This may not alter the company's bottom line (and managers may be told that it's none of their business), but employee transportation is as a good place as any to begin making changes because encouraging employees to use public transportation can significantly reduce the ecological rucksack and carbon footprint of a business. Additional waste-reduction suggestions include:[1]

- Encourage employees to walk or bike to work (to encourage the latter, ensure that employees have a safe place to put their bicycles).

- Begin a car-pooling program. Find out who lives on whose route to work and promote cooperation.
- Initiate a company vehicle inspection program. Ensure that all company vehicles are both efficient and well maintained. Encourage employees to be equally as vigilant and diligent with their vehicles.
- Determine if or how employees can work from home or, work out an alternative schedule that allows employees to stagger their schedules so they can work at home part-time.
- Encourage conference calls and/or videoconferencing instead of travelling to meetings.
- Share office space and equipment rather than purchasing separate items for every employee.

Making the most of office furnishings, computers and equipment

- Ensure all electrical equipment (even coffee makers) is energy-efficient. An Energy Star rated medium-sized copying machine, for example, can cut $50 or more off annual energy bills.
- Buy remanufactured, energy-efficient computers, copiers, fax machines, etc. instead of new models whenever possible. Remanufactured or refurbished equipment provides excellent value for money and no one will know the difference.
- Use laptops in place of desktop computers. Laptops use less electricity. (Remember to unplug the power cord when the laptop is not in use.)
- Turn equipment off when it's not needed. Computers, when left on overnight, can rack up $75 in energy costs per unit, per year.
- Unplug all electrical items when not in use. Most electrical equipment continues to draw power when it's turned off. Even an empty mobile phone charger draws electricity if it's plugged in. Especially ensure that equipment is unplugged during weekends (vending machines are a prime target).
- Enable the power management features on desktop computers (and monitors) to switch off when not in use. This can save up to $55 per monitor and $45 per computer annually.
- Use smaller computer monitors. A monitor that is 5 cm smaller than a larger model can reduce electricity consumption by as much as 30%.

- Don't use screen savers. Instead, switch the screen saver mode to 'blank screen' or 'none'.

- Buy used or remanufactured office furniture. Few people will notice the difference.

- Invest in high-quality equipment rather than cheap, shorter-life versions.

General energy reduction

- Insulate the building inside and out (paying particular attention to heat and cooling loss from doors, windows and walls). Improved insulation can save $800 or more a year in energy costs.

- Determine if the local power company provides sustainable energy alternatives. Some electricity providers invest in wind, solar or tidal energy and provide these options to their customers so they can cut CO_2 emissions.

- Set the office thermostat a few degrees lower in the winter and a few degrees higher in the summer. A 2% decrease during the day can cut energy bills by 2.5%.

- Don't heat or cool an unoccupied office (particularly during the evenings and weekends). Setting the thermostat back 10° at night can cut 15% off energy bills.

- Perform periodic maintenance of HVAC equipment (heating, ventilation, and air conditioning). Good maintenance can reduce heating bills by 5% and cut electrical bills by 2%.

- Replace all office light bulbs with energy-efficient alternatives. This not only saves money, the resulting drop in electricity reduces greenhouse gas emissions. If all Europeans changed their standard light bulbs to energy-efficient bulbs the resulting drop in carbon emissions would be equivalent to taking 70% of the continent's cars off the road.

- Turn off all lights when not needed (installing motion detectors can eliminate this problem). Keeping off unnecessary lights not only saves the money needed to power light bulbs, it also lowers cooling costs – and can shave up to 18% off an office energy bill.

- Turn off ventilation systems in unoccupied areas. This can lower HVAC costs by $300 annually.

- Pay bills electronically. If everybody in the USA paid his or her bills online, the nation's annual paper waste would be reduced by 1.6 tons and greenhouse gas emissions would be cut by 2.1 million tons.

Reduce paper consumption

Roughly 3% of world industrial production is spent on the creation of paper. Paper manufacturing also uses more water than any other industry (98 tons of water are needed to produce one ton of paper), releases the fourth most pollutants, and is considered the third most energy-intensive industry on Earth. In addition, around 900 million trees are cut down annually to meet the world's paper demands. Yet only 10% of the world's paper is ever utilized in the long term. Most is used and thrown away shortly after it's bought (the average office worker uses one sheet of paper every twelve minutes). With this in mind, the city government of Seattle, Washington, concluded that a 1% reduction in its $288,218 annual paper bill (which amounts to 73,902,000 sheets of paper) will save thousands of dollars in paper costs; 62 trees; 244,553 litres of water; 136 kilograms of water pollutants; 3,208 kilograms of solid waste; 9,298 kilograms of greenhouse gases and other pollutants; and 123,662 BTUs of energy. That being said, saving trees and reducing pollutants isn't all that minimal paper usage achieves.

The Brazilian business *Semco*, streamlined its operations years ago by, in part, reducing company paperwork. Upset with the fact that employees rarely talked to one another, company CEO Ricardo Semler decreed that all inter-office memos could be no more than one page in length. Employees therefore had no choice but to actually talk with each other. As a result, more work got done. In Australia, a business turn-around specialist once told me that virtually his entire secret to saving bankrupt companies was to 'forbid the writing of memos altogether' (for the same reason). *Oticon Inc.*, a hearing aid manufacturer in Denmark famously cut a hole in the roof of its multi-storey headquarters straight through the ceiling of the employee cafeteria and into a main collection site. A Plexiglas tube was inserted into the void and all discarded paper was continuously taken up to the roof and thrown down the tube – a powerful message directed at employees that paper waste would no longer be tolerated. Paper consumption in the company subsequently decreased by 50% and the business enjoyed a dramatic increase in productivity.

Suggestions for reducing paper use

- Establish a company mandate that demands paper use is reduced (then enforce the rule).
- Shorten the number of forms and papers customers must fill out (they'll love you for it).
- Store your business data (including employee manuals, policies, etc.) in an electronic format.

- Distribute memos via email or display them on a single sheet of paper in a central location.

- Use both sides of a sheet of paper and set photocopiers to do the same. This practice alone can cut 10%–40% off paper costs. Seagate Technology Inc., a computer disk drive manufacturing company in Scoots Valley, California, reduced its annual paper needs by four million sheets this way, thereby cutting its paper bill by $45,300.

- Set wider margins on documents so more words can be placed on each page.

- Use smaller font sizes so more text can be put on a single page.

- Use chlorine-free, recycled paper for all paper needs. Recycled paper requires 60% less energy to make than virgin paper. Every ton of recycled paper also saves 4,000 kilowatt-hours of electricity, 26,497 litres of water, and 17 trees (each of which has the capacity to filter 27 kilos of pollutants from the air).

- When printing or photocopying, adhere to the following: (1) always print in 'draft' mode, (2) avoid colour printing whenever possible, and (3) buy recycled toner and ink. Each of these practices saves ink.

- If recycled paper is unavailable, use paper made from sustainable sources such as ecologically treated bamboo or hemp.

- Place a paper recycling receptacle in a conspicuous place, encourage its use, and schedule a designated employee or cleaning crew member to arrange regular collection.

- Shred unwanted paper and use it as packing material.

- Reuse paper, envelopes, and boxes whenever possible. The Washington Suburban Sanitary Commission decided to replace its billing envelopes with send-and-return envelopes that could be used for both billing and receiving payments. As a result, 47 m^3 of warehouse space immediately became available and the cost of envelope purchases was reduced by $55,000.

- Replace paper towel dispensers in washrooms with energy-efficient air hand-dryers.

Water reduction measures

With offices using up to 12% or more of a nation's daily potable water, much can be done to reduce consumption without making sacrifices. For example:

- Install faucet aerators (low-flow devices) on all taps.
- Replace toilets and urinals with low-water or water-free models.

- Use filtered tap water rather than delivered bottled water – or use water straight from the tap. In many regions local tap water is better than bottled water in terms of cleanliness and quality.

Miscellaneous tips

- Ask office cleaning crew staff to use non-toxic cleaning products.
- Buy office supplies in bulk (which can save on packaging).
- Encourage the planting of trees or other indigenous foliage outside the office building.

Vehicle use cost-saving suggestions

In 2004, the *United Parcel Service* (UPS) began a policy designed to reduce the number of left turns made by its drivers. Having its vehicles stop and idle at traffic lights while waiting to turn against oncoming traffic was literally costing *UPS* millions of dollars in fuel losses so a software program was devised that mapped a customized route for each driver to minimize left turns. This practice not only saves the $3 million annually, it reduced 1,000 metric tons of CO_2 emissions during the first few years of trials.[2] Such is what happens when positive changes in behaviour are made.

To make your company's vehicles more efficient, first measure and record the amount of fuel they consume. Determine the efficiency rating of each vehicle, as well as how much pollution it produces per year. Visit the *U.S. Department of Energy* website and look up the year, make and model of the vehicle to obtain this information. Next, apply as many efficiency measures as possible (see below). Record how much was saved after one or two weeks then share the results with employees and encourage them to seek more ways to cut waste and costs. Some companies reward their most efficient drivers on a monthly basis, which instigates a healthy competition between employees. 'Just remember to keep encouraging everyone,' a shift supervisor told me, 'good ideas acquired with ease are just as easily discarded with ease.' Following are common ways a business can save fuel:

- Don't waste fuel idling. Large vehicles, like trucks and buses, consume huge amounts of fuel when idling – around 4 litres. Have drivers use auxiliary power units during rest periods
- Invest in hybrid vehicles. Hybrid cars and delivery vehicles are not only more fuel-efficient, they're gentler on the environment.

- Decrease the amount of time spent driving. Fill up trucks before sending them off (inform your customers how much money and CO_2 emissions they can save by having shipments delayed until delivery trucks are full). Combine errands or deliveries, car pool, take public transportation… do whatever is necessary to minimize driving time.

- Don't send out a big truck when a small one will suffice. This practice cut 21 million miles from Xerox's distribution network.

- Check tyre pressures. Try pushing a car with flat tyres and you'll discover why this is important. Keeping tyres properly inflated can increase fuel efficiency by 3% or more. According to the Rubber Manufacturers Association, 85% of people don't check their tyre pressure properly. Wal-Mart increases the efficiency of its fleet by 6% with fuel-efficient tyres.

- Clean and maintain engines. Clean or change the air filter regularly (two or three times a year), change the oil as recommended by the manufacturer (usually once or twice a year), check all fluids, and clean and replace spark plugs regularly.

- Plan journeys. Know every route in advance, which saves the time and expense of unnecessary travel or getting lost.

- Don't spill fuel when filling vehicles. A drop spilled is a drop wasted – and every drop adds up.

- Eliminate unnecessary weight. Don't carry around more items or equipment than is needed.

- Load up trucks to avoid making additional trips or to eliminate the need for two vehicles. Sentinel Transportation (a joint venture between DuPont and ConocoPhillips) have reduced the number of trucks leaving one site 55% by increasing payloads by 50%.

- Make vehicles more aerodynamic. Install wind skirts. Remove luggage carriers, roof racks and trailers when not needed (the air resistance these items create dramatically decreases fuel efficiency).

- Keep vehicle windows up. Open windows create drag and increase air resistance. Keep interior vents open instead.

- Turn off unneeded electrics. Although some manufacturers dispute it, air-conditioning can consume up to 10% of a vehicle's fuel.

- Observe the speed limit. The faster a vehicle is driven the more fuel is burned. Driving 113 kilometres an hour as opposed to 97 kilometres an hour consumes around 20% more fuel. Con-Way Freight estimates that lowering speed limits by 3 miles per hour will save the company 3.2 million gallons of fuel or $15 million annually.

- Don't ride the brake and don't brake hard. Many drivers brake more often than necessary, particularly when switching lanes. Unfortunately, heavy braking decreases fuel efficiency by as much as 30%.

- Coast on hills. Taking your foot off the accelerator when descending a hill reduces energy consumption.
- Reaffirm your commitment about sustainability and what it involves. After reading the end note below, re-read the introduction of this booklet and the first four sections.

Epilogue:
It's All or Nothing

Several years ago I was invited to Amsterdam to speak to a group of finance-event promoters about sustainability. After I explained the basics of waste elimination and resource extension, the group politely applauded, the chairwoman thanked me for coming, and the attendees began collecting their mobile phones as they rose from the table. 'Doesn't anyone have any questions?' I asked.

'No, thank you,' the chairwoman replied. A sympathetic expression creased her face as she stepped forward to shake my hand. 'Your talk was very interesting,' she said, 'but we're finance people and sustainability is obviously more of a manufacturing topic.' For several seconds I stood in silence, wondering where I had gone wrong. 'I though you said that you represented financial institutes, investment houses, banks and so forth,' I said.

'Yes,' she replied, 'that's correct.'

'Well, then: why does no one have any questions?' I continued. 'Fraud, unnecessary risk, damages, human error, weaknesses in processing systems, poor service, lawsuits, bad customer relations – all of these are forms of waste that should be eliminated and prevented in order for a business to become more sustainable. Just as important, are your financial customers interested in investing in businesses that are working toward eliminating their waste and becoming more profitable, or do they want to continue pouring money into businesses that are not?'

A sudden, stunned hush swept the room. Slowly, everyone returned to his or her seat. The question and answer session that followed lasted thirty minutes.

Several years later I was in Warsaw, Poland, discussing sustainability to the human resources director of a large multinational firm. 'This all sounds wonderful,' she said,' but it has nothing to do with my line of work so I can't say that I'm really interested.'

'I thought you said that you were a human resources director,' I replied.

'Yes, I am,' she answered.

'So what type of people do you want to hire?' I asked. 'People who can save a company hundreds of millions of dollars by doing the things I've just described, or people who can't?'

And so it goes, as otherwise intelligent people continue to believe that sustainability is someone else's responsibility or belongs in someone else's industry or profession. Even 'green' advocates sometimes make the same mistake by erroneously compartmentalizing their role in sustainability, placing their interests above the interests of others, or ignoring the bigger picture. For example, the use of ethanol as a fuel is sometimes promoted as a greener alternative to gasoline (petrol) because ethanol can be made from biological sources and be grown by sustainable means, thereby making it safer to process (no industrial spills, no mining accidents, etc.). In addition, ethanol emits fewer (and less harmful) pollutants when it is burned as a fuel.

All of that is true, however, in this case going green does not go far enough for the simple reason that the combustion engine is one of the most inefficient devices ever devised by human beings. Indeed, igniting a flammable liquid to produce kinetic energy, not to mention reconverting the energy down a transmission line to the wheels of a car, is ridiculously wasteful (indeed, most vehicles waste more than 80% of the fuel they consume due to these, and other, inefficiencies).

In other words, what is the point of changing from petroleum to ethanol if the ethanol is going to be put into a device where 80% of it will be wasted? Such is why a waste elimination (and prevention) program must work hand in glove with any resource extension idea (as explained in Chapter 9). Put another way, if you want to harness the capacity to continue into the long term, you have to look at the big picture.

In the Introduction of this publication I wrote that focusing only on one aspect of sustainability is both short-sighted and partial – not unlike claiming that good health is solely about vegetables. It is therefore difficult to expect progress in sustainability by focusing only on only one area of sustainability. The problem with focusing on only one aspect of sustainability (the empirical approach) is that once a few facts become clear it's tempting to believe that they possess an independence all their own and to rest in them and believe that they are the foundation of what is being sought (theologians call this 'idolatry'). Obviously, dividing the world into parts is something we all do to ease understanding, but in doing so something is always devalued – and what is diminished is often an awareness of and contact with that which can only function as a whole.

To do otherwise is merely robbing Peter to pay Paul. And that's not sustainable.

Before implementing the suggestions in this publication, please re-read the introduction of this book – then revert to Chapter 26 for a few basic ideas on how to get started. Then, once the easy targets have been hit it's time to lead rather than follow. Don't waste time 'greening' the wrong things. There is no point in making an unneeded production process more efficient or recycling an unnecessary packaging component. Take stock of the situation across you, delve deeper into the 7 Ps, involve more internal and external customers in making improvements, and go further. Drop the assumption that sustainability is a one-time-only endeavour; there is no finish line and it's not a good idea to wait for market shifts, or changes in regulations, or a return to bad habits to drive your next move. Stay ahead of the game. View oncoming laws, disruptive changes and other seismic shifts (many of which can be seen well in advance) as an opportunity rather than a threat.

After the 2008 economic collapse and the recession that followed, local and national governments – and the general public – are not in the mood to suffer through more business and finance community incompetence. Patience is wearing thin with businesses and industries that refuse to think in the long term and continue to cling to wasteful habits. Just as important, governments are on the prowl for new ways to fill empty coffers and customers around the globe are wising up to the hidden costs of short-term products and production processes – indeed, a growing number of people around the world are asking why a high quality of life today for a relative few should jeopardize everyone else's tomorrow.

What this means for businesses is that the entire risk–benefit spectrum is changing. Free rides are over. As you read this, domestic and imported products filled with toxins are increasingly being banned, system inefficiencies are being penalized, and cities are taking back tax breaks given to companies that promise jobs, but don't deliver. The message coming out of all of this is that sustainability is here to stay because sustainability just makes sense. It is not going away. Just as important, at some point, either as a manager or employee, you will have to decide whether or not to get involved – which means that *you* are the one who ultimately decides how painless or painful (and sustainable) your future is going to be.

Sustainability in Business:
It's All or Nothing

The Problem:

Every business specialty speaks its own language.
Every business specialty thinks its goals supersede the goals of others.

Endnotes

Introduction: What is Sustainability?

1. Fish, Stanley, 'Fathers, Sons and Motorcycles', *International Herald Tribune*, June 14, 2009 (www.iht.com).
2. Persig, Robert, *Zen and the Art of Motorcycle Maintenance*, Vintage Press, London, 1999.

1. Fundamentals

1. Kaufield, Rich, Malhotra, Abhishek, and Higgins, Susan, 'Green is a Strategy', *strategy + business* (www.strategy-business.com/article/00013?gko=e5d36). As reported in *Magee, David, Jeff Immelt and the New GE Way: Innovation, Transformation and Winning in the 21st Century*, McGraw-Hill, New York, 2009.
2. www.epa.gov
3. Winston, Andrew, *Green Recovery*, Harvard Business Press, Boston. MA, 2009.
4. searchsystemschannel.techtarget.com/generic/0,295582,sid99_gci1245328,00.html
5. Scott, Jonathan T., *Managing the New Frontiers*, MES Publishing, Panama City, FL, 2008.
6. See note 5 above.
7. See note 5 above.
8. See note 1 above.
9. See note 5 above.
10. See note 5 above.
11. See note 5 above.
12. Hawken, Paul, Lovins, Amory, and Lovins, Hunter, *Natural Capitalism*, Little, Brown & Company, Boston, MA, 1999.
13. Orzech, Dan, 'At Clean Plants, It's Waste Not', *Wired* (online), August 10, 2005 (http://www.wired.com/science/planetearth/news/2005/08/68448).
14. See note 5 above.
15. See note 5 above.
16. See note 5 above.
17. See note 5 above.
18. See note 5 above.
19. See note 5 above.

20. Kanal, Vijay, 'The Eight Biggest Myths about Sustainability in Business', *Green-Biz.com*, November 23, 2009 (www.greenbiz.com/blog/2009/11/23/8-myths-about-sustainability-business).

21. See note 3 above.

22. www.youtube.com/watch?v=iP9QF_lBOyA

23. www.tennantco.com

24. www.patagonia.com/web/us/home/index.jsp?OPTION=HOME_PAGE&assetid=1704

25. See note 3 above.

26. See note 9 above.

27. www.epa.gov/iaq/pubs/sbs.html

28. Zandonella, Catherine, 'Airborne Toxins', *National Geographic* ('The Green Guide 109'), July/August 2007 (www.thegreenguide.com/doc/109/toxin).

29. Kamrin, Michael, *Traces of Environmental Chemicals in the Human Body*, prepared for The American Council on Science and Health, May 2003.

30. EPA pamphlet, *Volunteer Estuary Monitoring: A Methods Manual* (EPA-842-B-06-003, 2nd edition), March 2006, ch. 12.

31. Johns Hopkins University, 'Prescription Drug Pollution May Harm Humans and Aquatic Life', *Science Daily* April 11, 2002 (www.sciencedaily.com).

32. Associated Press, 'Probe: Pharmaceuticals in Drinking Water', March 10, 2008, (www.cbsnews.com).

33. Luo, Michael, and Thee-Brennan, Megan, 'Poll Reveals Trauma of Joblessness in US', *New York Times*, December 14, 2009 (www.nytimes.com/2009/12/15/us/15poll.html?em&_r=1&).

34. Hart, Stuart, *Capitalism at the Crossroads*, Wharton School Publishing (Pearson), Upper Saddle River, NJ, 2005.

35. Easterly, Thomas, *The Elusive Quest for Growth*, MIT Press, Cambridge, MA, 2002.

36. Palley, Thomas, 'A New Development Paradigm: Domestic Demand-Led Growth', *Foreign Policy in Focus* September 1999 (www.fpif.org).

37. www.worldbank.org

38. Serwer, Andy, 'The 00's: Goodbye (at Last) to the Decade from Hell', *Time Magazine*, November 24, 2009 (www.time.com).

39. Baillie, Richard, 'Military Sets Its Sights on Sustainability', RenewableEnergyWorld.com, May 23, 2011 (www.renewableenergyworld.com/rea/news/article/2011/05/military-sets-its-sights-on-sustainability).

2. Understanding Waste

1. World Resources Institute (www.wri.org).

2. Ahuja, Gautam, 'Does It Pay to be Green? An Empirical Examination of the Relationship between Pollution Prevention and Firm Performance', *Business Strategy and the Environment* 5(1) (March 1996), pp. 30-37.

3. Institute of Medicine (IOM), 'Sustainable Business, Economy, and Health – A Case Study', *Rebuilding the Unity of Health and the Environment: A New Vision of Environmental Health for the 21st Century*, National Academies Press, Washington DC, 2001.

4. Courtesy of ESource (www.esource.com). Information confirmed 2012.

5. Epstein, Paul, 'Full Cost Accounting for the Life Cycle of Coal', *Annals of the New York Academy of Sciences*, Vol. 1,219, February 2011, pp. 73-98.

6. Slesinger, Scott, 'Two Year Anniversary of the Tennessee Coal Ash Spill', National Resources Defense Council, December 22, 2010 (switchboard.nrdc.org).

7. DeCanio, Stephan, 'The Economics of Climate Change', *Redefining Progress*, U.S. Bureau of the Census, San Francisco, CA, 1997.

8. Pielke, Roger A., 'Let There Be More Efficient Light', *International Herald Tribune*, March 10, 2011 (www.iht.com).

3. What the Reformer is Up Against

1.   Gertner, John, 'Why Isn't the Brain Green?', *The New York Times*, April 19, 2009 (www.nytimes.com).
2.   Kristof, Nicholas, 'When Our Brains Short-Circuit', *The New York Times*, July 1, 2009 (www.nytimes.com).
3.   Mlodinow, Leonard, 'The Limits of Control', *The International Herald Tribune* (www.iht.com), June 16, 2009.
4.   Langer, Ellen, and Rodin, Judith, 'Long-Term Effects of a Control Relevant Intervention with the Institutionalized Aged', *Journal of Personality and Social Psychology* 35 (December 1977), pp. 897-902.
5.   Dunn, D., and Wilson, T., 'When the Stakes are High: A Limit to the Illusion of Control Effect', *Social Cognition*, August 1990, pp. 305-323.
6.   Langer, Ellen, 'The Illusion of Control', *Journal of Personality and Social Psychology*, 32 (February 1975), pp. 311-328.
7.   Langer, Ellen, and Roth, J., 'Heads I Win, Tails It's a Chance: The Illusion of Control as a Function of the Sequence of Outcomes in a Purely Chance Task', *Journal of Personality and Social Psychology*, 34 (1975), pp. 191-198.
8.   See note 3 above.
9.   See note 1 above.
10.   See note 1 above.

4. Establishing Sustainability as an Objective

1.   Lovins, Hunter, *The Economic Case for Climate Change* (www.awarenessintoaction.com/article.php?url=the-economic-case-for-climate-action).
2.   Scott, Jonathan T., *Managing the New Frontiers*, MES Publications, Panama City, FL, 2008; Scott, Jonathan T., *The Entrepreneur's Guide to Building a Successful Business*, MES Publications, Panama City, FL, 2009.
3.   Mento, A.J., Steel, R.P. and Karren, R.J., 'A Meta-Analytic Study of the Effects of Goal Setting on Task Performance 1966–1984', *Organizational Behaviour and Human Decision Processes*, February 1987, pp. 52-83.
4.   Email correspondence with Ken Tannenbaum (formerly) of Dow Chemical, 2006.
5.   Bohan, Peter, 'EU Biotech Storm Plants Few Seeds', *Reuters News Service* (Chicago), April 22, 1999; *The Economist*, 'Genetically Modified Company', August 15, 2002 (posted on www.biotech-info.net/GMO_company.html).
6.   From email correspondence with the company.
7.   See note 1 above.
8.   De Blas, Alexandra, interview with Ray Anderson titled 'Sustainable Carpet Tiles', Australian Broadcasting Service (ABC Radio Network) (www.abc.net.au/rn/science/earth/stories/s28472.htm).
9.   Orzech, Dan, 'At Clean Plants, It's Waste Not', *Wired* (online) August 10, 2005 (www.wired.com/science/planetearth/news/2005/08/68448).
10.   This story was relayed to the author by one of his students.
11.   Parinello, Tony, 'Turning a Prospect's No Into a Yes', from the *Entrepreneur* magazine website, July 14, 2003 (www.entrepreneur.com/article/0,4621,309855,00.html).
12.   See note 11 above.
13.   See note 9 above.

5. Resource Extension Part 1: Service and the Performance Economy

1.   www.dow.com/safechem/about/story.htm
2.   www.cleanharbors.com

3. Perthen-Palmsino, B., and Jakl, T., 'Chemical Leasing: the Austrian Approach', 2004 (www.sustainable-chemistry.com).
4. Douglas, Ed, 'Better by Design: Battling the Throwaway Culture', *New Scientist* 2585 (January 4, 2007).
5. Nevius, C.W., 'Disposing with the Fix-It Guys', *The San Francisco Chronicle*, July 16, 2005.
6. White, Allen, Stoughton, Mark, and Feng, Linda, 'Servicizing: The Quiet Transition to Extended Product Responsibility' (DuPont case study), published by the Tellus Institute and the U.S. Environmental Protection Agency Office of Solid Waste, May 1999.

6. Resource Extension Part 2: Leasing and the Performance Economy

1. Hart, Stuart, *Capitalism at the Crossroads*, Wharton School Publishing (Pearson), Upper Saddle River, NJ, 2005.
2. Hawken, Paul, Lovins, Amory, and Lovins, Hunter, *Natural Capitalism*, Little, Brown & Company, Boston, MA, 1999.
3. Frenay, Robert, *Pulse*, Farrar, Straus & Giroux Publishing, New York, 2007.
4. White, Allen, Stoughton, Mark, and Feng, Linda, 'Servicizing: the Quiet Transition to Extended Product Responsibility' (DuPont case study), published by the Tellus Institute and the U.S. Environmental Protection Agency Office of Solid Waste, May 1999.
5. See note 2 above.
6. Fishbein, Bett, McGary, Lorraine, and Dillon, Patricia, 'Leasing: A Step toward Producer Responsibility', *Inform Inc.*, (N), 2000.

7. Cooperative Networking

1. Scott, Jonathan T., *The Entrepreneur's Guide to Building a Successful Business*, MES Publications, Panama City, FL, 2009.
2. See note 1 above.
3. Lotti, Ricardo, Mensing, Peter, and Valenti, David, 'A Cooperative Solution', *strategy + business* July 17, 2006 (www.strategy-business.com).
4. Batson, Daniel, 'How Social an Animal: The Human Capacity for Caring', *American Psychologist* 45(99) (April 1990), pp. 336-346.

8. Lean Thinking

1. Friedman, Thomas, *The World is Flat*, Penguin Books, London, 2006.
2. Cardiff Business School, 'What is Lean Thinking?', Lean Enterprise Research Centre, May 2007 (www.cardiff.ac.uk).
3. Alukal, George, and Manos, Anthony, 'How Lean Manufacturing Can Help Your Mold Shop', 2007 (www.moldmakingtechnology.com/articles/100204).
4. Lean Enterprise Institute, 'What is Lean Thinking?', 2007 (www.lean.org).
5. Womack, James, and Jones, Daniel, *Lean Thinking: Banish Waste and Create Wealth in Your Corporation*, Simon & Schuster, New York, 1996.
6. Environmental Protection Agency, 'Lean Thinking and Methods', *Lean Manufacturing and the Environment*, May 2007 (www.epa.gov/lean/thinking/index.htm).
7. See note 4 above.
8. See note 1 above.
9. See note 3 above.
10. See note 6 above.

11. Nave, Dave, 'How To Compare Six Sigma: Lean and the Theory of Constraints: A Framework for Choosing What's Best for Your Organization", *Quality Progress*, March 2002, pp. 73-78 (www.lean.org/Admin/KM%5Cdocuments/76dc2bfb-33cd-4ef2-bcc8-792c5b4ef6a6-ASQStoryonQualitySigmaAndLean.pdf).
12. Agency for Healthcare Research and Quality (AHRQ), 'Overview: What is Lean Thinking?', 2007 (www.ahrq.gov/qual/hroadvice/hroadviceapb.htm).

9. The Waste-First Rule: Resource Extension Begins with Waste Elimination

1. Interview with David Klockner, Vice President of ENERActive, June 2012.
2. *DuPont* examples provided by Dawn G. Rittenhouse, Business Sustainability & Product Stewardship Leader, DuPont SHE Excellence Center, Wilmington, DE, USA, July 2012.
3. Newman, Jared, 'Yet Another Promise of a Smart Phone Breakthrough', *Time* (online), November 2, 2012 (techland.time.com/2012/11/02/yet-another-promise-of-a-smartphone-battery-breakthrough).

10. Mapping the Waste-Elimination Process

1. Scott, Jonathan T., *Managing the New Frontiers*, MES Publications, Panama City, FL, 2008.
2. ESSP CLP, 'Product Stewardship through Life-cycle Analysis', Introduction to Sustainable Development for Engineering and Built Environment, 2007 (www.naturaledgeproject.net/ESSPCLP-Intro).
3. Nemes, Judith, 'Dumpster Diving from Garbage to Gold', *businessGreen.com*, January 16, 2009 (www.businessgreen.com/business-green/analysis/2234107/dumpster-diving-garbage-gold).
4. See note 3 above.
5. www.reuters.com/article/idUSN1943775220070419
6. Aster, Nick, 'ColdWater Tide: Provoking the Ah-Ha Moment at Procter & Gamble', November 13, 2009 (www.triplepundit.com/2009/11/coldwater-tide-provoking-the-ah-ha-moment-at-proctor-gamble).

11. Ongoing Measurement and Record-Keeping

1. Interview with Cheri Sustain (as recorded in: Scott, Jonathan T., *Managing the New Frontiers*, MES Publishing, Panama City, FL, 2008).
2. www.smallbusinessnotes.com/operating/finmgmt/recordkeeping.html
3. www.solovatsoft.com/outsourcing-green-development.html
4. www.snh.org.uk/publications/on-line/advisorynotes/45/45.htm
5. www.epa.gov/oecaerth/incentives/auditing/auditpolicy.html
6. www.britsafe.org/download/audits-advisories/5-star-environmental-brochure.pdf
7. See note 6 above.
8. Scott, Jonathan T., *Managing the New Frontiers*, MES Publishing, Panama City, FL, 2008.

12. Taxes and Legislation

1. 'Business Can Do It with Government's Help', *The Economist*, May 31, 2007 (www.economist.com).
2. Hoerner, Andrew, 'Tax Waste not Work', April 15, 2005 (www.tompaine.com).

3. 'Big Business Pushes Bush on Carbon Caps, Top US CEO's Tell President Action on Climate is Necessary', CBS news/AP, January 23, 2007 (www.cbsnews.com/stories/2007/01/23/business/main2387501.shtml?tag=contentMain;contentBody).

4. Butler, Jim, 'Hotel Lawyer: Why the SEC May Make You Go Green', September 30, 2007 (www.hotellawblog.com).

5. Kennard, Kenneth, 'Businesses Get a New Voice', 2007 (www.greenbiz.com, accessed March 2008).

6. Web, Toby, 'Sustainable Consumption: We Will if You Will Say Consumers', *Ethical Corporation*, July 21, 2006 (www.ethicalcorporation.com).

7. Romm, Joseph, 'Why We Never Need to Buy Another Polluting Power Plant', July 28, 2008 (www.salon.com).

13. The Perils of Greenwashing

1. Terrachoice Marketing, www.terrachoice.com/files/6_sins.pdf.

2. Ellison, Katherine, 'Shopping for Carbon Credits', July 2, 2007 (www.slaon.com).

3. Source Watch, 'Why Do Businesses Greenwash?' (www.sourcewatch.com).

4. Lovins, Amory, Lovins, Hunter, and Hawken, Paul, 'A Road Map for Natural Capitalism', *Harvard Business Review*, May-June 1999, pp. 145-158.

14. The Importance of Customers

1. 'How You Can Profit from a $600 Billion a Year Emerging Market', *CNBC European Business*, January/February 2007.

2. walmartstores.com/FactsNews/NewsRoom/6503.aspx

3. Saarte, Lynne, 'Things to Consider Before Going Green', www.articleblast.com/E-Commerce_and_Online_Businesses/General/Things_To_Consider_Before_Going_Green_. See also www.greenbiz.com.

4. Romm, J.J., and Browning, W.D., 'Greening the Building and the Bottom Line: Increasing Productivity through Energy Efficiency', Rocky Mountain Institute publication D94-27, 1994.

5. Winston, Andrew, *Green Recovery*, Harvard Business Press, 2009, pp. 10-11.

6. www.comcast.net/slideshow/finance-job-security/nugget-market

7. Edwards, L., and Torcellini, P., 'A Literature Review of the Effects of Natural Light on Building Occupants', National Renewable Energy Laboratory (Technical Report), Golden, CO, 2002.

8. 'Natural Light Facility Boosts Productivity 19% at DPC', *Manufacturing News*, July 11, 2002 (www.themanufacturer.com).

9. NRDC, 'Building Green: Increase Employee Satisfaction and Productivity', 2007 (www.nrdc.com).

10. See note 9 above.

11. Hart, Stuart, *Capitalism at the Crossroads*, Wharton School Publishing, Pennsylvania, 2005.

12. www.inclusivebusiness.org

15. Managing Change

1. Makower, Joel, 'Meeting Expectations', #884, November 29, 2005 (www.grist.org).

2. Communication with Ken Tannenbaum (formerly) of Dow Chemical.

3. Lewin, Kurt, *Field Theory in Social Science*, Harper Press, New York, 1951.

4. See note 3 above.
5. Band, William, *Creating Value from Customers*, John Wiley & Sons, New York, 1991.
6. Schein, E.H., 'Kurt Lewin's change theory in the field and in the classroom: Notes toward a model of managed learning', www.sol-ne.org/res/wp/10006.html (March 20, 2002); www.a2zpsychology.com/articles/kurt_lewin's_change_theory.htm (September 9, 2004)
7. Communication with Ken Tannenbaum (formerly) of Dow Chemical.

16. Putting a Team Together

1. MnTAP (Minnesota Technical Assistance Program), 'Building a Successful Pollution Prevention Team', University of Minnesota, 2007 (www.mntap.umn.edu); Ohio PPWM (Pollution Prevention and Waste Management), 'Organize the Pollution Prevention Program' (www.epa.state.oh.us/opp/guide/p2pch8.html).
2. Janus, Irving, 'Groupthink', *Psychology Today*, November 1971, pp. 43-46; Janus, Irving, *Victims of Groupthink*, Houghton Mifflin, Boston, 1982 (2nd edition).

17. Building Better Buildings

1. This information was graciously provided (and checked) by the *Rocky Mountain Institute* (www.rmi.org) for *Managing the New Frontiers* (2008) by Jonathan T. Scott, MES Publications, Panama City, FL, USA.
2. www.boma.org
3. See note 1 above.
4. NRDC, 'Building Green Increases Employee Satisfaction and Productivity,' July 2007 (www.nrdc.org).
5. Edwards, L., and Torcellini, P., 'A Literature Review of the Effects of Light on Building Occupants' (technical report sponsored by the *National Renewable Energy Laboratory*), NREL/TP-55-30769, July 2002.
6. Laudal, Terry, 'The Deeper Benefits of Going Green: More than Just Buildings', 2007 (www.greenbiz.com).
7. Parker, D., Fairey, P., and McIlaine, J., 'Energy Efficient Office Building Design for a Hot and Humid Climate: Florida's New Energy Center', (sponsored by) the Florida Energy Office, 1995.
8. Courtesy of *Energy Star* (www.energystar.gov).
9. See note 8 above.
10. Whitfield, Kermit, 'Green by Design: On Cars – Manufactured Products', *Look Smart*, Gardner Publications, 2003.
11. Copper Development Association, 'One Wire-Size Up Means Big Savings', 1996 (www.copper.org).

18. Saving Water

1. news.bbc.co.uk/2/hi/science/nature/3747724.stm
2. Gale, Sarah, 'Saving Every Last Drop', March 16, 2009 (www.greenbiz.com).
3. Proctor, Cathy, 'Building Owners are Flush with Big Drop in Water Bill', *The Denver Business Journal*, July 7, 2006.
4. T&L, 'Water Efficiency in the Textile and Leather Industry' (www.accepta.com/industry_water_treatment).
5. Crawford, Caroline, 'Good Things are Growing at Living Technologies Inc', *Business People – Vermont*, May 1999.

19. The Macro Advantages of Micro-power

1. Romm, Joseph, 'Peak Oil? Consider It Solved', March 28, 2008 (www.salon.com)
2. www.greenpower.govs.org
3. Seager, Ashley, 'Alternative Fuels: Now It's a New Game and Clean Energy is No Longer a Dream', *The Guardian* (London), November 7, 2007, p. 26.
4. Wee, Heesun, 'Buildings with Built-In Energy Savings', *Business Week Online*, August 27, 2001 (www.businessweek.com).
5. See note 3 above.

20. The Hidden History of Products

1. Paster, Pablo, 'What's SO Bad About Bottled Water Anyway?', January 14, 2008 (www.salon.com).
2. Schmidt-Bleek, Friedrich, 'Der Ökologische Rücksack', *Hirzel Verlag*, 2004.
3. This list was comprised by the author before it was pointed out that the Industrial Design Society of America comprised something similar 16 years earlier – long before the word 'sustainability' had entered the author's vocabulary. Credit is therefore due to the IDSA and its pioneering work in the field.
4. Hawken, Paul, Lovins, Amory, and Lovins, Hunter, *Natural Capitalism*, Little, Brown & Company, Boston, MA, 1999.
5. Beitz, W., 'Designing for Ease of Recycling', *Journal of Engineering Design* 4(1) (1993), pp. 11-23.
6. World Challenge, 'Fireproof Juice', 2006 (www.theworldchallenge.co.uk/fireproof.php).
7. Ventner, Craig, 'A DNA-Driven World', The Richard Dimbleby Lecture, December 2007.
8. GlaxoSmithKline, 'Eliminating Waste from Our Chemical Production Processes', 2003 (www.gsk.com).
9. Smith, Mark, Roy, Robin, and Potter, Stephen, 'The Commercial Impacts of Green Product Development', The Open University Design Innovation Group, DIG – 05, July 1996.

21. Minimizing Packaging

1. Fielding, Zoe, 'Manufacturers Accountable for Product Waste', *Manufacturers Monthly*, April 6, 2004.
2. 'Waste Prevention Pays Off: Companies Cut Waste in the Workplace', EPA/530-K-920-005, November 1993.
3. See note 2 above.

22. Reuse, Repair, Remanufacturing and Recycling

1. 'Waste Prevention Pays Off: Companies Cut Waste in the Workplace', EPA/530-K-920-005, November 1993.
2. Stahel, Walter, 'Caterpillar Case Study', 1995 (www.product-life.org).
3. 'Everything Old is New Again, *Business Week*, September 23, 2006 (www.businessweek.com).
4. 'Caterpillar Earns Green by Being Green', *Assembly Mag*, March 1 2003 (www.assemblymag.com).
5. See note 3 above.
6. 'Green Can Mean Different Things', *All Business* (Mississippi Business Journal), April 17, 2000 (www.allbusiness.com).

7. Lund, Robert, and Hauser, William, 'The Remanufacturing Industry: Anatomy of a Giant', Department of Manufacturing Engineering, Boston University, 2003.
8. See note 7 above.
9. Ferrer, Geraldo, and Whybark, Clay, 'From Garbage to Goods: Successful Remanufacturing Systems and Skills', *Business Horizons*, November 2000.
10. Orzech, Dan, 'At Clean Plants, It's Waste Not', *Wired* (online), August 10, 2005 (www.wired.com/science/planetearth/news/2005/08/68448).
11. Recycling Guide, www.recycling-guide.org
12. Institute for Local Self-Reliance, 'Waste to Health – Recycling Means Business', 2007 (www.ilsr.org).
13. EPA, 'Industrial Materials Recycling: Managing Resources for Tomorrow', RCC Fact Sheet (530-F-07-088), January 2007.

23. Sustainable Production Locations

1. Adapted from *Debert Eco-industrial Park: The Road Forward*, School for Resource & Environmental Studies, Dalhousie University, 2005.
2. Hollandar, Justin B., and Lowitt, Peter C., *Applying Industrial Ecology to Devens: A Report for the Devens Enterprise Council*, March 2000 (www.devensec.com/ecoreprt.html).
3. See note 2 above.
4. Jyrki, Heino, and Tuomo, Koskenkari, 'Industrial Ecology in the Metallurgy Industry: The Harjavalta Industrial Ecosystem', Roceeding of the Waste Minimization and Resources Use Optimization Conference, June 10, 2004, University of Oulu, Finland, Oulu University Press, pp. 143-151.

24. Clean Production

1. The Environmental Management Industry Association of Australia, 'Cleaner Production – Reuse, Recycle and Treatment Options – Banskia Food Product Pty Ltd' (www.emiaa.au, accessed 2007).
2. UNEP, 'Cleaner Production – Key Elements', 2007 (www.uneptie.org/pc/cp/understanding-cp/home.htm).
3. Smallbiz, 'What are the Benefits of Cleaner Production?', Department of State and Regional Development, New South Wales, Australia, 2007 (www.smallbiz.nsw.gov.au).
4. Washington State Department of Ecology, 'Toxic Reduction Successes', 07-01-032, Office of Communication and Education, July 2007.
5. Zelinski, Peter, 'Why Boeing is Big on Right-Size Machine Tools', Modern Machine Shop Online, September 2007 (www.mmsonline.com/articles/030601.htm).
6. Scott, Jonathan T., *Managing the New Frontiers*, MES Publishing, Panama City, FL, 2008.
7. Yu, Qian, Yun, Chen, Yanbin, Jiang, and Lijuan, Zhang, 'A Clean Production Process of Sodium Chlorite from Sodium Chlorate', *Journal of Cleaner Production* 15(10) (November 2007), pp. 920-926.
8. Energy Matters, 'Why Your Plant Should Be Efficient', U.S. Department of Energy (Energy Efficiency and Renewable Energy), 2007 (www.eere.government.org).
9. Energy Innovators Initiative, Office of Energy Efficiency, Natural Resources Canada, 2002 (oee.nrcan.gc.ca/eii).
10. White, Sue, 'Save Water, Save Waste, and Smell the Difference', *The Sydney Morning Herald*, September 26, 2007 (www.smh.au).
11. Korean NCPC (for more information contact: jaekim1@kitech.re.kr or jykang@kitech.re.kr, 2007).

25. Motors and Pumps

1. Hawken, Paul, Lovins, Amory, and Lovins, Hunter, *Natural Capitalism*, Little, Brown & Company, Boston, MA, 1999.
2. See note 1 above.
3. Energy Matters, 'Why Your Plant Should Be Efficient', US Department of Energy (Energy Efficiency and Renewable Energy), 2007 (www.eere.government.org).
4. See note 3 above.

26. Eliminating Waste at Work: Getting Started

1. AP Wire Service/CBS News, 'More Cities Taking Back Company Tax Breaks', www.cbsnews.com/stories/2010/01/02/business/main6047898.shtml. Thanks to www.ecomodder.com and the students at Kozminski University (Warsaw, Poland) for supplying many of the suggestions mentioned in this section.
2. Sayre, Caroline, 'Make One Right Turn After Another', *Time* magazine (online), 2007 (www.time.com/time/specials/2007/environment/article/0,28804,1602354_1603074_1603741,00.html).

About the author

Jonathan T. Scott (www.jonathantscott.com) is a lecturer, manager, entrepreneur and business leader with over 25 years of work experience in eight different countries. As a manager he was recognized for tripling productivity, reducing costs by up to 40%, and increasing net profits by over 55% at the companies where he worked. In the process he conducted three separate turn-arounds (the first occurred in a war zone; the second was described as 'the best of its kind in the country') and pioneered multi-million-dollar projects in parts of the world where they previously did not exist. Currently, Scott runs a business-education business. He is also the founder and director of the *Center for Industrial Productivity and Sustainability* (www.cipsfoundation.com) and *Wind Gateway* (www.windgateway. com). He serves, or has served, at the following business schools: *Kozminski University* (Warsaw, Poland), the *Rotterdam School of Management* (The Netherlands), the *Audencia Nantes School of Management* (Nantes, France) and *Bradford University* (Bradford, UK). He has also taught at the *University of Perugia* (Italy). In 2009, he was presented with an 'outstanding achievements in teaching' award. Scott's education includes attending *Brevard College* (Brevard, North Carolina) before graduating with a BSc degree from (Tallahassee). He has studied at the *Université de Bourgogne* (Dijon, France), earned an MBA (in management) from Western International University (at its former London, UK campus), received a teaching certification from *Oxford Brookes University* (Oxford, UK), and secured an MA (in management) from *Kozminski University* (Warsaw, Poland). Scott is the author of the following books (four of which are award-winning): *Fundamentals of Leisure Business Success* (1998), *The Concise Handbook of Management* (2005), *Managing the New Frontiers* (2008), *The Entrepreneur's Guide to Building a Successful Business* (2009), *The Sustainable Business* (2010), *New Standards for Long-Term Business Survival* (2011) and the action/adventure novel *On Wings* (2007). His specialty subjects include management, entrepreneurship, and sustainability.

Chief Editor

Walter R. Stahel (www.product-life.org) is the head of Risk Management at the *Geneva Association* (Switzerland), the insurance industry's most prestigious research body. He is also a respected business advisor and the founder and director of the *Product-Life Institute* (Geneva, Switzerland), Europe's oldest sustainability-based consultancy and think-tank. Stahel's pioneering research and collaborative work in the field of sustainability stretch back several decades – firmly establishing him as one of the subject's founders and appliers. He is a visiting professor at the Faculty of Engineering and Physical Sciences at the *University of Surrey* (UK) and is a regular guest lecturer (in the graduate department) at *Tohoku University* (Japan). Stahel is an alumnus of ETH, the Swiss Federal Institute of Technology (Zurich, Switzerland) and holds an honorary PhD from the University of Surrey. He is also the author of several prize-winning papers and pioneering academic books including: *Jobs for Tomorrow: The Potential for Substituting Manpower for Energy* (1976/1982), co-authored with Genevieve Reday; *The Limits of Certainty* (1989/1993), written with Orio Giarini and published in six languages; and *The Performance Economy* (2006/2010). He is a member of the Club of Rome.

Editors/reviewers of the 1st edition

Trained as a lawyer, **Hunter Lovins** (www.natcapsolutions.org) is the president and founder of *Natural Capitalism, Inc.* and co-creator of the Natural Capitalism concept. In 1982 she co-founded the *Rocky Mountain Institute* and led that organization as its CEO for Strategy until 2002. Under her leadership, RMI grew into an internationally recognized research centre, widely celebrated for its innovative thinking in energy and resource issues. She has managed international non-profits, created several corporations, and is in great demand as a speaker and consultant. Her areas of interest and expertise include Natural Capitalism, globalization, economic development, governance, land management, energy, water, green real-estate development and community economic development. She has taught at dozens of universities and is currently Professor of Business at the *Presidio School of Management* (the first accredited MBA program in Sustainable Management). Lovins has co-authored nine books, dozens of papers and has earned numerous awards including a 1982 Mitchell Prize, a 1983 Right Livelihood Award (often called the 'alternative Nobel Prize'), a 1993 Nissan Award, and the 1999 Lindbergh Award for Environment and Technology. She has several honorary doctorates, was named a "Hero for the Planet" by *Time* magazine in 2000, and received the Loyola University award for Outstanding Community Service. In 2001 she received the Leadership in Business Award and shared the Shingo Prize for Manufacturing Research. In addition she has served on the Boards of one government, three private corporations, and many public interest groups. In her spare time, Hunter is a volunteer fire-fighter and an EMT. She is also President of the *Nighthawk Horse Company* and is active training polocrosse horses, and competing at polocrosse and rodeo.

Professor **David Grayson** CBE joined the *Cranfield School of Management* as director of the new *Doughty Centre for Corporate Responsibility* in April 2007, after a 30-year career as a social entrepreneur and campaigner for responsible business, diversity and small business development. This included the chairmanship of the UK's National Disability Council and several other government bodies, as well as serving as a joint managing-director of Business in the Community. He is a visiting Senior Fellow at the *CSR Initiative* of the *Kennedy School of Government* (Harvard University). He has Master's degrees from the universities of Cambridge and Brussels, and an honorary doctorate from *London South Bank University*. He has been a Visiting Fellow at several UK and American business schools. His books include: *Corporate Social Opportunity: Seven Steps to Make Corporate Social Responsibility Work for Your Business* (Greenleaf, 2004; www.greenleaf-publishing.com) and *Everybody's Business* (2001) – both co-authored with Adrian Hodges. He currently chairs *Housing 21* – one of the leading providers of sheltered and extra care housing and care for older people (www.housing21.co.uk).

Index

THE SUSTAINABLE BUSINESS WORKBOOK

WASTE ELIMINATION

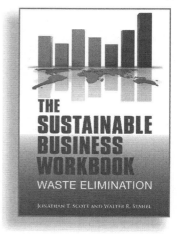

Relevance · Reliability · Results

With the specific intent of saving your business money, increasing its efficiency and competitiveness, and boosting its ability to profit from myriad worldwide future challenges, authors Jonathan T. Scott and Walter R. Stahel (with a combined total of over 40 years of experience working with students and businesses in dozens of countries), walk managers, employees and students through the beginning stages of the waste elimination process.

The aim is to help you transform your business into a performance-based powerhouse that optimizes resources, eliminates waste, and dramatically reduces future costs.

Whether you're a manager looking to strengthen or build the foundation of a results-orientated employee training program, or a business school administrator searching for an application-based program to add to your curriculum, *The Sustainable Business Workbook: Waste Elimination* is for you.

January 2013   30 pp   297 x 210 mm
£9.95   12.95 $17.95
ISBN 978-1-906093-84-6 (wiro-bound)
ISBN 978-1-909493-07-0 (PDF)
www.greenleaf-publishing.com/tsb_workbook